T0210456

Lecture Notes in Computer Science 9128

Commenced Publication in 1973
Founding and Former Series Editors:
Gerhard Goos, Juris Hartmanis, and Jan van Leeuwen

More information about this series at http://www.springer.com/series/7408

Manuel Núñez · Matthias Güdemann (Eds.)

Formal Methods
for Industrial
Critical Systems

20th International Workshop, FMICS 2015
Oslo, Norway, June 22–23, 2015
Proceedings

 Springer

Editors
Manuel Núñez
Universidad Complutense de Madrid
Madrid
Spain

Matthias Güdemann
Systerel
Aix-en-Provence
France

ISSN 0302-9743   ISSN 1611-3349   (electronic)
Lecture Notes in Computer Science
ISBN 978-3-319-19457-8   ISBN 978-3-319-19458-5   (eBook)
DOI 10.1007/978-3-319-19458-5

Library of Congress Control Number: 2015940351

LNCS Sublibrary: SL2 – Programming and Software Engineering

Springer Cham Heidelberg New York Dordrecht London

Printed on acid-free paper

Springer International Publishing AG Switzerland is part of Springer Science+Business Media
(www.springer.com)

Preface

This volume contains the papers presented at FMICS 2015, the 20th International Workshop on Formal Methods for Industrial Critical Systems, which was held during June 22–23, 2015, in Oslo, Norway. The FMICS 2015 workshop took place as a collocated event of the 20th International Symposium on Formal Methods, FM 2015.

The aim of the FMICS workshop series is to provide a forum for researchers who are interested in the development and application of formal methods in industry. In particular, FMICS brings together scientists and engineers who are active in the area of formal methods and interested in exchanging their experiences in the industrial usage of these methods. The FMICS workshop series also strives to promote research and development for the improvement of formal methods and tools for industrial applications. The topics of interest include, but are not limited to:

- Design, specification, code generation, and testing based on formal methods
- Methods, techniques, and tools to support automated analysis, certification, debugging, learning, optimization, and transformation of complex, distributed, dependable, real-time systems, and embedded systems
- Verification and validation methods that address shortcomings of existing methods with respect to their industrial applicability, e.g., scalability and usability issues
- Tools for the development of formal design descriptions
- Case studies and experience reports on industrial applications of formal methods, focusing on lessons learned or identification of new research directions
- Impact of the adoption of formal methods on the development process and associated costs
- Application of formal methods in standardization and industrial forums

This year we received 20 submissions. Each of these submissions went through a rigorous review process in which each paper received at least three reports. We selected 12 papers for presentation during the workshop and inclusion in these proceedings. The workshop also featured invited talks by Kim G. Larsen (Aalborg University, Denmark) and by Marielle Petit-Doche (Systerel, France). In addition, two invited talks by Dino Distefano (Queen Mary University, UK and Facebook) and José Meseguer (University of Illinois, USA) organized by the Workshop on Automated Specification and Verification of Web Systems were open to FMICS participants.

We would like to thank the ERCIM FMICS working group coordinator Radu Mateescu (Inria Grenoble and LIG) for his counselling and support during the organization of FMICS 2015. We would like to thank the FM 2015 workshops chairs Marieke Huisman and Volker Stolz for their help with the local arrangements in Oslo. We would like to thank the chairs of the 11th Workshop on Automated Specification and Verification of Web Systems, Maurice H. ter Beek (ISTI-CNR, Pisa, Italy) and Alberto Lluch Lafuente (Technical University of Denmark), for the generous offer to share their invited speakers with FMICS attendants. Finally, we would like to thank the Program Committee members and external reviewers for their useful and detailed reviews and discussions, all authors for their submissions, and all attendees of the workshop.

June 2015   Manuel Núñez
                                                       Matthias Güdemann

Organization

Programm Committee Chairs

Manuel Núñez   Universidad Complutense de Madrid, Spain
Matthias Güdemann   Systerel, France

Programm Committee

María Alpuente	Universitat Politècnica de Valencia, Spain
Alvaro Arenas	IE University, Spain
Jiri Barnat	Masaryk University, Czech Republic
Jean-Paul Blanquart	Astrium Satellites, France
Eckard Böde	Offis, Germany
Mario Bravetti	University of Bologna, Italy
Michael Dierkes	Rockwell Collins, France
Cindy Eisner	IBM Research - Haifa, Israel
Alessandro Fantechi	Università di Firenze, Italy
Francesco Flammini	Ansaldo, Italy
María del Mar Gallardo	University of Málaga, Spain
Stefania Gnesi	ISTI-CNR, Italy
Matthias Güdemann	Systerel, France
Clément Houtmann	Google, Switzerland
Frédéric Lang	Inria and LIG, France
Luis Llana	Universidad Complutense de Madrid, Spain
Alberto Lluch	DTU, Denmark
Paqui Lucio	University of the Basque Country, Spain
Tiziana Margaria	University of Potsdam, Germany
Jasen Markovski	GN ReSound Benelux, The Netherlands
Radu Mateescu	Inria and LIG, France
David Mentré	Mitsubishi Research, France
Manuel Núñez	Universidad Complutense de Madrid, Spain
Charles Pecheur	Université Catholique de Louvain, Belgium
Ralf Pinger	Siemens AG, Germany
Jaco van de Pol	University of Twente, The Netherlands
Wendelin Serwe	Inria and LIG, France
Hans Svensson	Quviq, Sweden
Anton Wijs	Technical University of Eindhoven, The Netherlands
Fatiha Zaïdi	Université Paris-Sud XI, France

Additional Reviewers

Emilie Balland
Demis Ballis
Marcello M. Bersani
Paul Brauner
Laura Carnevali
Marcus Gerhold
Jeroen Meijer

Invited Talks

Formal Verification of Industrial Critical Software

Marielle Petit-Doche

Systerel, Les portes de l'Arbois, Bâtiment A — 1090, rue René Descartes
13857 Aix-en-Provence CEDEX 3, France
marielle.petit-doche@systerel.fr
www.systerel.fr

Abstract. In this talk I will review the challenges for using formal verification based on automatic tools, like model-checkers, in the industrial development process of safety critical systems is discussed. This usage must be integrated into an appropriate process and must allow for independent result-checking.

Our approach is illustrated with a case study from the openETCS ITEA2 research project using the Systerel Smart Solver S3, a modern SAT-based model-checker for equivalence checking and safety properties analysis of SCADE, C or Ada programs.

This work was partially funded by the "Direction Générale de la compétitivité, de l'industrie et des services" (DGCIS) (Grant No. 112930309) within the ITEA2 project openETCS.

From Timed Automata
to Stochastic Hybrid Games
Model Checking, Performance Evaluation, Synthesis and Optimization

Kim G. Larsen

Department of Computer Science, Aalborg University, Denmark
kgl@cs.aau.dk

Abstract. Timed automata [1] and games [3,7], priced timed automata [2,4] and energy automata [6] have emerged as useful formalisms for modeling real-time and energy-aware systems as found in several embedded and cyber-physical systems. During the last 20 years the real-time model checker UPPAAL has been developed allowing for efficient verification of hard timing constraints of timed automata. Moreover a number of significant branches exists, e.g. UPPAAL CORA providing efficient support for optimization, and UPPAAL TIGA allowing for automatic synthesis of strategies for given safety and liveness objectives. In the beginning of this decade the branch UPPAAL SMC [10,11] has been released, providing a highly scalable new engine that supports (distributed) statistical model checking of stochastic hybrid automata (and games).

The most recent branch of the UPPAAL family is the tool UPPAAL STRATEGO [8,9], that combines all of the above tools and extend the with techniques from machine learning, in order to generate, optimize, compare and explore consequences and performance of strategies synthesized for stochastic priced timed games in a userfriendly manner. In particular, UPPAAL STRATEGO allows for generation of strategies that simultaneously satisfy a number of hard real-time constraints, while having near optimal expected performance properties.

The various branches of UPPAAL have been applied in concerted fashions to a range of real-time and cyber-physical examples including schedulability and performance evaluation of mixed criticality systems, modeling and analysis of biological systems, energy-aware wireless sensor networks, synthesis and performance evaluation of smart grids and energy-aware buildings and battery-aware scheduling.

References

1. Alur, R., Dill, D.L.: A theory of timed automata. Theor. Comput. Sci. 126(2), 183–235 (1994)
2. Alur, R., La Torre, S., Pappas, G.J.: Optimal paths in weighted timed automata. In: Benedetto and Sangiovanni-Vincentelli [5], pp. 49–62, http://dx.doi.org/10.1007/3-540-45351-2_8
3. Behrmann, G., Cougnard, A., David, A., Fleury, E., Larsen, K.G., Lime, D.: Uppaal-tiga: Time for playing games! In: CAV. pp. 121–125 (2007)
4. Behrmann, G., Fehnker, A., Hune, T., Larsen, K.G., Pettersson, P., Romijn, J., Vaandrager, F.W.: Minimum-cost reachability for priced timed automata. In: Benedetto and Sangiovanni-Vincentelli [5], pp. 147–161, http://dx.doi.org/10.1007/3-540-45351-2_15

This work has been supported by the projects IDEA4CPS, SENSATION and CASSTING.

5. Benedetto, M.D.D., Sangiovanni-Vincentelli, A.L. (eds.): Hybrid Systems: Computation and Control, 4th International Workshop, HSCC 2001, Rome, Italy, March 28-30, 2001, Proceedings, Lecture Notes in Computer Science, vol. 2034. Springer (2001)
6. Bouyer, P., Fahrenberg, U., Larsen, K.G., Markey, N., Srba, J.: Infinite runs in weighted timed automata with energy constraints. In: Cassez, F., Jard, C. (eds.) Formal Modeling and Analysis of Timed Systems, 6th International Conference, FORMATS 2008, Saint Malo, France, September 15-17, 2008. Proceedings. Lecture Notes in Computer Science, vol. 5215, pp. 33–47. Springer (2008), http://dx.doi.org/10.1007/978-3-540-85778-5_4
7. Cassez, F., David, A., Fleury, E., Larsen, K.G., Lime, D.: Efficient on-the-fly algorithms for the analysis of timed games. In: CONCUR. pp. 66–80 (2005)
8. David, A., Jensen, P.G., Larsen, K.G., Legay, A., Lime, D., Sørensen, M.G., Taankvist, J.H.: On time with minimal expected cost! In: Cassez, F., Raskin, J. (eds.) Automated Technology for Verification and Analysis - 12th International Symposium, ATVA 2014, Sydney, NSW, Australia, November 3-7, 2014, Proceedings. Lecture Notes in Computer Science, vol. 8837, pp. 129–145. Springer (2014), http://dx.doi.org/10.1007/978-3-319-11936-6_10
9. David, A., Jensen, P.G., Larsen, K.G., Mikucionis, M., Taankvist, J.H.: Uppaal stratego. In: Baier, C., Tinelli, C. (eds.) Tools and Algorithms for the Construction and Analysis of Systems - 21st International Conference, TACAS 2015, Held as Part of the European Joint Conferences on Theory and Practice of Software, ETAPS 2015, London, UK, April 11-18, 2015. Proceedings. Lecture Notes in Computer Science, vol. 9035, pp. 206–211. Springer (2015), http://dx.doi.org/10.1007/978-3-662-46681-0_16
10. David, A., Larsen, K.G., Legay, A., Mikucionis, M., Poulsen, D.B., van Vliet, J., Wang, Z.: Statistical model checking for networks of priced timed automata. In: Fahrenberg, U., Tripakis, S. (eds.) Formal Modeling and Analysis of Timed Systems - 9th International Conference, FORMATS 2011, Aalborg, Denmark, September 21-23, 2011. Proceedings. Lecture Notes in Computer Science, vol. 6919, pp. 80–96. Springer (2011), http://dx.doi.org/10.1007/978-3-642-24310-3_7
11. David, A., Larsen, K.G., Legay, A., Mikucionis, M., Wang, Z.: Time for statistical model checking of real-time systems. In: Gopalakrishnan, G., Qadeer, S. (eds.) Computer Aided Verification - 23rd International Conference, CAV 2011, Snowbird, UT, USA, July 14-20, 2011. Proceedings. Lecture Notes in Computer Science, vol. 6806, pp. 349–355. Springer (2011), http://dx.doi.org/10.1007/978-3-642-22110-1_27

Contents

Applications

Protocols

Specification and Analysis

Verification

Formal Verification
of Industrial Critical Software

Marielle Petit-Doche[(✉)], Nicolas Breton, Roméo Courbis,
Yoann Fonteneau, and Matthias Güdemann

Systerel, Les portes de l'Arbois, bâtiment A — 1090,
rue René Descartes, 13857 Aix-en-Provence CEDEX 3, France
{marielle.petit-doche,nicolas.breton,romeo.courbis,
yoann.fonteneau}@systerel.fr, matthias@guedemann.org
www.systerel.fr

Abstract. In this paper, the challenges for using formal verification based on automatic tools, like model-checkers, in the industrial development process of safety critical systems is discussed. This usage must be integrated into an appropriate process and must allow for independent result-checking.

Our approach is illustrated with a case study from the openETCS ITEA2 research project using the Systerel Smart Solver S3, a modern SAT-based model-checker for equivalence checking and safety properties analysis of SCADE, C or Ada programs.

1 Introduction

Railway and aerospace critical software require rigorous design, verification and validation processes. These can be achieved by the use of formal methods as recommended by the standards in these domains [7,13].

One possibility is to apply formal methods from the early stage of the design to produce "correct-by-construction" software. Numbers of success stories have already been described, for example in the railway industry with the B method [4,2,8]. Another approach is to introduce formal methods later, during an independent verification and validation phase: starting from an informal specification, the properties to verify are identified and formally specified in parallel to the software design activities. Then, they are automatically checked on an executable model or the code.

In the following we describe how this second approach can be applied using the Systerel Smart Solver S3, a model-checking tool based on SAT technologies, dedicated to automatic proof of properties on SCADE, C or Ada code. This approach has been successfully applied on industrial critical software, for example [6].

M. Güdemann—This work was partially funded by the "Direction Générale de la compétitivité, de l'industrie et des services" (DGCIS) (Grant No. 112930309) within the ITEA2 project openETCS.

© Springer International Publishing Switzerland 2015
M. Núñez and M. Güdemann (Eds.): FMICS 2015, LNCS 9128, pp. 1–11, 2015.
DOI: 10.1007/978-3-319-19458-5_1

In the sequel we illustrate the approach on a part of the on-board unit software of the European Train Control System (ETCS), developed in SCADE for the openETCS project[1].

The paper is structured as follows: In Section 2 S3 model-checker is introduced and show how it can be used for certifiable formal verification. Section 3 gives an overview of the openETCS project which serves as a case study for the S3 application explained in Section 4. Section 5 concludes the paper.

2 Introduction to Systerel Smart Solver

2.1 Principles of S3

Systerel Smart Solver (S3) is a SAT-based model checker for safety properties analysis.

The High Level Language (HLL), the input language of S3, is a stream oriented declarative data-flow language which can be used to model:

- the system behavior
- the environment
- the formal expression of the properties.

S3 proceeds to the analyses of properties on the traces of the HLL models following one of these two strategies:

- Induction to prove a property (see [14]);
- Bounded model checking (BMC) to falsify a property or generate test cases (see [5,1]).

Thus S3 can be applied on different ways to verify and validate a critical industrial system.

2.2 Application of S3: Static Analysis

S3 adds some proof obligations to assess that the HLL model is correctly defined:

- Indexes of arrays belong to their ranges
- Latch definition range check
- No division by 0
- No overflow and no underflow on arithmetic expressions
- Output and constraint initialization check

Besides, the translators from a language to HLL can also generate proof obligations to be analyzed by S3, to check that the code does not have undefined behavior with respect to the source language.

For example the C-translator adds some proof obligations to ensure conformance with the C99 standard.

---

[1] http://openetcs.org/

2.3   Application of S3: Verification of Safety Properties

Safety Properties are of the form *always* ϕ meaning that the Boolean predicate ϕ holds Globally, *i.e.*, in every state reachable from the initial state. S3 can be used to verify safety properties as shown in the process in Fig. 1.

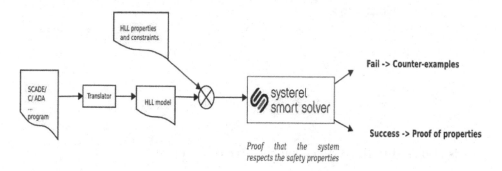

Fig. 1. Safety Property Verification

First the source program in either C, SCADE, Ada,... is translated into HLL format via a translator; this HLL system model is then combined with safety properties expressed in HLL to form a verification model. Environment hypotheses and constraints can be added if a property does not hold based only on the formal model of the software and requires additional hypotheses about the overall system and/or its environment.

Finally the properties are verified using S3.

A good approach is to first use the BMC strategy with a rather large depth (depending on the system). After, if there is no counter-example, the induction strategy can be launched.

2.4   Application of S3: Equivalence Verification of Different Models

There are different areas where the formal verification of equivalence is required. One such example is the verification of equivalence of two different tool chains for the same task in an approach based on diversification. Such an approach is often used in the development of safety critical systems, to decrease the probability of errors. In general, two different versions of a software are developed independently, using different programming languages, different approaches and also separate teams.

The equivalence of the two resulting system models is then verified using S3.

To prove equivalence between two HLL models, we make the hypothesis that the inputs of the two HLL models are equal and we want to prove that the outputs are equal (see Fig. 2).

The equivalence could also be used to prove that a code is equivalent to a specification: the code is translated into HLL and the specification is written in HLL.

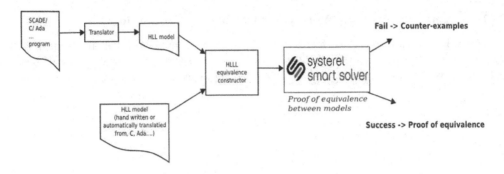

Fig. 2. Equivalence Check

It is also used in the certification flow (see section 2.6).

2.5   Application of S3: Test Case Generation

S3 can also be used for test case generation:

- In the case of functional black-box testing, the main difficulty in writing of test scenario is to define the values of the outputs to observe as a function of the input values, as the analysis of the functionality can be complex.
- In the case of white-box verification, the difficulty is to define the right input values to cover a function, a branch or a condition.

As an alternative, for black box-testing, S3 shall allow to determine easily test oracle. For white-box testing, we can easily write a test objective in HLL that states exactly the objective of the test (e.g. the desired output values). Applying a BMC strategy, we obtain all the desired scenario with the expected values of the inputs.

2.6   Certifiable Systerel Smart Solver

In order to conform to industrial standards requirements for critical systems [7,13], we propose a certifiable formal verification solution with S3 (see Fig.3).

When building certifiable formal verification solutions, the certifiable Systerel Smart Solver (cS3) approach relies on three different techniques:

Diversification of the Translation Chain: the translation of a model to HLL is done twice[2], with two translators being developed by two independent teams in two independent programming language (for instance one in C the other in Ocaml).

---

[2] When applicable, these diversified translations are performed from differentiated sources.

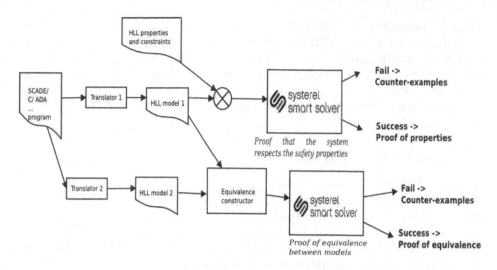

Fig. 3. Certifiable solution

Equivalence-check of the Translated Models: the outputs of the two diversified translation chains are compared using equivalence checking. S3 is used together with an equivalence-constructor to check if the two translated models are *sequentially equivalent, i.e.*, if given the same scenario on their inputs, they would produce the same outputs.

Record of Results in a Verifiable Proof-log: when a proof is validated or an equivalence between model established, the result of the S3 is not a simple "OK" answer, but a *proof-log* file that contains an encoding of the proof of this claim in a sound and complete proof-system. An independent checker is run *a-posteriori* to check the correctness of this proof.

3   The openETCS Project

The openETCS (http://openetcs.org/) project aims at providing an open-source formal model for the European Train Control System (ETCS), an automatic train protection system. The goal is to produce an open reference model which can be verified following an open-proof [12] approach.

3.1   European Train Control System

The ETCS is an automatic train protection system, targeted at providing a common standard for European cross-border railway. It allows for automatic train protection for high-speed trains up to 500 km/h. The ETCS is divided in on-board subsystems and trackside subsystems.

The main function of ETCS trackside system is to calculate and provide the movement authority of all the trains present in a section of tracks, in such a way that signals are obeyed and collision between trains avoided.

The main function of ETCS on-board system is to ensure that the train runs in an authorized portion of track and never exceeds its authorized speed. In order to be able to move, a train receives a movement authority (MA) which authorizes the train to move until a certain position on the track, with potential speed restrictions.

The technical specifications of the system are provided by the European Railway Agency [9][3]

3.2   OpenETCS Case Study

The openETCS project partners have decided to provide SysML and SCADE models of some on-board kernel functions [11]. Use of different formal methods have been proposed to verify or validate these models [10].

In this context, we have used S3 to verify some properties and validate parts of the functional behavior. We focused our work on the on-board sub-function which is in charge of mode and level management.

Mode and Level Management. Depending on the equipment of the track and the train, and way of interaction between them, five ETCS levels are define: **Level 1, 2 and 3** are applied when both tracks and trains are equipped to communicate together following the ETCS protocol; **Level 0** is used when the tracks are not equipped, and **Level STM/NTC**, when the tracks are equipped with a national signalization system, *e.g.*, German PZB/LZB, Dutch ATB or French.

During a mission, a train can cross trackside sections equipped in different levels, thus the on-board system shall manage the different levels in order to manage correctly communication with trackside and apply the adapted supervision function.

Besides the levels, 17 modes are defined to identify the functional behavior of the on-board system: some are related to nominal modes with execution of supervision functions, some are related to passive behaviors (for example for coupling engines) or failure or dangerous behaviors. The current mode of the system is a criteria to select activation or not of on-board functions (as supervision, driver interface management, ...).

4   Use of Systerel Smart Solver in the openETCS Project

4.1   Model Verification

At first, the formal verification of the model was used to find bugs in the developed model. This comprises two parts:

- A set of basic properties are automatically verified to check that the SCADE model is well defined as described in section 2.2.

---

[3] See   http://www.era.europa.eu/Core-Activities/ERTMS/Pages/Current-Legal-Reference.aspx for more details.

- Specific safety properties can be defined to complete this verification; Typically in our example, properties allow us to confirm the good implementation of priority criteria in the selection of modes and levels.

4.2   Validation of Safety Properties

Then S3 can be used to validate the functional aspects of the model.

In our study we focused on validation, by an independent expert of functional behavior specified in the informal input specification [15].

But as we are focusing on a sub-function it is difficult to identify safety properties to check on the whole model as described in section 2.3. An example of such properties is that a safety failure detected by any other functions is immediately taken into account: the software shall immediately switch in "Safety Failure Mode".

4.3   Functional Validation by Equivalence of Models

Thus we focus on validating informal specification description (for example as flowchart) on our SCADE model in an independent way: informal description is specified in HLL and then equivalence of models is shown as described in section 2.4.

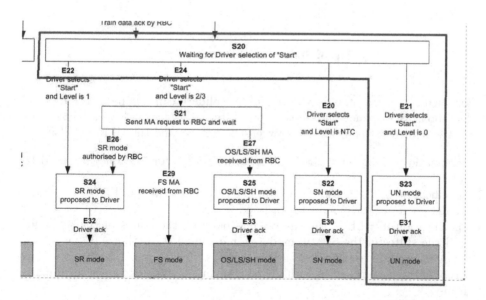

Fig. 4. Start of mission in Level 0 in the Subset 26 input specification (§ 5.4.4)

For example, when a train starts a mission, the train is at standstill, on-board system is in Stand-by mode (SB), and train data (identification numbers, length,..) are validated. As soon as the driver pushes the start of mission button, the on-board system sends him a request for acknowledgment message, then waits reception of this acknowledgment to switch to the appropriate mode. In Fig. 4, as level 0 is selected, the on-board system shall switch to Unfitted mode (UN).

This expected scenario is described in figure 5.

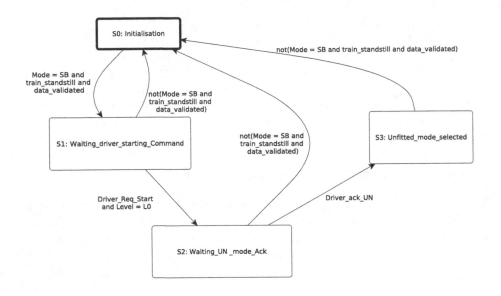

Fig. 5. Start of mission in Level 0

For such a scenario, the SCADE model to validate can not be considered as a black-box, as for safety properties, but internal state shall be analyzed to explicitly defined the equivalence between the SCADE and the HLL models:

1. automatic translation of the SCADE model (Fig. 6 for example) to an HLL model;
2. specification of a scenario (for example the one described in Fig. 5) in aHLL model (or in a SCADE model translated in HLL);
3. specification in HLL of the equivalence between the states of the scenario and the states of the SCADE model (for example state "Level_0" in Fig. 6 shall correspond to state "S2" in Fig. 5);
4. proof of these equivalences with the S3 tool and analysis of counter-examples if any.

A counter-example contains specific input values which lead to disprove the equivalence. However, it can be due to unrealistic input values. In this case it is possible to add constraints to our HLL model. In our example, we can assume that during the mode management the level input value stays constant with value "L0" and that train data stay unchanged and valid.

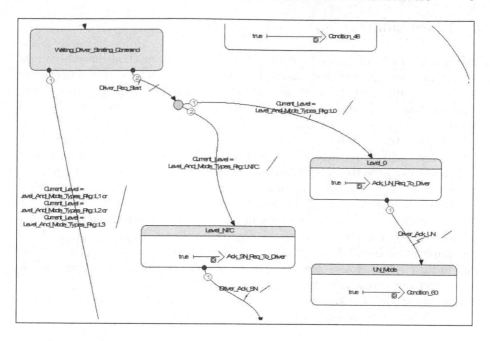

Fig. 6. Start of mission — SCADE model — Zoom

In a verification process, adding constraints leads to add new properties to be verified on another part of the system (*i.e.* the part which is connected to our model inputs).

Other hypotheses can be integrated in the property to verify: the proof goal P is replaced by the proof goal $H \Rightarrow P$ where H are the hypotheses. Other properties shall be introduced to cover the case where H is false, and no external verification is required. Typically, these hypotheses are defined to eliminate possible behaviors, not directly related to the topic of verification. In our example, we assume that system failure is not detected in input of the models, and then we do not consider all the behaviors which drive to system failure mode, to check switch to unfitted mode. The occurrence of a system failure has been covered by another properties.

In this context, proof shows, that under given constraints on inputs, and hypotheses, behaviors of both state machines are equivalent.

Models in SCADE and HLL and set of proofs are available for further analyses on the openETCS website[4].

---

[4] In the modelisation repository for the SCADE model
https://github.com/openETCS/modeling/tree/master/model/Scade/System/ObuFunctions/ManageLevelsAndModes and in the validation repository for the HLL proof files https://github.com/openETCS/validation/blob/master/VnVUserStories/VnVUserStorySysterel/04-Results/e-Scade_S3/Scade_S3_VnV.pdf

5   Discussion

Thanks to our experience in the railway industry, formal methods have been first used to produce "correct-by-construction" software. Now, to open the market of critical software products, they are also used to verify and validate, a posteriori, configuration data [3] or software developed without formal methods as presented in this paper.

Such an activity needs selection or development of tools, which respond to certification criteria requested by standards such as [7,13]. Moreover, methods and processes to use this tools in an industrial context shall be explicitly defined in view to reinforce quality of critical systems.

Besides, in the context of the openETCS project, as described in this paper, this SAT-based model checking solution has been shown to be particularly efficient in proving the safety of the Computer Based Interlocking (CBI) or Communication-Based Train Controler (CBTC) systems developed by the railway industry. It had also been used to generate test cases for an aeronautic subsystem and verify its parametrization process.

Benefits of formal methods in an a posteriori verification process of critical systems has been recognized by our industrial customers:

- Contrarily to a human generated test-based verification solution, a formal safety verification is intrinsically complete. It is equivalent to search for every possible falsification.
- It clearly identifies the complete list of assumptions upon which the safety relies.
- A certified solution allows for a reduction of the testing and review efforts (only the generic safety specification has to be reviewed).
- The use of formal verification in the qualification of critical software sends a strong and positive message to the market, and is sometime even a requirement for some customers.

References

1. Amla, N., Du, X., Kuehlmann, A., Kurshan, R.P., McMillan, K.L.: An analysis of SAT-based model checking techniques in an industrial environment. In: Borrione, D., Paul, W. (eds.) CHARME 2005. LNCS, vol. 3725, pp. 254–268. Springer, Heidelberg (2005)
2. Badeau, F., Amelot, A.: Using B as a High Level Programming Language in an Industrial Project: Roissy VAL. In: Treharne, H., King, S., C. Henson, M., Schneider, S. (eds.) ZB 2005. LNCS, vol. 3455, pp. 334–354. Springer, Heidelberg (2005)
3. Badeau, F., Doche-Petit, M.: Formal data validation with event-b. Proceeding of DS-Event 2012, CoRR abs/1210.7039 (2012)
4. Behm, P., Benoit, P., Faivre, A., Meynadier, J.-M.: Météor: A successful application of B in a large project. In: Wing, J.M., Woodcock, J. (eds.) FM 1999. LNCS, vol. 1708, pp. 369–387. Springer, Heidelberg (1999)

5. Biere, A., Cimatti, A., Clarke, E., Zhu, Y.: Symbolic model checking without bDDs. In: Cleaveland, W.R. (ed.) TACAS 1999. LNCS, vol. 1579, pp. 193–207. Springer, Heidelberg (1999)
6. Boulanger, J.L.: Safety Demonstration for a Rail Signaling Application in Nominal and Degraded Modes Using Formal Proof (2014)
7. CENELEC–EN 50128: Railway applications –Communication, signalling and processing system –Software for railway control and protecton system. DIN (October 2011)
8. Essamé, D., Dollé, D.: B in Large-Scale Projects: The Canarsie Line CBTC Experience. In: Julliand, J., Kouchnarenko, O. (eds.) B 2007. LNCS, vol. 4355, pp. 252–254. Springer, Heidelberg (2006)
9. European Union: Commission decision of 25 january 2012 on the technical specification for interoperability relating to the control-command and signalling subsystems of the trans- european rail system - 2012/88/EU, official journal of the european union, pp. l51/1-l51/65 (2012)
10. Marielle Petit-Doche, WP7 participants: Report on all aspects of secondary tooling. Report D7.2, openETCS (2014)
11. Jastram, M., Petit-Doche, M.: WP7 participants: Report on the Final Choice of the Primary Toolchain. Report D7.1, openETCS (October 2013)
12. openETCS: Project Outline Full Project Proposal Annex openETCS open proofs methodology for the european train control system. Requirements v2.2 (2011)
13. RTCA, EUROCAE: Software Considerations in Airborne Systems and Equipment Certification. RTCA DO-178 (2011)
14. Sheeran, M., Singh, S., Stålmarck, G.: Checking safety properties using induction and a SAT-solver. In: Johnson, S.D., Hunt Jr., W.A. (eds.) FMCAD 2000. LNCS, vol. 1954, pp. 108–125. Springer, Heidelberg (2000)
15. UNISIG: SUBSET-026 System Requirements Specification, version 3.3.0 (2012)

Applications

A Case Study on Formal Verification of the Anaxagoros Hypervisor Paging System with Frama-C

Allan Blanchard[1,3](✉), Nikolai Kosmatov[1],
Matthieu Lemerre[1], and Frédéric Loulergue[2,3]

[1] CEA, LIST, Software Reliability Laboratory, PC 174, 91191,
Gif-sur-Yvette, France
{firstname.lastname}@cea.fr
[2] Inria πr^2, PPS, University Paris Diderot, CNRS, Paris, France
[3] INSA Centre Val de Loire, University Orléans, LIFO EA, 4022, Orléans, France
{firstname.lastname}@univ-orleans.fr

Abstract. Cloud hypervisors are critical software whose formal verification can increase our confidence in the reliability and security of the cloud. This work presents a case study on formal verification of the virtual memory system of the cloud hypervisor Anaxagoros, a microkernel designed for resource isolation and protection. The code under verification is specified and proven in the FRAMA-C software verification framework, mostly using automatic theorem proving. The remaining properties are interactively proven with the Coq proof assistant. We describe in detail selected aspects of the case study, including parallel execution and counting references to pages, and discuss some lessons learned, benefits and limitations of our approach.

Keywords: Deductive verification · Interactive proof · Cloud hypervisor · FRAMA-C · Specification · Concurrency

1 Introduction

Recent years have seen a huge trend towards mobile and Internet applications. Well known applications are moving to the cloud to become "software as a service" offers. At the same time, more and more of our data is in the cloud. It is thus necessary to have reliable, safe and secure cloud environments.

Certification of programs in critical systems is an old concern, while a recent trend in this area is to *formally verify* the programs, the tools used to produce them [1,2] (and even the tools used to analyze them), and the operating system kernel [3] used to execute them. This formal verification is mostly done using interactive theorem provers, and sometimes automated provers.

This work has been partially funded by the CEA project CyberSCADA and the EU FP7 project STANCE (grant 317753).

© Springer International Publishing Switzerland 2015
M. Núñez and M. Güdemann (Eds.): FMICS 2015, LNCS 9128, pp. 15–30, 2015.
DOI: 10.1007/978-3-319-19458-5_2

Anaxagoros [4] is a secure microkernel that is also capable of virtualizing pre-existing operating systems, for example Linux virtual machines, and can therefore be used as a hypervisor in a cloud environment. One distinctive feature of Anaxagoros is that it is capable of securely executing hard real-time tasks or operating systems, for instance the PharOS real-time system [5], simultaneously with non real-time tasks, on a single chip or on a multi-core processor. Our goal is to formally verify the prototype C implementation of Anaxagoros, starting with its most critical components. In this paper we focus on the virtual memory system of Anaxagoros and use the FRAMA-C toolset [6] for conducting the verification.

FRAMA-C is a platform for static analysis, deductive verification and testing of critical software written in C. It offers a collection of plugins for source code analysis. These plugins could be used in cooperation for a particular verification task. They interact through a common specification language for C programs: ACSL [6,7]. In this work, the specifications are written in ACSL, and the weakest precondition calculus plugin WP of FRAMA-C together with SMT solvers are used to provide automatic proof for most properties. Some remaining proof obligations (that were not proven automatically) are proven in the interactive proof assistant COQ [8].

The Contributions. of this paper include a case study on formal verification of a critical module of a Cloud hypervisor. Assuming a sequentially consistent memory model, we performed the verification for both sequential and concurrent execution for one of the key parts of the virtual memory module related to setting new page mappings. We show how a simulation-based approach allows us to take into account concurrent execution using the FRAMA-C plugin WP that does not natively support parallel programs. One advantage of its usage is the possibility to perform the proof for most specified properties *automatically* with a very reasonable effort. Only a few lemmas in this case study have to be proven manually, and WP allows the user to conveniently complete their proofs in the interactive proof assistant Coq, where the Coq statements to be proven are automatically extracted based on the specified code.

Moreover, the verification in this case study can be considered completely formal under the hypothesis that other functions do not interfere on the same variables (memory page mappings) with the function that we verify. That is realistic given that these mappings can be changed only by a couple of functions that can be included into the case study. On the other hand, we argue that, even seen as a partial formal verification, such a study of a critical module in isolation can still be quite efficient to avoid security issues. Finally, we argue that, even done under the assumption that the memory model is sequentially consistent, the presented case study remains valid for weak memory models.

Outline. The paper is organized as follows. Section 2 presents the Anaxagoros hypervisor and its virtual memory system. The verification of this system is described in Section 3, where we detail particular issues of the case study including simulation of parallel execution (Section 3.1), counting references to pages (Section 3.2), automatic proof with FRAMA-C (Section 3.3) and interactive proof with COQ (Section 3.4). Section 4 provides a discussion of the approach, some lessons learned and axes of improvement. Finally, Section 5 presents related work, while Section 6 gives a conclusion and future work.

2   The Anaxagoros Virtual Memory System

Anaxagoros [4,9] is a secure microkernel and hypervisor developed at CEA LIST, that can virtualize preexisting operating systems, for example, Linux virtual machines. It puts a strong emphasis on security, notably resource security, so it is able to provide both quality-of-service guarantees and an exact accounting (billing) of CPU time and memory provided to virtual machines, thus satisfying requirements of cloud users.

A critical component to ensure security in Anaxagoros is its *virtual memory system* [9]. The x86 processor (as many other high-end hardware architectures) provides a mechanism for *virtual memory translation*, that translates an address manipulated by a program into a real physical address. One of the goals of this mechanism is to help to organize the program address space, for instance, to allow a program to access big contiguous memory regions. The other goal is to control the memory that a program can access. The physical memory is split into equally sized regions, called *pages* or *frames*. Pages can be of several types: `data`, `pagetable`, `pagedirectory`. Basically, page directories contain mappings (i.e. references) to page tables, that in turn contain mappings to data pages. The page size is 4kB on standard x86 configurations.

Anaxagoros does not decide what is written to pages; rather, it allows tasks to perform any operations on pages, provided that this does not affect the security of the kernel itself, and of the other tasks in the system. To do that, it has to ensure only two simple properties. The first one ensures that a program can only change a page that it "owns". The second property states that pages are used according to their types.

Indeed, the hardware does not prevent a page table or a page directory from being also used as a data page. Thus, if no protection mechanism is present, a malicious task can change the mappings and, after realizing a certain sequence of modifications, it can finally access (and write to) any page, including those that it does not own.

The virtual memory module should prevent such unauthorized modifications. It relies on recording the type of each page and maintaining counters of mappings to each page (i.e. the number of times the page is referred to as a data page, page table, or page directory). The module ensures that pages can be used only according to their type. In addition, to allow dynamic reuse of memory, the module should make it possible to change the type of a page. To avoid possible attacks, changing the page type requires some complex additional properties. (Simplified) examples of properties include: page contents should be cleaned before any type change; still referred pages cannot be cleaned; the cleaning should

```
1  int set_entry(int fn, int idx, int new){
2      // Step 1 -> read_map_new
3      int c_n = mappings[new];
4      // Step 2 -> test_map_new
5      if(c_n >= MAX) return 1;
6      // Step 3 -> CAS_map_new
7      if(!compare_and_swap(&mappings[new], c_n, c_n+1))
8          return 1;
9      // Step 4 -> EXCH_entry
10     page_t p = get_frame(fn);
11     int old = atomic_exchange(&p[idx], new);
12     // Step 5 -> test_map_old
13     if(!old) return 0;
14     // Step 6 -> FAS_map_old
15     fetch_and_sub(&mappings[old], 1);
16     return 0;
17 }
```

Fig. 1. Function `set_entry` writes page reference `new` into page `fn` at index `idx`

be correctly resumed after an interruption; the counters of mappings (references) should be correctly maintained; cleaned pages are never referred to; etc.

For instance, in Anaxagoros, the function that sets a mapping to a page inside a page table (illustrated in Fig. 1 and described below) has to update the counters of mappings taking into account the ones it sets and removes. The counters are maintained by an array storing the state of every page, including the number of times it is mapped. The goal is to ensure that for every page, the real number of mappings to it is at most equal to the value of the counter. Thus, checking if the counter is equal to zero allows us to ensure that the page is no longer referred to before it is cleaned and its type is changed. This prevents possible attacks.

The algorithm also has to take care of the memory management unit cache called the translation lookaside buffer (TLB), which has to be flushed before repurposing a page. Indeed, an entry left in this cache could allow a user program to change a page after it has been cleaned by the kernel. As TLB flushes are costly, the algorithm should avoid them whenever possible, i.e. when we can ensure that there are no entries left in the TLB for a page. We have currently excluded modeling of the TLB from the verification study.

This case study focuses on a simplified version of the virtual memory module that includes most of its key aspects such as data pages and page tables used with respect to the page type, setting new mappings to data pages, maintaining correct counters of mappings and concurrent execution. Simplifications include the replacement of bitfields used in page descriptors by a set of arrays of separate variables, and the fact that we do not take into account the multiple levels of hierarchy of pagetables in the considered properties. Another characteristic of the simplified version is that it splits some functions into smaller ones, and therefore allows to treat a more fine-grained concurrency than the original one.

3   Formal Verification

As any OS, Anaxagoros is inherently concurrent, so we have to deal with concurrency in this case study. Frama-C does not currently treat concurrency, and there are no concurrency primitives available in the considered version of C. Dealing with concurrency becomes even more difficult nowadays because of weak memory models. In this section, we assume a sequentially consistent memory model.

Since no concurrency primitives are available, we consider two classes of functions. The first one is the low-level functions that are atomic, so we verify them as sequential code. We specified all low-level functions of the virtual memory module in ACSL (15 functions, ≈500 lines of annotated C code) and successfully proved them in FRAMA-C, with the WP plugin and the SMT solvers Z3, CVC3 and CVC4. This proof is automatic and takes about 90 seconds. This part of the case study was mostly standard and is not presented here in detail.

The second class is higher-order functions that are not atomic, so we decompose them as sequences of atomic instructions for which we *simulate* concurrency. We focus here on the most crucial function of the module that is in charge of setting mappings between pages. The rest of this section presents how we simulate parallelism by modeling the execution context of each thread and creating interleavings, introduces the main properties we want to verify, and describes their proof.

3.1   Simulating Parallel Execution

To take into account parallel execution of code by several threads and to be able to verify it in FRAMA-C, we simulate parallel execution by sequential code. Let us illustrate it for the C function set_entry given at Fig. 1. It sets a mapping (i.e. a reference) to a data page of index new into the element of index idx of the page table of index fn, that can be seen as writing new into the corresponding page table element. It has to maintain a correct number of mappings to new in the counter mappings[new] to remain resistant to attacks. In addition, special care must be taken in case of parallel execution by several threads.

At Step 1 (line 2–3 of Fig. 1), the current number of mappings to new is stored in c_n. It must be less than the maximal value to avoid an overflow, otherwise the operation is aborted (Step 2, line 4–5). At Step 3 (lines 6–8), the counter is incremented, but only after checking that its value is the same as the one previously read, using an atomic compare_and_swap (CAS) operation (note that it could have been modified several times, the only thing that matters is that it must be the same). Step 4 (lines 9–11) retrieves a pointer to the page table of index fn (using get_frame function), then atomically, again to avoid concurrent access issues, writes new into its element at index idx and stores the old value in old. Step 5 (line 12–13) checks if the old value was a mapping, that is, nonzero, and in that case Step 6 (line 14–15) atomically decrements the number of mappings to old, since one mapping has now been replaced by a new one. Notice that if new is equal to old, the same counter is first incremented and then decremented, as the mapping actually remains the same.

For the sake of verification with FRAMA-C, we simulate parallel execution of set_entry as shown in Fig. 2. Every single step is simulated by a separate simulating function (cf. comments in Fig. 1) that takes a thread number, performs the step for this thread and sets the number of the next step to be executed.

```
1  #define NOF   2048 //nb of frames          31  void EXCH_entry(uint th){      // Step 4
2  #define THD   1024 //max nb of threads      32    page_t p = get_frame(fn[th]);
3  #define MAX    256 //max nb of mappings     33    old[th] = p[idx[th]];
4  #define SIZE  1024 //size of a page          34    p[idx[th]] = new[th];
5  uint mappings[NOF];                         35    //@ghost ref[th] = old[th];
6  uint new[THD], idx[THD], fn[THD];           36    pct[th] = 5;
7  uint old[THD], c_n[THD];                    37  }
8  uint pct[THD];                              38  void test_map_old(uint th){    // Step 5
9  //@ghost uint ref[THD];                     39    pct[th] = (!old[th])? 0 : 6;
10                                             40  }
11 page_t get_frame(uint fn);                  41  void FAS_map_old(uint th){     // Step 6
12 void gen_args(uint th){        // Step 0    42    mappings[old[th]]--;
13   /* generate function args */              43    //@ghost ref[th] = 0;
14   pct[th] = 1;                              44    pct[th] = 0;
15 }                                           45  }
16 void read_map_new(uint th){ // Step 1       46  void interleave(){
17   c_n[th] = mappings[new[th]];              47    while(true){
18   pct[th] = 2;                              48      int th = choose_a_thread();
19 }                                           49
20 void test_map_new(uint th){ // Step 2       50      switch(pct[th]){
21   pct[th] = (c_n[th] < MAX)? 3 : 0;         51      case 0 : gen_args(th); break;
22 }                                           52      case 1 : read_map_new(th); break;
23 void CAS_map_new(uint th){    // Step 3     53      case 2 : test_map_new(th); break;
24   if(mappings[new[th]] == c_n[th]){         54      case 3 : CAS_map_new(th); break;
25     mappings[new[th]] = c_n[th]+1;          55      case 4 : EXCH_entry(th); break;
26     //@ghost ref[th] = new[th];             56      case 5 : test_map_old(th); break;
27     pct[th] = 4;                            57      case 6 : FAS_map_old(th); break;
28   }                                         58      }
29   else pct[th] = 0;                         59    }
30 }                                           60 }
```

Fig. 2. Simplified simulation of parallel execution for function set_entry of Fig. 1

Step 0 simply generates input values for the arguments being passed to set_entry function. When the execution reaches the end of the function, we assume it goes to Step 0 and can start again with new arguments. Error cases are treated in the same way. Parallelism is simulated by an infinite loop (lines 47–59) that, at each iteration, randomly selects a thread and makes it execute one step.

Values of input and local variables of different threads are kept in arrays (fn, idx, new, c_n, old) that associate to each thread number the value of the corresponding variable for this thread. The array pct stores the current step (program counter) of each thread. Atomic instructions such as compare_and_swap, atomic_exchange and fetch_and_sub can be simulated by standard C instructions in the corresponding simulating functions (since each simulating function is already supposed to be an atomic step in our simulation approach).

3.2   Counters of Mappings and Global Invariant

One of the key properties ensured by Anaxagoros states that the actual number of mappings to any valid page p is at most the value of the corresponding counter mappings[p]. Along with the property that this counter is under a certain limit, it ensures that the real number of mappings is also under this limit. Notice that we do not count mappings to the page 0 since, in this model, the value 0 in a page table stands for the absence of mapping.

Let Occ_a^v denote the number of occurrences of the value v in an array a (that can be also a page), and Occ^v the number of occurrences of v in all page tables in memory. We can formalize the global invariant in the following form:

$$\forall e, \mathtt{validpage}(e) \Rightarrow \mathrm{Occ}^e \leq \mathtt{mappings}[e] \leq \mathtt{MAX\_MAPPINGS}.$$

But, while this property is easily proven as maintained by the set_entry function after each instruction in monoprocess mode (as this function is not preemptible), it is not precise enough to be used in a multi-threaded context. Indeed, this invariant cannot easily ensure that before we decrement a counter (cf. Step 6 in Fig. 1) it is always greater than 0.

To keep track of values more precisely, we use an invariant in the following form:

$$\forall e, \mathtt{validpage}(e) \Rightarrow \exists k, 0 \leq k \wedge \mathrm{Occ}^e + k = \mathtt{mappings}[e] \leq \mathtt{MAX\_MAPPINGS},$$

where k can be defined as the gap between the real number of mappings to (that is, occurrences of) e in page tables and the value indicated by its counter. This gap comes from the mappings already counted but not yet effectively set (between Steps 3 and 4 in Fig. 1), and from the valid mappings already removed whose counter is not yet decremented (between Steps 4 and 6 in Fig. 1). In other words, a thread executing set_entry creates a gap of 1 for the mappings to new at Step 3, then Step 4 removes this gap and creates one for the mappings to old (if old was a valid mapping, i.e. nonzero), and finally Step 6 removes the last gap (if old was not a valid mapping, Step 5 exits the execution before this last step). Therefore, any thread can only create a gap of at most 1 for at most one mapping at the same time.

To model the gap in our simulation approach, we add a ghost array ref that associates to each thread number the entry for which the thread creates a gap, and 0 if the thread provokes no gap at the moment. This ghost array is updated by ghost statements at lines 26, 35 and 43 in Fig. 2. This allows to ensure the desired property for ref formalized by the ACSL predicate of Fig. 5.

The precise definition for k is $\mathrm{Occ}_{\mathtt{ref}}^e$, and the final global invariant is

$$\mathcal{I}: \forall e, \mathtt{validpage}(e) \Rightarrow \mathrm{Occ}^e + \mathrm{Occ}_{\mathtt{ref}}^e = \mathtt{mappings}[e] \leq \mathtt{MAX\_MAPPINGS}.$$

To express and prove assertions invoking the number of occurrences of a value e in memory pages, we define in ACSL two logic functions with related axioms to count occurrences of e over a range of indices [from,to[in one page referred by t (Fig. 3), and over a range of page tables [from,to[(Fig 4). The left bound of the range is included, while the upper bound is excluded. The label L defines the program point where the values are considered. For example, the value Occ^e at label L can be now expressed as occ_m{L}(e,0,NOF-1), where NOF denotes the number of frames.

The axioms of Fig. 3 define the following cases: the range [from,to[is empty so there are no occurrences (axiom end_occ_a), or it is non-empty and there are two cases, the rightmost element contains e, so the result is one plus the number of

```
axiomatic OccArray{
logic integer occ_a{L}(integer e, uint* t,
                       integer from, integer to);

axiom end_occ_a{L}:
\forall integer e, uint* t, integer from, to;
  from >= to ==> occ_a{L}(e,t, from, to) == 0;
axiom iter_occ_a_true{L}:
\forall integer e, uint* t, integer from, to;
  (from < to && t[to-1] == e) ==>
    occ_a{L}(e,t,from,to) == occ_a{L}(e,t,from,to-1) + 1;
axiom iter_occ_a_false{L}:
\forall integer e, uint* t, integer from, to;
  (from < to && t[to-1] != e) ==>
    occ_a{L}(e,t,from,to) == occ_a{L}(e,t,from,to-1);
}
```

Fig. 3. Simplified logic function `occ_a` counting occurrences in a subarray

```
axiomatic OccMemory{
logic integer occ_m{L}(integer e,integer from,integer to);

axiom end_occ_m{L}:
\forall integer e, integer from, to;
  from >= to ==> occ_m{L}(e, from, to) == 0;
axiom iter_occ_m_true{L}:
\forall integer e, integer from, to;
  from < to && pagetable[to-1] == true ==>
    occ_m{L}(e,from,to) == occ_a{L}(e,frame(to-1),0,SIZE)
                         + occ_m{L}(e,from,to-1);
axiom iter_occ_m_false{L}:
\forall integer e, integer from, to;
  from < to && pagetable[to-1] != true ==>
    occ_m{L}(e,from,to) ==  occ_m{L}(e,from,to-1);
}
```

Fig. 4. Simplified logic function `occ_m` counting occurrences over a range of pages

occurrences over the reduced range [from,to-1[(axiom `iter_occ_a_true`), or it does not, and this is simply the number of occurrences on the reduced range (axiom `iter_occ_a_false`). Similarly, the axioms of Fig. 4 define how to count the number of occurrences of `e` in all page tables, hence we need an additional condition: we count occurrences in a page only if it is a page table.

3.3   Proof with the Wp Plugin of Frama-C

WP [6] is a weakest precondition calculus plugin integrated to FRAMA-C. Given a C program specified in ACSL, WP generates proof obligations in the WHY3 language that can be discharged with automatic or interactive provers.

To use WP, we first write ACSL annotations to define the contract of each function as well as a few lemmas (detailed in Sec. 3.4) to help automatic provers. For the code of Fig. 2, our main goal is to ensure that for every simulating function, if the global invariant $\mathcal{I}$ holds before its execution, it is maintained after.

```
predicate pct_imply_for_thread(integer th) =
    (pct[th] <= 3 ==> ref[th] == 0         ) &&
    (pct[th] == 4 ==> ref[th] == new[th]) &&
    (pct[th] == 5 ==> ref[th] == old[th]) &&
    (pct[th] == 6 ==> ref[th] == old[th] && old[th] != 0);
```

Fig. 5. Predicate defining the link between the program counter and the array ref

Thus, $\mathcal{I}$ is formalized as an ACSL predicate that appears both in the precondition and the postcondition of the contract.

Other clauses include some routine properties, for example, bounding local variables to the range of authorized values, or defining the relationship between ref and the thread's program counter illustrated by the predicate in Fig. 5.

The verified prototype simulating parallel execution of the set_entry function contains about 610 lines of code including 530 lines of ACSL annotations. 140 lines are needed for the axioms and lemmas related to occurrence counting. We also define some predicates to express the bounds of the different simulated local variables (about 50 lines). The remaining lines contain function contracts and some assertions necessary to guide the proof. In the function contracts, 200 lines are just duplicates of the actual invariant (about 10 lines), and could be auto-generated (cf. Section 4.2).

The specification of this function, the adaptation of the invariant for the model of concurrency, and the addition of the relation between the program counter and the ghost variable, together with the determination of the assertion needed to guide the proof took about a month for a junior verification engineer.

From the function contracts, WP generates about 320 proof goals, including 190 for the interleaving loop. Except the lemmas, all generated goals are successfully discharged by Z3 (v.4.3.1) or CVC4 (v.1.3) within about 65 sec. on a QuadCore Intel Core i7-4800QM @2.7GHz. We have also investigated if the constant values used for the size of a page (SIZE), the number of frames (NOF) or the maximal number of threads (THD), have an impact on the time needed to discharge the proof obligations. An experiment shows that this time does not depend on these values. Indeed, the axiomatic definition of logical functions prevents the provers from unrolling the recursion when properties involve the number of occurrences of values in arrays.

3.4   Proof of Lemmas in Coq

To facilitate the proof of formulas using the logic functions of Fig. 3 and 4, we state simple lemmas in ACSL that express useful properties of these logic functions. For each function, we have three lemmas that express the same idea at the corresponding level: for a single page and for all page tables. The proof of these lemmas requires careful induction, paying attention to the right usage of the induction hypothesis and axioms, so they cannot be automatically proven by Z3 and CVC4. WP allows us to complete the proof of goals using COQ.

```
lemma occ_a_separable{L}:
\forall integer e, uint* t, integer from, cut, to;
  from <= cut <= to ==>
    occ_a{L}(e,t,from,to) ==
      occ_a{L}(e,t,from,cut)+occ_a{L}(e,t,cut,to);
```

Fig. 6. Example of a lemma in ACSL for counting over two sub-ranges

So we first use WP to automatically extract the goals for the lemmas from ACSL into the CoQ format, and then perform their proof interactively in CoQ.

A good example of a lemma about counting occurrences in a single array is the property shown in Fig. 6. It states that we can split a range [from,to[of page elements on which we want to count into two subranges [from,cut[and [cut,to[, count separately on each of them, and then take the sum to obtain the number of occurrences over the complete range. This is a very useful property as it allows us to partition ranges in order to keep only smaller subranges that changed between two points, saying that "all other elements did not change". The proof of this lemma consists in an induction on to compared to from and a case analysis on cut, the most complex case being proven using the axioms iter_occ_a_false and iter_occ_a_true.

Another interesting lemma says that if in a range of array elements, none of them changed between two program points, then for any value, the number of its occurrences over the range did not change. The proof is done by a simple induction.

The last lemma says that if only one array element changed to a different value between two labels, the number of occurrences decreases by 1 for the old value, increases by 1 for the new value, and all other values have the same number of occurrences. Its proof uses the two preceding lemmas. We use the first lemma to separate the subrange that changed from those that did not. Then we use the second lemma to prove that the number of occurrences did not change in the unmodified subrange, and finally prove that at the modified location, the number of occurrences respects the desired property.

For the level of all page tables (function occ_m), we define similar lemmas and use similar proof ideas. The complete proofs totalize about 300 lines of CoQ code and took about 4 days to be written by a junior verification engineer.

4   Discussion

4.1   Weak Memory Model Compliance

The approach we applied to simulate concurrent execution of the function set_entry is based on the assumption that it respects an interleaving semantics. Actually, none of modern multi-processors respect this assumption, implementing *weak* (or *relaxed*) memory models that authorize memory access reordering [10]. It can lead to "strange" behavior, like shown in Fig. 7 where "|" stands for parallel composition of threads.

```
1    R0 = R1 = [x] = [y] = 0          Authorized behaviors :
2                                      R0 = 1 /\ R1 = 1
3   // Thread 1:        Thread 2:      R0 = 0 /\ R1 = 1
4    [x] <- 1       |   [y] <- 1       R0 = 1 /\ R1 = 0
5    R0  <- [y]     |   R1  <- [x]     R0 = 0 /\ R1 = 0  (*)
```

Fig. 7. Example of a two-thread program and its possible weak memory behavior

Indeed, we cannot find an interleaving that exhibits the (*) behavior. However, it can happen on weak memory for two possible reasons. First, as in the first thread there is no dependency between the write of x (line 4) and the read of y (line 5), these instructions could be reordered by the compiler or the processor itself. A similar reordering can occur for the second thread. So the reads would be performed before the writes, setting 0 to both R0 and R1. The second reason is that memory writes are added into a store buffer before accessing the real shared memory. So each thread could register its write in its buffer and then read the global shared memory before the write of the other thread hits it, thus reading 0 instead of 1.

For a weak memory model, what is called the "Fundamental Property" by Saraswat et al. [11], is the fact that any program whose sequentially consistent executions do not have any *data race* must only have executions that are sequentially consistent. Any reasonable memory model should have this property. It allows to reason about programs in a weak memory model using sequential consistency. Of course this property should have been proved for the weak memory model, and indeed it has been done for most weak memory models (e.g. [12]).

A data race is a pair of conflicting operations, i.e. two accesses to the same memory address, one of them being a write, that are concurrent, i.e. without any temporal dependencies between them. There are several ways to formalize what it means for two events to be concurrent. One of them is to use a happens-before relation, which is a transitive, irreflexive partial order: one event happens-before another one if they belong to the same thread, and synchronizations introduce pairs in this relation for events in different threads. Concurrent events are events that are not related with a happens-before relation. Thus, if we want to analyze concurrent programs by generating interleavings, we first need to justify that these programs are race-free.

There are several methods to ensure data-race freedom. For example by automatic static analysis [13], or by respecting a programming discipline that adds to a program the guarantee that its execution will respect sequentially consistent behavior by construction [14]. One way to enforce such a programming discipline is to prove the correctness of the program with a program logic such as concurrent separation logic [15].

Actually, for the function set_entry of Fig. 1 such justification is trivial as every shared memory access is performed by an atomic routine that flushes write caches, thus introduces a synchronization: we use compare_and_swap to increment the mapping counter, atomic_exchange to swap the page entry, and fetch_and_sub to decrement the mapping counter. Thus, this program does not contain data-races.

We can also justify an (almost) total ordering on the instructions. The function call with argument passing (simulated by Step 0) comes necessarily first. Then, the next three steps (read, test and CAS) are ordered by their control or data dependencies. In the x86 model, the fence between the CAS (Step 3) and the atomic exchange (Step 4) is implicit, while in a model that does not place this fence (e.g. Power or ARM) we would need to add it explicitly. The test on `old` (Step 5) is in data-dependency with the atomic exchange (Step 4). Finally, the counter decrementation at Step 6 is control-dependent on the test at Step 5.

The read `page_t p = get_frame(fn)` is the only instruction that could be re-ordered everywhere between the function call (Step 0) and the atomic exchange (Step 4). Since it actually only depends on a static array (used in the implementation of `get_frame`) and the parameter `fn` which are never assigned after the function call, possible reorderings of this read do not change anything in the execution , so we chose to place it near the atomic exchange (cf. Step 4 in Fig. 2).

Consequently, in this case, this simulation-based approach is sound and remains valid for weak memory models. We aimed to know what can be done for concurrent programs with FRAMA-C provided that they are correctly and fully synchronized. Currently, ensuring that the programming discipline is respected is not done by a dedicated tool, a future work would be to automate this verification.

4.2   Lessons Learned, Benefits and Limitations of the Approach

This case study confirms that an obvious benefit of deductive verification based on automatic theorem provers, combined when necessary with interactive proof, is its cost efficiency. Indeed, most specified properties are proven automatically by modern SMT solvers. The possibility to easily complete unsuccessful proofs afterwards in the interactive proof assistant Coq offered by the WP plugin appears to be very convenient and allows the verification engineer to focus on really difficult properties, leaving routine proofs to automated tools. The time needed to complete interactive proofs in this study appeared to be much less than the overall effort of code specification.

Another lesson learned in this work is the ability of this approach to treat concurrent code in FRAMA-C/WP that originally does not offer this possibility. Moreover, the effort needed to model concurrent context remains reasonable against the specification effort, at least for short functions.

One could argue that this verification study remains valid only if this function is the only one able to access and modify page tables and their properties. Actually, another function, responsible for cleaning pages before changing their type, can also modify them. Its algorithm is however very simple: "for any entry, replace its value by null (we do not count references to the null page) and decrement the counter for the old value", so we can perform simulation for this part as we did for the `set_entry` function. The proof can be performed in a similar way.

This work also suggests a generic verification approach that can be summed up as follows. Given a concurrent program that respects an interleaving semantic, and a shared region of data that needs to respect a particular invariant, we analyze in isolation the group of functions that might access it. We model every local variable by an array associating to each thread the corresponding value, while the position of each thread in its execution is modeled by an array of program counters. Every single atomic action should be modeled by a separate simulating function. The interleavings are modeled by a loop that randomly executes a step of a thread. Finally, the global invariant is attached both to the loop and the functions in their contracts.

Since writing the specified simulating program by hand is error-prone, the next step is to make this approach automatic. The program transformation described above is quite simple. Its automation would require to extend ACSL in order to allow more precise specification of concurrent properties (e.g. when some part of the invariant depends on the position of some thread in its execution, cf. the argument leading to the definition of $\mathcal{I}$ in Sec. 3.2) that could be then translated into simulating function contracts and interleaving loop invariant in the simulating program.

We expect this verification approach to have a limited scalability on complete real-sized programs. Indeed, the interleaving loop is very short in our case. Treating numerous functions can require to track a great number of local variables globally, that can make the automatic proof more difficult, typically for the contract associated to the interleaving loop that would become much bigger. Nevertheless, thanks to the automation perspective of the program transformation and the cost-efficiency of deductive verification, conducting in-depth verification of critical algorithms by extracting the interesting part and analyzing it in isolation can still be a practical approach to identify potential problems.

5   Related Work

Klein et al. [3] present formal verification for seL4, a microkernel allowing devices running it to achieve the EAL7 level of the Common Criteria. Another formal verification of a microkernel is described in [16]. Both projects take into account concurrency between the processor and the devices (represented by their drivers), whereas our aim here is to treat the multi-processor concurrency of a particular function. Their verification uses interactive, machine-assisted and machine-checked proof with the theorem prover Isabelle/HOL.

Another recent work on verification of a virtual memory manager [17] relies on the fact that virtual memory managers are constructed in layers, and uses this to structure the proof by successive small refinements, making it easier to achieve and to maintain. A framework is provided to lighten the work needed for refinement and layers definition. The proof is also done interactively, with the CoQ proof assistant.

[18] presents a verification of a model of virtualization. Both implementation and verification are done in CoQ. Being relatively far from a real implementation, it allows reasoning about isolation between guests on an axiomatic basis modeling hypervisor behavior including caches and TLB. In contrast, our work is interested in low-level details of the real implementation.

Unlike the aforementioned projects, we aim to maximize the amount of automatic proof in our work.

The formal verification of a simple hypervisor [19] uses VCC, an automatic first-order logic based verifier for C. The underlying architecture is precisely modeled and represented in VCC, where the mixed-language system software is then proven correct. Unlike [3] and [16], this technique is based on automated methods. The verification consists in verifying that the invariant of the system is respected by an infinite loop of steps. While VCC is intrinsically concurrent, FRAMA-C is not. Our goal is to investigate what has to be done to achieve concurrent program proof with FRAMA-C/WP, in particular, in order to benefit from the multiple analysis plugins available in the toolset.

In [20], Alkassar et al. report on verification of the translation lookaside buffer (TLB) virtualization, a core component of modern hypervisors. As devices, like memory management units (MMUs), run in parallel with software, they require concurrent program reasoning even for single-threaded software. Their work gives a general methodology for verifying virtual device implementations, and demonstrates the verification of TLB virtualization code in VCC.

As we mentioned previously, [14] presents a programming discipline to write concurrent programs that allow only sequentially consistent behaviors. [21] points out that this method is not sufficient to deal with programs that edit their own page tables and proposes an extension to complete the programming discipline. Instead of considering a precise model of the x86 memory management unit (MMU) [20], it proposes an abstract MMU model that allows to verify that the MMU of a thread will not access page tables of another one. As we explained in Section 2, our analysis does not yet consider the MMUs nor the TLB, and could be extended with a similar approach.

Formal verification nowadays remains very expensive. [22] estimates that the verification of the seL4 microkernel took around 25 person-years, and required highly qualified experts. seL4 contains only about 10,000 lines of C code, and verification cost is about $700 per line of code.

Our present work continues the previous efforts and presents a case study on formal verification of a critical module of a hypervisor in FRAMA-C. To minimize the verification cost, we use automatic theorem proving as much as possible, complete it by interactive proof when necessary and apply a sound simulation-based approach compliant with weak memory models to deal with parallelism.

The only previous work [23] on verification of Anaxagoros presented partial formal verification, completed by test generation for unproven functions, did not consider parallel execution and did not use interactive proof.

6   Conclusion and Future Work

One of the most critical modules in the Anaxagoros hypervisor is its virtual memory mechanism. We present here the formal verification of a slightly simplified version of it for a sequentially consistent memory model. In this component, the low-level functions are atomic and we verified them as sequential functions. The ACSL specifications were automatically proven in FRAMA-C using its weakest precondition calculus plugin WP, and the proof obligations discharged by Z3, CVC3 and CVC4.

Higher level functions are no longer atomic. To deal with concurrency we simulated parallelism: the execution context of each thread and interleavings. The verification of its key part, the function that sets mappings between pages, has been performed using this technique. Again, the specifications were written in ACSL and the proofs conducted by Z3 and CVC4. However, in order to write the specifications, we introduced axiomatized functions. Basic results about these functions were needed to allow the SMT solver to conclude, but these lemmas themselves cannot be proven by automatic provers. We used the proof assistant CoQ to prove them.

This case study illustrates formal verification of a critical module in isolation, that can be still quite efficient to detect various functionality and security issues such as the recent Heartbleed bug[1] in OpenSSL. The main benefits of our approach include the possibility to conduct most proofs automatically, to reduce interactive proof to a minimum, and to take into account parallel execution.

In order to prove the actual code of Anaxagoros, we should deal with bit vectors. To avoid the need for a lot of interactive proofs, it would be interesting to design a library of basic results for bit vectors that could be then used automatically by automated provers. While the simulation approach was sufficient to deal with this case study, we do not expect it to scale to the whole hypervisor. Therefore, it would be interesting to be able to deal directly with parallelism in FRAMA-C, in particular in the case of weak memory models.

Acknowledgment. The work of the first author was partially funded by a Ph.D. grant of the French Ministry of Defence. The authors thank the FRAMA-C team for providing the tools and support. Special thanks to François Bobot and Loïc Correnson, the main author of WP, for many fruitful discussions, suggestions and advice. Many thanks to the anonymous referees for their helpful comments.

References

1. Leroy, X.: A formally verified compiler back-end. Journal of Automated Reasoning 43(4), 363–446 (2009)
2. Leroy, X.: Verified squared: does critical software deserve verified tools? In: POPL 2011. ACM (2011)
3. Klein, G., Andronick, J., Elphinstone, K., Murray, T.C., Sewell, T., Kolanski, R., Heiser, G.: Comprehensive formal verification of an OS microkernel. ACM Trans. Comput. Syst. 32(1) (2014)
4. Lemerre, M., David, V., Vidal-Naquet, G.: A communication mechanism for resource isolation. In: IIES 2009 (2009)

---

[1] http://blog.regehr.org/archives/1125

5. Lemerre, M., Ohayon, E., Chabrol, D., Jan, M., Jacques, M.B.: Method and Tools for Mixed-Criticality Real-Time Applications within PharOS. In: AMICS 2011 (2011)
6. Cuoq, P., Kirchner, F., Kosmatov, N., Prevosto, V., Signoles, J., Yakobowski, B.: Frama-C: A software analysis perspective. In: Eleftherakis, G., Hinchey, M., Holcombe, M. (eds.) SEFM 2012. LNCS, vol. 7504, pp. 233–247. Springer, Heidelberg (2012)
7. Baudin, P., Cuoq, P., Filliâtre, J.C., Marché, C., Monate, B., Moy, Y., Prevosto, V.: ACSL: ANSI/ISO C Specification Language, http://frama-c.cea.fr/acsl.html
8. The Coq Development Team: The Coq Proof Assistant, http://coq.inria.fr
9. Lemerre, M., David, V., Vidal-Naquet, G.: A dependable kernel design for resource isolation and protection. In: IIDS 2010 (2010)
10. Adve, S.V., Gharachorloo, K.: Shared memory consistency models: A tutorial. IEEE Computer 29(12), 66–76 (1996)
11. Saraswat, V.A., Jagadeesan, R., Michael, M.M., von Praun, C.: A theory of memory models. In: PPoPP, pp. 161–172. ACM (2007)
12. Boudol, G., Petri, G.: Relaxed memory models: an operational approach. In: POPL 2009 (2009)
13. Dabrowski, F., Pichardie, D.: A Certified Data Race Analysis for a Java-like Language. In: Berghofer, S., Nipkow, T., Urban, C., Wenzel, M. (eds.) TPHOLs 2009. LNCS, vol. 5674, pp. 212–227. Springer, Heidelberg (2009)
14. Cohen, E., Schirmer, B.: From total store order to sequential consistency: A practical reduction theorem. In: Kaufmann, M., Paulson, L.C. (eds.) ITP 2010. LNCS, vol. 6172, pp. 403–418. Springer, Heidelberg (2010)
15. Brookes, S.D.: A semantics for concurrent separation logic. In: Gardner, P., Yoshida, N. (eds.) CONCUR 2004. LNCS, vol. 3170, pp. 16–34. Springer, Heidelberg (2004)
16. Alkassar, E., Paul, W.J., Starostin, A., Tsyban, A.: Pervasive verification of an OS microkernel. In: Leavens, G.T., O'Hearn, P., Rajamani, S.K. (eds.) VSTTE 2010. LNCS, vol. 6217, pp. 71–85. Springer, Heidelberg (2010)
17. Vaynberg, A., Shao, Z.: Compositional verification of a baby virtual memory manager. In: Hawblitzel, C., Miller, D. (eds.) CPP 2012. LNCS, vol. 7679, pp. 143–159. Springer, Heidelberg (2012)
18. Barthe, G., Betarte, G., Campo, J.D., Chimento, J.M., Luna, C.: Formally verified implementation of an idealized model of virtualization. In: TYPES 2013(2013)
19. Alkassar, E., Hillebrand, M.A., Paul, W., Petrova, E.: Automated verification of a small hypervisor. In: Leavens, G.T., O'Hearn, P., Rajamani, S.K. (eds.) VSTTE 2010. LNCS, vol. 6217, pp. 40–54. Springer, Heidelberg (2010)
20. Alkassar, E., Cohen, E., Kovalev, M., Paul, W.J.: Verification of TLB virtualization implemented in C. In: Joshi, R., Müller, P., Podelski, A. (eds.) VSTTE 2012. LNCS, vol. 7152, pp. 209–224. Springer, Heidelberg (2012)
21. Chen, G., Cohen, E., Kovalev, M.: Store buffer reduction with MMUs: Complete paper-and-pencil proof. Technical report, Saarland University, Saarbrücken (2013)
22. Klein, G.: From a verified kernel towards verified systems. In: Ueda, K. (ed.) APLAS 2010. LNCS, vol. 6461, pp. 21–33. Springer, Heidelberg (2010)
23. Kosmatov, N., Lemerre, M., Alec, C.: A case study on verification of a cloud hypervisor by proof and structural testing. In: Seidl, M., Tillmann, N. (eds.) TAP 2014. LNCS, vol. 8570, pp. 158–164. Springer, Heidelberg (2014)

Intra-procedural Optimization
of the Numerical Accuracy of Programs

Nasrine Damouche[1,2(✉)], Matthieu Martel[1,2], and Alexandre Chapoutot[3]

[1] University of Perpignan Via Domitia, DALI Team-Project, Perpignan, France
[2] University of Montpellier II and CNRS, LIRMM, UMR, 5506, Montpellier, France
[3] ENSTA ParisTech, Palaiseau, France
nasrine.damouche@univ-perp.fr

Abstract. Numerical programs performing floating-point computations
are very sensitive to the way formulas are written. These last years, several techniques have been proposed concerning the transformation of
arithmetic expressions in order to improve their accuracy and, in this article, we go one step further by automatically transforming larger pieces
of code containing assignments and control structures. We define a set
of transformation rules allowing the generation, under certain conditions
and in polynomial time, of larger expressions by performing limited formal computations, possibly among several iterations of a loop. These
larger expressions are better suited to improve the numerical accuracy
of the target variable. We use abstract interpretation-based static analysis techniques to over-approximate the roundoff errors in programs and
during the transformation of expressions. A prototype has been implemented and experimental results are presented concerning classical numerical algorithm analysis and algorithm for embedded systems.

Keywords: Program transformation · Floating-point numbers · Static
analysis · IEEE754 standard

1 Introduction

These last years, as the complexity of the floating-point computations [1,23] carried out in embedded systems and elsewhere increased, numerical accuracy has
become a more and more sensitive subject in computer science. Due to the important impact of accuracy on the reliability of embedded systems, many industries
and companies encourage research to validate [5,10,14,13] and improve [16,21]
their software in order to avoid failures and eventually disasters in aeronautics,
automotives, robotics, etc.

In this article, we focus on the transformation [6,8] of intra-procedural pieces
of code in order to automatically improve their accuracy. For automatic transformation of single arithmetic expressions, several techniques have already been
proposed. We can mention [16] which introduces a new intermediary representation (IR) that manipulates in a single data structure a large set of equivalent
arithmetic expressions. This IR, called APEG [16,17] for Abstract Program Expression Graphs, succeeds to reduce the complexity of the transformation in

© Springer International Publishing Switzerland 2015
M. Núñez and M. Güdemann (Eds.): FMICS 2015, LNCS 9128, pp. 31–46, 2015.
DOI: 10.1007/978-3-319-19458-5_3

polynomial size and time. Starting from this state of the art, we aim at going a step further by automatically transforming larger pieces of code. Our interest is to transform automatically sequences of commands that contain assignments and control structures in order to improve their numerical accuracy. This transformation consists in optimizing a target variable with respect to some given ranges for the input variables of the program. Accuracy bounds are computed by abstract interpretation [7] techniques for the floating-point arithmetic [13].

We start by motivating our work with a case study concerning an algorithm frequently used in robotics for odometry. We show how to rewrite it into another program which is more accurate numerically but equivalent semantically (in the sense that both programs compute the same function in exact arithmetic). This transformation operates by simplifying and developing the expressions and inlining them into other expressions. This allows one to generate new formulas and to reduce the number of operations in programs. We also rewrite the codes by unfolding the body of loops, manner to have more computations on a single iteration. The transformation of the odometry program and the rewriting rules used to automatically rewrite codes are the main contribution of this article. These rules are presented as sequents containing conditions under which the transformation may be applied without breaking the semantical equivalence between the source and target programs. In addition, these rules are applied deterministically, yielding a polynomial time transformation. This work is completed by experimental results involving the transformation of codes coming from multiple domains of science.

This article is organized as follows. Section 2 is consecrated to our case study about odometry and Section 3 introduces related work concerning the analysis and transformation of arithmetic expressions. In Section 4, we give the set of transformation rules for commands together with the conditions required to conserve the semantical equivalence of programs. Section 5 presents experimental results and shows various experimentations obtained using our prototype. Finally, Section 6 concludes.

2   Case Study: Odometry

In this section, we are interested in an example widely used in embedded systems, taken from robotics and whose code is given in Figure 2. It concerns the computation of the position of a two wheeled robot by odometry. Given the instantaneous rotation speeds s_l and s_r of the left and right wheels, we aim at computing the position of the robot in a cartesian space (x, y). Let C be the circumference of the wheels of the robot and L the length of its axle (see Figure 1). We assume that s_l and s_r are updated by the system, by side-effect. The computation of the position is given by

$$x(t+1) = x(t) + \Delta d(t+1) \times \cos\left(\theta(t) + \frac{\Delta\theta(t+1)}{2}\right), \tag{1}$$

$$y(t+1) = y(t) + \Delta d(t+1) \times \sin\left(\theta(t) + \frac{\Delta\theta(t+1)}{2}\right), \tag{2}$$

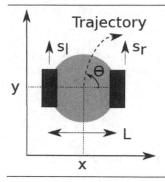

It	x (Odometry₁)	x (Odometry₂)
1	8.681698	8.444116
2	17.038230	16.589474
3	24.756744	24.147995
4	31.549016	30.852965
5	37.163761	36.469708
6	41.398951	40.806275
7	44.114126	43.724118
8	45.242707	45.148775

Fig. 1. Left: Parameters of the two-wheeled robot. Right: Values of x in Odometry₁ and Odometry₂ at the first iterations.

```
sl = [0.52,0.53]; sr = 0.785398163397;
theta = 0.0; t = 0.0; x = 0.0; y = 0.0; inv_l = 0.1; c = 12.34;
while (t < 100.0) do {
  delta_dl = (c * sl) ;
  delta_dr = (c * sr) ;
  delta_d = ((delta_dl + delta_dr) * 0.5) ;
  delta_theta = ((delta_dr - delta_dl) * inv_l) ;
  arg = (theta + (delta_theta * 0.5)) ;
  cos = (1.0 - ((arg * arg) * 0.5)) + ((((arg * arg)* arg)* arg) / 24.0);
  x = (x + (delta_d * cos)) ;
  sin = (arg - (((arg * arg)* arg)/6.0))
      + (((((arg * arg)* arg)* arg)* arg)/120.0);
  y = (y + (delta_d * sin));
  theta = (theta + delta_theta) ;
  t = (t + 0.1) }
```

Fig. 2. Listing of the initial Odometry program.

with

$$\theta(t+1) = \theta(t) + \Delta\theta(t), \quad \Delta d(t) = \big(\Delta d_r(t) + \Delta d_l(t)\big) \times 0.5, \qquad (3)$$

$$\Delta\theta(t) = \big(\Delta d_r(t) - \Delta d_l(t)\big) \times \frac{1}{L}, \quad \Delta d_l(t) = s_l(t) \times C, \quad \Delta d_r(t) = s_r(t) \times C. \qquad (4)$$

In equations (1) to (4), $\theta(t)$ is the direction of the robot, $d(t)$ is the elementary movement of the robot at time t and $d_l(t)$, $d_r(t)$ are the elementary movements of the left and right wheels. We assume that cos and sin, not computed by a library, are obtained by a Taylor Series development as shown in Equation (5).

$$\cos(x) \approx 1 - \frac{x^2}{2!} + \frac{x^4}{4!}, \qquad \sin(y) \approx x - \frac{x^3}{3!} + \frac{x^5}{5!}. \qquad (5)$$

We aim at rewriting the initial program Odometry₁ into a better program Odometry₂ which improves the numerical accuracy of the computed position.

```
sl = [0.52,0.53] ; theta = 0.0 ; y = 0.0 ; x = 0.0 ; t = 0.0 ;
while (t < 100.0) do {
  TMP_6 = (0.1 * (0.5 * (9.691813336318980 - (12.34 * sl)))) ;
  TMP_23 = ((theta + (((9.691813336318980 - (sl * 12.34)) * 0.1) * 0.5))
          * (theta + (((9.691813336318980 - (sl * 12.34)) * 0.1) * 0.5))) ;
  TMP_25 = ((theta + TMP_6)*(theta + TMP_6))*(theta
          + (((9.691813336318980 - (sl * 12.34)) * 0.1) * 0.5)) ;
  TMP_26 = (theta + TMP_6) ;
  x = ((0.5 * (((1.0 - (TMP_23 * 0.5)) + ((TMP_25 * TMP_26) / 24.0))
      * ((12.34 * sl) + 9.691813336318980)))) + x) ;
  TMP_27 = ((TMP_26 * TMP_26) * (theta + (((9.691813336318980
          - (sl * 12.34)) * 0.1) * 0.5))) ;
  TMP_29 = (((TMP_26 * TMP_26) * TMP_26) * (theta + (((9.691813336318980
          - (sl * 12.34)) * 0.1) * 0.5))) ;
  y = (((9.691813336318980 + (12.34 * sl)) * (((TMP_26 - (TMP_27 / 6.0))
      + ((TMP_29 * TMP_26) / 120.0)) * 0.5)) + y) ;
  theta = (theta + (0.1 * (9.691813336318980 - (12.34 * sl)))) ;
  t = t + 0.1 ; }
```

Fig. 3. Listing of the transformed Odometry program.

The speed of the left wheel is assumed to belong to an interval of $[0.52, 0.53]$ radians per second. Our prototype develops and simplifies the expressions δ_d, cos and sin and then inline them within the loop, in x and y. In addition, it creates new intermediary variables, called TMP, in order to avoid to have too large expressions. This process makes it possible to produce constant formulas and, in the same time, reduces the number of operations in the program. Furthermore, the resulting expressions are rewritten using existing techniques for the transformation of arithmetic expressions based on the use of Abstract Program Equivalence Graphs [16,21]. We obtain the final program given in Figure 3. If we compare the resulting values x_1 and x_2 of Odometry$_1$ and Odometry$_2$, we observe that the transformation leads to a significant difference in the accuracy of the program as shown in Figure 1. The results show an important difference on the third or even on the second digit of the decimal values of the result. The difference in the computed trajectory (x, y) of the robot is shown in Figure 4.

3   Transformation of Expressions

This section introduces related work concerning the static analysis of the accuracy and the transformation of expressions. The syntax of expressions is

$$\text{Expr} \quad \ni \quad e ::= id \mid cst \mid e + e \mid e - e \mid e \times e \mid e \div e. \tag{6}$$

Expressions in Equation (6) are made of variables $id \in \mathcal{V}$ with $\mathcal{V}$ a finite set, constants $cst \in \mathbb{F}$ with $\mathbb{F}$ the set of floating-point numbers and of the four elementary operations $+$, $-$, $\times$ and $\div$.

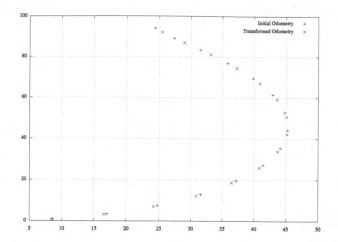

Fig. 4. Computed trajectories by the initial and the transformed odometry programs

3.1 Static Analysis of the Accuracy

In order to compute safe bounds on the accuracy of arithmetic expressions, an abstract value is defined by a pair of intervals representing the range of the floating-point value seen by the program and the range of the error i.e., the difference between the floating-point and the exact value [22]. An abstract value is denoted by $(x^\sharp, \mu^\sharp) \in E^\sharp$ where $x^\sharp$ is the interval of values of the input and $\mu^\sharp$ is the interval of errors on the input. It abstracts a set of concrete values $\{(x, \mu) \; : \; x \in x^\sharp \text{ and } \mu \in \mu^\sharp\}$ by intervals in a component-wise way. When working with arithmetic expressions, the propagation of roundoff errors is given by the following semantics. We denote by $\uparrow_\circ^\sharp (x^\sharp)$ the approximation of an interval with real bounds by an interval with floating-point bounds. The bounds are rounded to the nearest to reflect the fact this first interval corresponds to the approximated values seen by the program.

$$\uparrow_\circ^\sharp [(\underline{x}, \overline{x})] = [\uparrow_\circ (\underline{x}), \uparrow_\circ (\overline{x})] \tag{7}$$

where $\uparrow_\circ (x)$ denotes the rounding of x in the IEEE754 Standard [1] rounding mode $\circ \in \{-\infty, +\infty, 0, \sim\}$.

Conversely, the function $\downarrow_\circ^\sharp$ abstracts the concrete function $\downarrow_\circ$ which computes the exact error $\downarrow_\circ (x) = x - \uparrow_\circ (x)$. That means that for all $x \in [\underline{x}, \overline{x}]$ we have $\downarrow_\circ (x) \in \downarrow_\circ^\sharp [(\underline{x}, \overline{x})]$. We have

$$\downarrow_\circ^\sharp [(\underline{x}, \overline{x})] = [-y, y] \quad \text{with} \quad y = \begin{cases} \frac{1}{2}\mathtt{ulp}\big(max(|\underline{x}|, |\overline{x}|)\big) & \text{if} \quad \circ = \sim \\ \mathtt{ulp}\big(max(|\underline{x}|, |\overline{x}|)\big) & \text{otherwise.} \end{cases} \tag{8}$$

Note that the *unit in the last place* $\mathtt{ulp}(x)$ is the weight of the least significant digit of the floating-point number x. A sample of the elementary operations over $E^\sharp$ are defined in equations (9) to (10), for other operations see [22].

$$(x_1^\sharp, \mu_1^\sharp) + (x_2^\sharp, \mu_2^\sharp) = (\uparrow_\circ^\sharp (x_1^\sharp + x_2^\sharp), \mu_1^\sharp + \mu_2^\sharp + \downarrow_\circ^\sharp (x_1^\sharp + x_2^\sharp)), \tag{9}$$

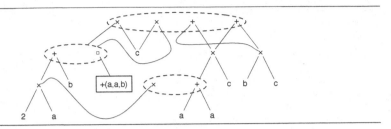

Fig. 5. APEG for the expression $e = ((a + a) \overset{\cdot}{+} b) \times c$

$$(x_1^\sharp, \mu_1^\sharp) \times (x_2^\sharp, \mu_{2,}^{\sharp}) = (\uparrow_\circ^\sharp (x_1^\sharp \times x_2^\sharp), x_2^\sharp \times \mu_1^\sharp + x_1^\sharp \times \mu_2^\sharp + \mu_1^\sharp \times \mu_2^\sharp + \downarrow_\circ^\sharp (x_1^\sharp \times x_2^\sharp)). \tag{10}$$

For example, if we add two numbers, the errors on the operands are added to the error due to the roundoff of the result. For the product, the semantic consists of the development of $(x_1^\sharp + \mu_1^\sharp) \times (x_2^\sharp + \mu_2^\sharp)$.

Note that more efficient abstract domains exist, e.g., [5,14,13] as well as complementary techniques [3,4]. Let us also mention that other methods exist to transform, synthesize or repair arithmetic expressions in the integer or fixed arithmetic [12,20].

3.2 Accuracy Improvement of Expressions

Here, we briefly present former work [16,21,24] to semantically transform arithmetic expressions using Abstract Program Expression Graph (APEG). This data structure remains in polynomial size while dealing with an exponential number of equivalent expressions. To prevent any combinatorial problem, APEGs hold in abstraction boxes many equivalent expressions up to associativity and commutativity. A box containing n operands can represent up to $1 \times 3 \times 5 ... \times (2n-3)$ possible formulas. In order to build large APEGs, two algorithms are used (propagation and expansion algorithms). The first one searches recursively in the APEG where a symmetric binary operator is repeated and introduces abstraction boxes. Then, the second algorithm finds a homogeneous part and inserts a polynomial number of boxes. In order to add new shapes of expressions in an APEG, one propagates recursively subtractions and divisions into the concerned operands, propagate products, and factorizing common factors. Finally, an accurate formula is searched among all the equivalent formulas represented in an APEG using the abstract semantics of Section 3.1.

Example 1. An example of APEG is given in Figure 5. When an equivalence class (denoted by a dotted ellipse) contains many APEGs $p_1, \ldots, p_n$ then one of the p_i, $1 \leq i \leq n$, may be selected in order to build an expression. A box $\boxed{*(p_1, \ldots, p_n)}$ represents any parsing of the expression $p_1 * \ldots * p_n$. For instance, the APEG p of Figure 5 represents all the following expressions:

$$\mathcal{A}(p) = \left\{ \begin{array}{l} ((a + a) + b) \times c, \ ((a + b) + a) \times c, \ ((b + a) + a) \times c, \\ ((2 \times a) + b) \times c, \ c \times ((a + a) + b), \ c \times ((a + b) + a), \\ c \times ((b + a) + a), \ c \times ((2 \times a) + b), \ (a + a) \times c + b \times c, \\ (2 \times a) \times c + b \times c, \ b \times c + (a + a) \times c, \ b \times c + (2 \times a) \times c \end{array} \right\}. \tag{11}$$

For this example, the last step of transformation would consist of evaluating all the expressions in $\mathcal{A}(p)$ with the abstract semantics of Section 3.1 in order to select the most accurate one.   □

4   Transformation of Commands

In this section, we introduce the formal rules used to transform intra-procedural pieces of code. The syntax of commands is given in Equation (12). It corresponds to the core of an imperative language.

$$\text{Com} \quad \ni \quad c ::= id = e \mid c_1 \; ; \; c_2 \mid \text{if}_\Phi \; e \; \text{then} \; c_1 \; \text{else} \; c_2 \mid \text{while}_\Phi \; e \; \text{do} \; c \mid \text{nop}. \quad (12)$$

The command language is made of assignments $id = e$, sequences of instructions, the void operation nop, a conditional statement $\text{if}_\Phi \; b \; \text{then} \; c_1 \; \text{else} \; c_2$ and a loop statement $\text{while}_\Phi \; b \; \text{do} \; c$. Programs are assumed to be written in SSA form [9] and the Φ variables attached to conditional and while statements denote their sets of Φ nodes. The Φ node $\Phi(id, id_1, id_2)$ is understood as an assignment of form $id = \Phi(id_1, id_2)$ where $\Phi(id_1, id_2) = id_1$ or $\Phi(id_1, id_2) = id_2$ depending on the control flow. The construction of Φ-nodes is classical and is left to the reader [2,9].

The transformation defined by the rules of Figure 6 uses states of the form $\langle c, \delta, C, \nu, \beta \rangle$ where:

- c is a command, as defined in Equation (12),
- δ is an environment $\delta : \mathcal{V} \to \text{Expr}$ which maps variables to expressions. Intuitively, this environment, fed by Rule $(A1)$, records the expressions assigned to variables in order to inline them later on in larger expressions thanks to Rule $(A2)$,
- $C \in \text{Ctx}$ is a single hole context [15] defined in Equation (13). It records the program englobing the current expression to be transformed and which is intended to fit in the hole denoted by $[]$.

$$\text{Ctx} \ni C ::= [] \mid id = e \mid C_1 \; ; C_2 \mid \text{if}_\Phi \; e \; \text{then} \; C_1 \; \text{else} \; C_2 \mid \text{while}_\Phi \; e \; \text{do} \; C \mid \text{nop}. \quad (13)$$

- let $\nu \in \mathcal{V}$ denote the reference variable that we aim at optimizing.
- let $\beta \subseteq \mathcal{V}$ be a list of assigned variables that should not be removed from the source program. Initially, $\beta = \{\nu\}$, i.e., the target variable ν must not be removed. The set β is modified by rules $(C1), (C2), (C4)$ and $(W2)$.

Let us now describe the rules of Figure 6. Rule $(A1)$ allows one to discard an assignment $id = e$ by memorizing in δ the formal expression e in order to inline it later, in a larger expression. The function $Var(e)$ returns the set of variables occurring in the expression e while $Dom(\delta)$ denotes the domain of definition of δ. When using Rule $(A1)$, to get a semantically equivalent program, we must respect some restrictions. The first one requires that the variables occurring in e do not meet the domain of δ (otherwise we would break some data dependencies). Finally, Rule $(A1)$ requires that the transformation is done if the identifier id does not belong to the set β of variables which may not be removed.

$$\frac{\delta' = \delta[id \mapsto e] \quad Var(e) \cap Dom(\delta) = \emptyset \quad id \notin \beta}{\langle id = e, \delta, C, \nu, \beta \rangle \to \langle \mathsf{nop}, \delta', \beta \rangle} \quad (A1)$$

$$\frac{e' = \delta(e) \quad \sigma^\sharp = [\![C[c]]\!]^\sharp \iota^\sharp \quad \langle e', \sigma^\sharp \rangle \leadsto e''}{\langle id = e, \delta, C, \nu, \beta \rangle \to \langle id = e'', \delta, \beta \rangle} \quad (A2)$$

$$\frac{\langle c, \delta, C, \nu, \beta \rangle \to \langle c', \delta', \beta' \rangle}{\langle \mathsf{nop} \; ; \; c, \delta, C, \nu, \beta \rangle \to \langle c', \delta', \beta' \rangle} \quad (S1)$$

$$\frac{\langle c, \delta, C, \nu, \beta \rangle \to \langle c', \delta', \beta' \rangle}{\langle c \; ; \; \mathsf{nop}, \delta, C, \nu, \beta \rangle \to \langle c', \delta', \beta' \rangle} \quad (S2)$$

$$\frac{\langle c_1, \delta, C[[]; c_2], \nu, \beta \rangle \to^* \langle c_1', \delta', \beta' \rangle \quad C' = C[c_1'; []]}{\langle c_2, \delta', C', \nu, \beta' \rangle \to^* \langle c_2', \delta'', \beta'' \rangle}{\langle c_1 \; ; \; c_2, \delta, C, \nu, \beta \rangle \to \langle c_1' \; ; \; c_2', \delta'', \beta'' \rangle} \quad (S3)$$

$$\frac{\sigma^\sharp = [\![C[\mathsf{if}_\Phi \; e \; \mathsf{then} \; c_1 \; \mathsf{else} \; c_2]]\!]^\sharp \iota^\sharp \quad [\![e]\!]^\sharp \sigma^\sharp = \mathsf{true}}{\beta' = \beta \cup Assigned(c_1) \quad \langle c_1, \delta, C, \nu, \beta' \rangle \to^* \langle c_1', \delta', \beta'' \rangle}{\langle \mathsf{if}_\Phi \; e \; \mathsf{then} \; c_1 \; \mathsf{else} \; c_2, \delta, C, \nu, \beta \rangle \to \langle c_1', \delta', \beta'' \rangle} \quad (C1)$$

$$\frac{\sigma^\sharp = [\![C[\mathsf{if}_\Phi \; e \; \mathsf{then} \; c_1 \; \mathsf{else} \; c_2]]\!]^\sharp \iota^\sharp \quad [\![e]\!]^\sharp \sigma^\sharp = \mathsf{false}}{\beta' = \beta \cup Assigned(c_2) \quad \langle c_2, \delta, C, \nu, \beta' \rangle \to^* \langle c_2', \delta', \beta'' \rangle}{\langle \mathsf{if}_\Phi \; e \; \mathsf{then} \; c_1 \; \mathsf{else} \; c_2, \delta, C, \nu, \beta \rangle \to \langle c_2', \delta', \beta'' \rangle} \quad (C2)$$

$$\frac{Var(e) \cap Dom(\delta) = \emptyset \quad \beta' = \beta \cup Assigned(c_1) \cup Assigned(c_2)}{\langle c_1, \delta, C, \nu, \beta' \rangle \to^* \langle c_1', \delta_1, \beta_1 \rangle \quad \langle c_2, \delta, C, \nu, \beta' \rangle \to^* \langle c_2', \delta_2, \beta_2 \rangle \delta' = \delta_1 \cup \delta_2}{\langle \mathsf{if}_\Phi \; e \; \mathsf{then} \; c_1 \; \mathsf{else} \; c_2, \delta, C, \nu, \beta \rangle \to \langle \mathsf{if}_\Phi \; e \; \mathsf{then} \; c_1' \; \mathsf{else} \; c_2', \delta', \beta' \rangle} \quad (C3)$$

$$\frac{V = Var(e) \quad c' = AddDefs(V, \delta) \quad \delta' = \delta_{|Dom(\delta) \setminus V}}{\langle c'; \mathsf{if}_\Phi \; e \; \mathsf{then} \; c_1 \; \mathsf{else} \; c_2, \delta', C, \nu, \beta \cup V \rangle \to^* \langle c'', \delta', \beta' \rangle}{\langle \mathsf{if}_\Phi \; e \; \mathsf{then} \; c_1 \; \mathsf{else} \; c_2, \delta, C, \nu, \beta \rangle \to \langle c'', \delta', \beta' \rangle} \quad (C4)$$

$$\frac{Var(e) \cap Dom(\delta) = \emptyset \quad C' = C[\mathsf{while}_\Phi \; e \; \mathsf{do} \; []] \quad \langle c, \delta, C', \nu, \beta \rangle \to^* \langle c', \delta', \beta' \rangle}{\langle \mathsf{while}_\Phi \; e \; \mathsf{do} \; c, \delta, C, \nu, \beta \rangle \to \langle \mathsf{while}_\Phi \; e \; \mathsf{do} \; c', \delta', \beta' \rangle} \quad (W1)$$

$$\frac{V = Var(e) \cup Var(\Phi) \quad c' = AddDefs(V, \delta) \quad \delta' = \delta_{|Dom(\delta) \setminus V}}{\langle c'; \mathsf{while}_\Phi \; e \; \mathsf{do} \; c, \delta', C, \nu, \beta \cup V \rangle \to^* \langle c'', \delta', \beta' \rangle}{\langle \mathsf{while}_\Phi \; e \; \mathsf{do} \; c, \delta, C, \nu, \beta \rangle \to \langle c'', \delta', \beta' \rangle} \quad (W2)$$

Fig. 6. Transformation rules used to improve the accuracy of programs

Rule $(A2)$ offers an alternative way of processing assignments, when the conditions of Rule $(A1)$ are not fulfilled. The action of substituting the variables of e by their definitions in δ is denoted by $\delta(e)$. Rule $(A2)$ transforms the expression $e' = \delta(e)$ into an expression e'' by a call $\langle e', \sigma^\sharp \rangle \leadsto e''$ to the tool based on APEGs and which transforms expressions, as described in Section 3. The abstract environment $\sigma^\sharp : \mathcal{V} \to E^\sharp$ used for this transformation results from a static analysis using the domain $E^\sharp$ also introduced in Section 3. As mentioned earlier, in Rule $(A2)$, $\iota^\sharp$ denotes the user-defined initial environment which binds the free variables of the program to intervals. For example, in Section 2, the variable $\mathtt{s1}$ is set to $[0.52, 0.53]$ in $\iota^\sharp$. The program given to the static analyzer is $C[c]$, i.e. the program obtained by inserting the command c into the context C. Accordingly to these notations, the expression e' is transformed into an expression e'' by $\langle e', \sigma^\sharp \rangle \leadsto e''$ which transforms the source expression into a more accurate one for the environment σ. In our implementation this corresponds to a call to the APEG tool [16,17]. The returned expression e'' is inserted in the new assignment $id = e''$.

Remark that by inlining expressions in variables when transforming programs, we create large formulas. In our implementation, in order to facilitate their manipulation, we slice these formulas at a defined level of the syntactic tree on several sub-expressions and we assign them to intermediary variables. Finally, we inject these new assignments into the main program.

Example 2. To explain the use of rules $(A1)$ and $(A2)$, let us consider the example of Equation (14) in which three variables x, y and z are assigned. In this example, ν consists of the variable z that we aim to optimize and $a = 0.1$, $b = 0.01$, $c = 0.001$ and $d = 0.0001$ are constants.

$$\langle \mathsf{x} = \mathsf{a} + \mathsf{b}; \mathsf{y} = \mathsf{c} + \mathsf{d}; \mathsf{z} = \mathsf{x} + \mathsf{y}, \ \delta, [], \nu, \emptyset \rangle$$
$$\xrightarrow[(A1)]{} \langle \mathsf{nop}; \mathsf{y} = \mathsf{c} + \mathsf{d}; \mathsf{z} = \mathsf{x} + \mathsf{y}, \delta' = \delta[\mathsf{x} \mapsto \mathsf{a} + \mathsf{b}], [], \nu, \emptyset \rangle$$
$$\xrightarrow[(A1)]{} \langle \mathsf{nop}; \mathsf{nop}; \mathsf{z} = \mathsf{x} + \mathsf{y}, \delta'' = \delta'[\mathsf{y} \mapsto \mathsf{c} + \mathsf{d}], [], \nu, \emptyset \rangle \qquad (14)$$
$$\xrightarrow[(A2)]{} \langle \mathsf{nop}; \mathsf{nop}; \mathsf{z} = ((\mathsf{d} + \mathsf{c}) + \mathsf{b}) + \mathsf{a}, \delta'', [], \nu, \emptyset \rangle$$

In Equation (14), initially, the environment δ is empty. If we apply the first rule $(A1)$, we may remove the variable x and memorize it in δ. So, the line corresponding to the variable discarded is replaced by nop and the new environment is $\delta = [x \mapsto a+b]$. We then repeat the same process by using $(A1)$ on the variable y. For the last step, we may not apply $(A1)$ to z because the condition is not satisfied $(z = \nu)$. Then we use $(A2)$, we substitute x and y by their value in δ and we transform the expression.   □

Rules $(S1)$ to $(S3)$ deal with sequences. Rules $(S1)$ and $(S2)$ are special cases enabling the system to discard the nop statements while the general rule for sequences is $(S3)$. The first command c_1 is transformed into c_1' in the current environment δ, C, ν and β and a new context C' is built which inserts c_1' inside C. Then c_2 is transformed into c_2' using the context $C[c_1'; []]$, the formal environments δ' and the list β' resulting from the transformation of c_1. Finally, the state $\langle c_1' \ ; \ c_2', \delta'', \beta'' \rangle$ is returned.

Rules $(C1)$ to $(C4)$ concern conditionals. The first two rules correspond to a partial evaluation of the program [18], when the test evaluates to true or false in the environment $\sigma^\sharp$ which is computed by static analysis, $\sigma^\sharp = [\![C[\mathrm{if}_\Phi \ e \ \mathrm{then} \ c_1 \ \mathrm{else} \ c_2]\!]^\sharp \iota^\sharp$. In rules $(C1)$ and $(C2)$, the conditional is replaced by the branch c_1 or c_2. In this case, the reference variable ν does not appear necessarily in c_1 or c_2 but the variables assigned in these branches are used in the Φ nodes. Consequently, they may not be removed from c_1 or c_2 and we have to transform the command with $\beta' = \beta \cup Assigned(c_i)$, for $i = 1$ or 2. Here, $Assigned(c)$ denotes the set of identifiers assigned in the command c.

Example 3. Let us consider the program, in SSA form.

$$x_1 = 0; \text{ if}_{\Phi(x_3,x_1,x_2)} \text{ cond then } x_2 = a + b \text{ else } y_1 = c + d; \nu = x_3. \qquad (15)$$

Depending on the value of the test, we transform this program into

$$\begin{cases} \nu = a + b & \text{if } cond, \\ \nu = 0 & \text{if } \neg cond. \end{cases} \qquad (16)$$

However, when *cond* is *true*, without the blacklist, Rule $(A1)$ would store x_2 in δ during the transformation of the branch. The Φ-node $\Phi(x_3,x_1,x_2)$ would be wrong. $\qquad\square$

Rule $(C3)$ is the general rule for conditionals. The then and else branches are transformed, assuming that the variables of the condition do not meet the variables of δ. As for rules $(C1)$ and $(C2)$, the variables assigned in the branches have to be added to β and the environment δ' resulting from the transformation joins the environments of both branches (note that thanks to the SSA form, the variables assigned in both branches are distinct). Finally, Rule $(C4)$ is used when the conditions for Rule $(C3)$ do not hold. In this case, $Var(e) \cap Dom(\delta) \neq \emptyset$ and we need to reinsert the common variables into the source code. Let $Var(e)$ be the list of variables occuring in the expression e. Firstly, a new command c' corresponding to sequences of assignments of the form $id = \delta(id)$ is built for all the variables $id \in Var(e)$ by $AddDefs(V, \delta)$ and, secondly, the variables of $Var(e)$ are removed from the domain of δ, yielding δ'. The resulting command is the command c'' obtained by transforming c'; if$_\Phi$ e then c_1 else c_2 with δ' and $\beta \cup Var(e)$.

Example 4. Let us take another example to explain the Rules $(C3)$ and $(C4)$.

$$x_1 = 0; \text{ if}_{\Phi(y_3,y_1,y_2)} x_1 > 1 \text{ then } y_1 = x_1 + 2; \text{ else } y_2 = x_1 - 1; \nu = y_3. \qquad (17)$$

By rule $(A1)$, x_1 is stored in δ. Then, we transform recursively the new program

$$\text{if}_{\Phi(y_3,y_1,y_2)} x_1 > 1 \text{ then } y_1 = x_1 + 2; \text{ else } y_2 = x_1 - 1; \nu = y_3. \qquad (18)$$

This program is semantically incorrect since the test is undefined. However, $Var(e) \cap Dom(\delta) \neq \emptyset$ and we cannot apply Rule $(C3)$. Instead Rule $(C4)$ is used to reinject the statements $x_1 = 0$ in the program and to add x_1 to the blacklist β in order to avoid an infinite loop in the transformation. $\qquad\square$

The last two rules $(W1)$ and $(W2)$ are for the while statements. Rule $(W1)$ makes it possible to transform the body c of the loop assuming that the variables of the condition e have not been stored in δ. In this case, c is optimized in the context $C[\text{while}_\Phi \ e \ \text{do} \ []]$ where C is the context of the loop. Rule $(W2)$ first builds the list $V = Var(e) \cup Var(\Phi)$ where $Var(\Phi)$ is the list of variables read and written in the Φ nodes of the loop. The set V is used to achieve two tasks: firstly, it is used to build a new command c' corresponding to the sequence of assignments $id = \delta(id)$, for all $id \in V$ (as for Rule $(C4)$). Secondly, the variables of V are removed from the domain of δ and added to β. The resulting command is the command c'' obtained by transforming c'; while$_\Phi$ e do c with δ' and $\beta \cup V$.

We end this section with complexity considerations. At each step of the transformation of a program p, only one rule of Figure 6 can be selected. Consequently, the transformation would be linear in the size n of the program if we would not reinject assignments. However, a given assignment cannot be removed twice, so the transformation is quadratic. Finally, the entire transformation of a program p is repeated until nothing changes, that is at most n times. Hence, the global complexity for the transformation of a program of size n is $\mathcal{O}(n^3)$.

5   Experimental Results

In this section, we evaluate the efficiency of the transformation presented in Section 4 through a series of experiments using our prototype. We have chosen several algorithms coming from various application fields (avionics, chemistry, mathematics, etc.) In each case, we compare the numerical accuracy of the sample program with the accuracy of the generated code. The upper bounds on the rounding errors are computed as in Section 3.1. We optimize the value of the reference variable, named ν in Section 4. The original and the transformed codes are shown in Figure 9 and their accuracy is given in Figure 8. This transformation is achieved almost instantaneously (less than one second) on a standard laptop (Intel Core i5 with 4 Go memory).

5.1   Control Algorithms

In this section, we consider three classical algorithms from control theory, namely a PID Controller, Lead-Lag Compensator and the running example of Odometry.

PID. The PID Controller [6] is an algorithm widely used in embedded and critical systems, like aeronautic and avionic systems. It keeps a physical parameter at a specific value known as the *setpoint*. In other words, it tries to correct a measure by maintaining it at a defined value. To compute this correction, the controller incorporates three terms: the integral term i and the derivative term d of the error, as well as a proportional error term p. The error e is the difference between the setpoint c and the measure m. We have $e = c - m$,

$$p = k_p \times e, \quad i = i + k_i \times e \times dt \quad \text{and} \quad d = k_d \times (e - e_{old}) \times \frac{1}{dt}.$$

The weighted sum of these terms contributes to improve the reactivity, the robustness and the speed of the program. We assume that $m \in [4.5, 9.0]$.

Lead-Lag System. A second test has been performed on a dynamical system illustrated in Figure 7. This system includes a single mass and a single spring and is governed by an automatically synthesized controller [11] which tries to move the mass from the initial position y to the desired one y_d. The main variables in this algorithm are: x_c consists of the discrete-time controller state, y_c is the bounded output tracking error and u presents the mechanical system output. We assume that the position y of the mass m $\in [2.1, 17.9]$.

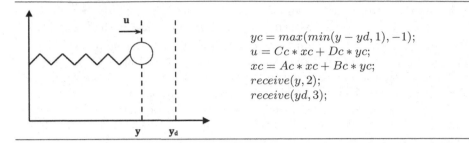

$$yc = max(min(y - yd, 1), -1);$$
$$u = Cc * xc + Dc * yc;$$
$$xc = Ac * xc + Bc * yc;$$
$$receive(y, 2);$$
$$receive(yd, 3);$$

Fig. 7. Left: The lead-lag system of section 5.1. Right: Parameters of the system.

5.2 Numerical Algorithms

Runge-Kutta Methods. This example concerns Runge-Kutta methods [19]. We consider an order 2 and an order 4 method. They are employed to solve the equation describing the dynamics of a chemical reaction $A + B \to C$. The order 2 method integrates a differential equation whose solution is $y(t)$. The second order method uses the derivative on the starting point x_i in order to find the intermediary point. Then, it uses this intermediary point to have the next value of the function. The derivative of $y(x)$ at the points x_i and $x_i + \frac{h}{2}$ are

$$k_1 = (\frac{dy}{dx}) = h \times f(x_i, y_i) \quad \text{and} \quad k_2 = (\frac{dy}{dx}) = h \times f(x_i + \frac{h}{2}, y_i + \frac{h}{2}). \quad (19)$$

Finally, we have $y_{i+1} = y_i + k_2 + O(h^3)$. We assume that initially, $y_0 \in [-10.1, 10.1]$. For the order 4 method, we obtain as final formula:

$$y_{i+1} = y_1 + \frac{1}{6}[k_1 + 2 \times k_2 + 2 \times k_3 + k_4] \times h. \quad (20)$$

The Trapezoidal Rule. This example concerns with an algorithm for the trapezoidal rule [19], well known in numerical analysis to approximate the definite integral $\int_a^b f(x) \, dx$. This trapezoidal rule works by approximating the region between x and $x + h$ under the graph of the function f(x) as a trapezoid and calculates its area. Here, we compute the integral $\int_{0.25}^{5000} g(x) dx$ of some function:

Code	Initial Error	New Error	s	%
PID	$0.453945103062736 \times 10^{-14}$	$0.440585745442590 \times 10^{-14}$	5	2.94
Odometry	$0.106578865995068 \times 10^{-10}$	$0.837389354639250 \times 10^{-11}$	5	21.43
RK2	$0.750448486755706 \times 10^{-7}$	$0.658915054553695 \times 10^{-7}$	5	12.19
RK4	$0.201827996912328 \times 10^{-1}$	$0.169791306481639 \times 10^{-1}$	5	15.87
Lead-Lag	$0.294150262243136 \times 10^{-11}$	$0.235435212105148 \times 10^{-11}$	10	19.96
Trapezoid	$0.536291684923368 \times 10^{-9}$	$0.488971110442931 \times 10^{-9}$	20	8.82

Fig. 8. Initial and new errors on the examples programs of Section 5

$$g(x) = \frac{u}{0.7x^3 - 0.6x^2 + 0.9x - 0.2}. \tag{21}$$

We assume that u is a user defined parameter in the range $[1.11, 2.22]$. In addition, we have unfold the body of the loop twice to obtain better results with our prototype.

Code	Source Code	Optimized Code

PID $\nu = m$	`m = [4.5,9.0]; ki = 0.69006; kp = 9.4514;`
	`kd = 2.8454; t = 0.0; i = 0.0; c = 5.0;`
	`dt = 0.2; invdt = 5.0; eold = 0.0;`
	
	`while (t < 20.0) do {`
	`  e = c - m ;`
	`  p = kp * e ;`
	`  i =  i + ((ki * dt) * e) ;`
	`  d = ((kd * invdt) * (e - eold)) ;`
	`  r = ((p + i) + d) ;`
	`  m = m + (0.01 * r) ;`
	`  eold = e ; t = t + dt }`
		`m = [4.5,9.0]; t = 0.0; eold = 0.0;`
		`i = 0.0;`
		
		`while (t < 20.0) do {`
		`  i = (i + (0.138012 * (5.0 - m))) ;`
		`  eold = (5.0 - m) ;`
		`  m = (m + (0.01 * (((((5.0 - m)`
		`    * 9.4514) + i) + (((5.0 - m)`
		`    - eold) * 14.227)))) ;`
		`  t = t + 0.2 }`

Lead-Lag $\nu = xc_1$	`y = [2.1,17.9] ; xc0 = 0.0 ; xc1 = 0.0`
	`; t = 0.0 ; yd = 5.0; Ac00 = 0.499;`
	`Ac01 = -0.05; Ac10 = 0.01; Ac11 = 1.0;`
	`Bc0 = 1.0; Bc1 = 0.0; Cc0 = 564.48;`
	`Cc1 = 0.0; Dc = -1280.0;`
	
	`while (t < 5.0) do {`
	`  yc = (y - yd) ;`
	`  if (yc < -1.0) then {yc = -1.0} ;`
	`  if (1.0 < yc) then {yc = 1.0} ;`
	`  xc0 = (Ac00*xc0)+(Ac01*xc1)+(Bc0*yc);`
	`  xc1 = (Ac10*xc0)+(Ac11*xc1)+(Bc1*yc);`
	`  u = (Cc0* xc0)+(Cc1* xc1)+(Dc* yc);`
	`  t = (t + 0.1) }`
		`y = [2.1,17.9]; t = 0.0; xc1 = 0.0;`
		`xc0 = 0.0;`
		
		`while (t < 5.0) do {`
		`  yc = (-5.0+y) ;`
		`  if (yc < -1.0) then {yc = -1.0} ;`
		`  if (1.0< yc) then {yc = 1.0} ;`
		`  u = (((564.48*xc0)+(0.0*xc1))`
		`    +(-1280.0*yc)) ;`
		`  xc0 = ((((-0.05*xc1)+(1.0*yc))`
		`    +(0.499*xc0)) ;`
		`  xc1 = ((((0.01*xc0)+(0.0*yc))`
		`    +(1.0*xc1)) ;`
		`  t = (t + 0.1) }`

Fig. 9. Original and optimized codes for the examples of Section 5.1

5.3   Results

Our prototype consists of an implementation of the rules described in Section 4 coupled to the APEG tool for the transformation of expressions. For the demonstration of its efficiency, we evaluate through it the examples described previously in this section. Our tool takes as input an initial program and intervals for some parameters and returns another program mathematically equivalent but numerically more accurate as long as the parameters remain in the given ranges. We compare then the initial error and the new error of each program before and after transformation. Figures 9 and 10 show the source and target program as well as how much our tool improves the numerical accuracy of these programs. For example, if we take the case of **odometry**, we observe that we optimize it by 21.43%. If we compare the implementation of Runge-Kutta method, we remark that the order four methods is improved of 15.87%. The Lead-Lag system is optimized by 19.96%. The improvement of the error is given in Figure 8, where

Code	Source Code	Optimized Code
| RK4<br>$\nu$ =<br>$y_{n+1}$ | ```
yn = [-10.1,10.1]; t = 0.0; k = 1.2;
c = 100.1; h = 0.1;
while (t < 1.) do {
    k1 = (k*(c-yn))*(c-yn) ;
    k2 = (k*(c-(yn+((0.5*h)*k1))))
        *(c-(yn+((0.5*h)*k1)));
    k3 = (k*(c-(yn+((0.5*h)*k2))))
        *(c-(yn+((0.5*h)*k2)));
    k4 = (k*(c-(yn+(h*k3))))
        *(c-(yn+(h*k3)));
    yn+1 = yn+((1/6*h)*(((k1+(2.0*k2))
        +(2.0*k3))+k4));
    t = (t + h) }
``` | ```
yn = [-10.1,10.1] ; t = 0.0 ;
while (t < 1.0) do {
    TMP_7 = (1.2 * (100.099 - yn)) ;
    TMP_8 = (100.099 - yn) ;
    TMP_13 = (1.2*(100.099-(yn+(0.05*((1.2
        * (100.099-(yn+(0.05*(TMP_7*TMP_8)))))
        * (100.099-(yn+((1.2*TMP_8)
        * (100.099-yn))))))))) ;
    TMP_14 = (100.099-(yn+(0.05*((1.2*(100.099
        - (yn+(0.05*(TMP_7*TMP_8)))))*(100.099
        - (yn+(0.05*TMP_8)*(100.099-yn));
    TMP_18 = (yn+(0.05*((1.2*(100.099-(yn+(0.05
        * (TMP_7*TMP_8)))))*(100.099-(yn+(0.05
        * ((1.2*TMP_8)*(100.099-yn)))))))));
    TMP_28 = ((1.2*(100.099-(yn+(0.05*(TMP_7
        * TMP_8)))))*(100.099-(yn+(0.05*((1.2
        * TMP_8)*(100.099-yn))))));
    TMP_38 = ((TMP_14*TMP_13)*0.1) + yn ;
    TMP_40 = 0.1*((1.2*TMP_14)*(100.099-TMP_18));
    yn_plus_1 = (yn+(0.016666667*(((((TMP_7*TMP_8)
        + (2.0*TMP_28))+(2.0*(TMP_13*TMP_14)))
        +((1.2*(100.099-TMP_38))*(100.099-(yn
        +TMP_40)))))); + [...] ;
    t = (t + 0.1) }
``` |
| Trapeze<br>$\nu$ = r | ```
u = [1.11, 2.22]; a = 0.25; b = 5000.0;
n = 25.0 ; r = 0.0 ; xa = 0.25 ;
h = ((b - a) / n) ;
while (xa < 5000.0) do {
    xb = (xa + h) ;
    if (xb > 5000.) then { xb = 5000.0 };
    gxa = (u / (((((0.7 * xa) * xa) * xa)
        - ((0.6*xa) * xa))+(0.9*xa))-0.2));
    gxb = (u / (((((0.7 * xb) * xb) * xb)
        - ((0.6*xb)* xb))+(0.9*xb))-0.2));
    r = (r + (((gxb + gxa) * 0.5) * h));
    xa = (xa + h) }
``` | ```
u = [1.11, 2.22] xa = 0.25; r = 0.0;
while (xa < 5000.) do {
    TMP_1 = (0.7 * (xa + 199.99)) ;
    TMP_2 = (xa + 199.99) ;
    TMP_9 = (((((0.7*xa)*xa)*xa)-((0.6*xa)*xa))
        + (0.9*xa));
    TMP_11= (((199.99+xa)*(TMP_2*TMP_1))-((199.99
        + xa)*(TMP_2*0.6)))+(0.9*TMP_2);
    r = (r +((((u/(TMP_11-0.2))+(u/(TMP_9-0.2)))
        * 0.5)*199.99));
    xa = (xa + 199.99)
}
``` |

Fig. 10. Original and optimized codes for the examples of Section 5.2

s is the slice size, i.e., the parameter defining at which height of the syntactic tree we cut the expressions.

6   Conclusion

In our search for automatic transformation of programs, we have developed a tool which rewrites codes to improve their numerical accuracy. More precisely, we have shown how to perform intra-procedural rewritings of commands and how to transform assignments. In the rules of Figure 6, correctness conditions have been defined to guarantee that the dependencies are respected and to ensure the correctness of the rewritings in conditions and loops. In order to validate our tool, we have chosen a set of representative programs taken from various fields of science and engineering. We have automatically tuned them and analyzed their accuracy before and after transformation.

The further research directions consists of generalizing our techniques to other kinds of programming patterns like for loops, arrays and, specially functions in order to obtain an intra-procedural program transformation with function refactoring and specialization with respect to the values of arguments. Another extension looks at extending our approach to optimize several reference variables simultaneously. A difficulty is that the optimization of one variable may decrease the accuracy of other variables. Compromises have to be done. Finally, our transformation relies on a static analysis of the source codes. Indeed, we select the optimized program by using the abstract semantics in Section 3.1, we compute certified error bounds which can be over-approximated. We would like to improve it by using more accurate relational domains in order to obtain finer error bounds completed by statistical results on the actual accuracy gains on concrete executions.

References

1. ANSI/IEEE. IEEE Standard for Binary Floating-Point Arithmetic. SIAM (2008)
2. Appel, A.-W.: Modern Compiler Implementation in ML. Cambridge University Press (1998)
3. Barr, E.-T., Vo, T., Le, V., Su, Z.: Automatic detection of floating-point exceptions. In: Symposium on Principles of Programming Languages, POPL 2013, pp. 549–560. ACM (2013)
4. Benz, F., Hildebrandt, A., Hack, S.: A dynamic program analysis to find floating-point accuracy problems. In: Programming Language Design and Implementation, PLDI 2012, pp. 453–462. ACM (2012)
5. Bertrane, J., Cousot, P., Cousot, R., Feret, F., Mauborgne, L., Miné, A., Rival, X.: Static analysis by abstract interpretation of embedded critical software. ACM SIGSOFT Software Engineering Notes 36(1), 1–8 (2011)
6. Chapoutot, A., Damouche, N., Martel, M.: Automatic transformation of a PID controller. In: International Workshop on Numerical Software Verification (2014)
7. Cousot, P., Cousot, R.: Abstract interpretation: A unified lattice model for static analysis of programs by construction or approximation of fixpoints. In: Principles of Programming Languages, pp. 238–252 (1977)
8. Cousout, P., Cousot, R.: Systematic design of program transformation frameworks by abstract interpretation. In: Principles of Programming Languages, pp. 178–190. ACM (2002)
9. Cytron, R., Gershbein, R.: Efficient accomodation of may-alias information in SSA form. In: Programming Language Design and Implementation (PLDI), pp. 36–45. ACM (1993)
10. Delmas, D., Goubault, E., Putot, S., Souyris, J., Tekkal, K., Védrine, F.: Towards an industrial use of FLUCTUAT on safety-critical avionics software. In: Alpuente, M., Cook, B., Joubert, C. (eds.) FMICS 2009. LNCS, vol. 5825, pp. 53–69. Springer, Heidelberg (2009)
11. Feron, E.: From control systems to control software. IEEE Control Systems Magazine 30(6), 50–71 (2010)
12. Gao, X., Bayliss, S., Constantinides, G.-A.: SOAP: structural optimization of arithmetic expressions for high-level synthesis. In: Field-Programmable Technology, FPT, pp. 112–119. IEEE (2013)
13. Goubault, E.: Static analysis by abstract interpretation of numerical programs and systems, and FLUCTUAT. In: Logozzo, F., Fähndrich, M. (eds.) SAS 2013. LNCS, vol. 7935, pp. 1–3. Springer, Heidelberg (2013)

14. Goubault, E., Putot, S.: Static analysis of finite precision computations. In: Jhala, R., Schmidt, D. (eds.) VMCAI 2011. LNCS, vol. 6538, pp. 232–247. Springer, Heidelberg (2011)
15. Hankin, E.: Lambda Calculi A Guide For Computer Scientists. Clarendon Press, Oxford (1994)
16. Ioualalen, A., Martel, M.: A new abstract domain for the representation of mathematically equivalent expressions. In: Miné, A., Schmidt, D. (eds.) SAS 2012. LNCS, vol. 7460, pp. 75–93. Springer, Heidelberg (2012)
17. Ioualalen, A., Martel, M.: Synthesizing accurate floating-point formulas. In: Application-Specific Systems, Architectures and Processors, ASAP, pp. 113–116 (2013)
18. Jones, N.-D.: An introduction to partial evaluation. ACM Computing Surveys 28(3), 480–503 (1996)
19. Kendall, A.: An Introduction to Numerical Analysis. John Wiley & Sons (1989)
20. Logozzo, F., Ball, T.: Modular and verified automatic program repair. In: Conference on Object-Oriented Programming, Systems, Languages, and Applications, OOPSLA, pp. 133–146. ACM (2012)
21. Martel, M.: Accurate evaluation of arithmetic expressions (invited talk). Electr. Notes Theor. Comput. Sci. 287, 3–16 (2012)
22. Martel, M.: Semantics of roundoff error propagation in finite precision calculations. Higher-Order and Symbolic Computation 19(1), 7–30 (2006)
23. Muller, J.-M., Brisebarre, N., De Dinechin, F., Jeannerod, C.-P., Lefèvre, V., Melquiond, G., Revol, N., Stehlé, D., Torres, S.: Handbook of Floating-Point Arithmetic. Birkhäuser (2010)
24. Tate, R., Stepp, M., Tatlock, Z., Lerner, S.: Equality saturation: A new approach to optimization. Logical Methods in Computer Science 7(1) (2011)

Formal Analysis and Testing of Real-Time Automotive Systems Using UPPAAL Tools

Jin Hyun Kim[1]([⊠]), Kim G. Larsen[2], Brian Nielsen[2], Marius Mikučionis[2],
and Petur Olsen[2]

[1] INRIA/IRISA, Rennes Cedex, France
jin-hyun.kim@inria.fr
[2] Department of Computer Science, Aalborg University, Aalborg, Denmark

Abstract. Many safety-concerned standards and regulations for real-time embedded systems, e.g., ISO 26262 for automotive electric/electronic systems, recommends the use of formal techniques to achieve the required safety level. This paper presents a method for formal analysis of real-time embedded systems. The method allows properties to be statistically checked early and quickly with high confidence, and may also produce a formal proof when required. This environment exploits UPPAAL tools consisting of a symbolic model checker (UPPAAL MC) and a statistical model checker (UPPAAL SMC), and a model-based testing environment (UPPAAL Yggdrasil), all of which are based on a formal model in timed automata. We demonstrate our method on an industrial case, an automotive Turn Indicator System, showing how the design of the system at the early phase of system development may be efficiently checked against the defined system requirements.

1 Introduction

Embedded and cyber-physical systems must implement an ever increasing number of increasingly advanced and intelligent features that are distributed onto a larger number of hardware and software components. A typical example is found in automotive systems where not only novel individual electric/electronic components are supplied at a rapid race, but also advanced driver assistance systems are added—heading towards autonomous driving systems in the foreseeable future. Unfortunately existing industrial verification and validation techniques (primarily testing based) does not scale with this increase in functionality and system environments and usage scenarios. Consequently it is getting more difficult and costly to guarantee their correctness, including safety and reliability.

For this reason, standards such as ISO 26262 [13] and IEC 615087 [12] for automotive electric/electronic systems require the analysis of the components and system corresponding to their Safety Integrity Level (SIL). In particular, ISO 26262 recommends the use of formal analysis techniques for development of a component that should meet the highest SIL standard.

The research presented in this paper has been partially supported by EU Artemis Projects CRAFTERS and MBAT.

© Springer International Publishing Switzerland 2015
M. Núñez and M. Güdemann (Eds.): FMICS 2015, LNCS 9128, pp. 47–61, 2015.
DOI: 10.1007/978-3-319-19458-5_4

Techniques, methods, and tools for model-based development and formal analysis have progressed significantly during the last decade. In addition to advancing classical modeling, symbolic model-checking (MC), and simulation techniques also novel techniques like statistical model-checking (SMC) and model-based test generation (MBT) have emerged.

This paper presents our recent progress in developing a method and supporting integrated tool environment for formal modeling and analysis of critical embedded real-time systems. Our work is based on the UPPAAL tool which has unique support for analysis of real-time properties of behavioral models described as extended timed automata (TA). It offers a graphical editor for UP-PAAL timed automata and accompanying a symbol and concrete state animator, a symbolic model checker (UPPAAL MC), an SMC facility (UPPAAL SMC), and a model-based test generator (UPPAAL Yggdrasil). SMC and Yggdrasil are novel additions that recently have been integrated into the main tool and made accessible via their own tab in the GUI, making them easier to access for industrial users. Through this integration and our method for using them together, formal analysis becomes easier to use by industrial engineers and fits better to their way of working where simulations, visualizations, and light verification are used intensively in the beginning prior to time consuming exhaustive analysis.

As requirements are formalized and as the first models are constructed, our method emphasize early and quick verification by exploiting SMC to generate and visualize system runs and perform sound probabilistic verification of the required properties. Once the formulated properties and models have stabilized, critical requirements may be fully model-checked. When the model has been thoroughly analyzed, it may be used for system construction, test-case generation, or additional performance analysis or design space exploration.

The main contributions of the paper are

- We outline a method describing how our integrated UPPAAL environment for model-based analysis and testing may be efficiently employed for early formal analysis of embedded real-time systems.
- We illustrate the analysis method and UPPAAL tool environment on an automotive subsystem, a Turn Indication System.

The rest the paper is organized as follows: Section 2 introduces MC, SMC and MBT using the UPPAAL environment. Section 3 presents our analysis method. Sections 4, 5, and 6.1 introduce the case study and apply our method and tools. Finally, Section 7 compares with related work, and Section 8 concludes.

2   Background

2.1   UPPAAL **Symbolic Model Checking**

UPPAAL symbolic model checking (MC) uses symbolic reachability analysis to check whether a system model (represented as a network of timed automata[3]) satisfies temporal properties (represented as Timed-CTL (Computational Tree Logic)).

UPPAAL MC explores all states of a system in a model to determine if a property to be analyzed is satisfied by the model all the time. If any undesirable state is identified, UPPAAL MC generates a trace i.e. a counterexample that leads the system to the undesirable state, so that the model can be corrected based on the counterexample.

2.2 UPPAAL Statistical Model Checking

UPPAAL SMC (SMC) [10] exploits the statistics theory to give a statistically quantitative proof that a system satisfies a specified property [7][9]. The SMC returns the analysis results in less time relative to the symbolic model checking technique and produces the result even though it does not guarantee a property of a system with the 100% certainty [15].

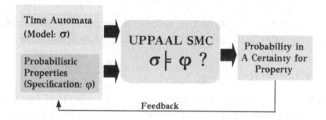

Fig. 1. UPPAAL SMC

As shown in Fig. 1, UPPAAL SMC reads a network of timed automata and probabilistic property specification, similar with CTL but including a probability quantifier, as inputs. Differently from MC, SMC returns a probability regarding a property in a specific certainty. UPPAAL SMC supports five different analysis methods: *Hypothesis testing, Probability evaluation, Probability comparison, Expected value*, and *Simulations*. Below we use N to denote a natural number, P to denote a probability, and *expr* to denote an expression.

- **Statistical Evaluation:** SMC estimates the probability of the state property being satisfied. For instance, the following query computes a probability confidence interval where simulation time is limited up to N time units:

$$Pr[<=N](<> \ expr) \tag{1}$$

- **Hypothesis Testing:** SMC checks if the property is satisfied within a certain probability. For instance, the query

$$Pr[<=N](<> \ expr) >= P \tag{2}$$

asks whether the probability of meeting the state property "expr" is greater than or equal to given probability value P while checking (simulating) the system under analysis up to N time units. This type of query yields less information than an estimated confidence interval above, but it is more efficient as it requires fewer simulation runs.

– **Statistical Comparison:** SMC compares the satisfaction possibilities over two properties. For instance, the query can be in the form of

$$\text{Pr[<=N\_1](<> expr1) >= Pr[<=N\_2](<> expr2)} \tag{3}$$

– **Expected Value:** SMC computes the maximal or minimal value of a certain variable while checking the system. For instance, the query

$$\text{E[<=N; M](min: expr)} \tag{4}$$

asks what the average of the minimal values of the variable in "expr" is when simulating the system up to N time units by M rounds.

– **Simulations:** SMC simulates a system multiple times and computes trajectories of specified expressions over time. Query

$$\text{simulate M [<=N] \{expr\_1, expr\_2\}} \tag{5}$$

requires UPPAAL SMC to show the values of "expr_1," and "expr_2" expressions over time when running M simulations up to N time units.

2.3   UPPAAL **Yggdrasil**

UPPAAL Yggdrasil is an off-line test case generator. The tool takes models created in UPPAAL and creates a suite of test cases that aim at covering all syntactic transitions in the model (edge coverage). By using a special syntax within UPPAAL that allows user defined code to be output upon transition execution, and location entry or exit, the generated test suite can take the format of a test script in any desired language that can be used as input to test execution engines. The user defined code can both be used for stimuli generation and for checking functions defining the test oracle.

The test generation procedure progresses in three phases, each adding to the coverage achieved in preceding *phases*. For *phase one*, the test engineer may (optionally) formulate requirements based test-purposes for which a test case must be generated. The test purposes are formulated as UPPAAL reachability properties. During *phase two* the procedure automatically generates random test cases to improve coverage. The user must set a parameter defining the desired test case length. As a heuristic for when to stop generating test cases, the procedure continues until a new test case does not add new coverage. Finally, *phase three* tries to create a single test case for each of the coverage items that might still be uncovered. For phases one and three the algorithm uses the normal UPPAAL search and for phase two a random depth-first search algorithm is used.

Yggdrasil generates symbolic test cases in terms of UPPAAL traces. Concrete test cases are created by annotating the model with test code. Since these annotation are plain text, any test execution back-end can be used.

Yggdrasil has been integrated into the UPPAAL GUI. A new tab has been made available with the features of Yggdrasil. A list of generated traces is shown. Selecting a trace will show the statistics of that trace. Double clicking a trace will load it in the simulator for inspection. The statistics for the total coverage can be viewed and uncovered edges are available.

3 Formal Analysis Framework

In this paper, a real-time embedded software system is analyzed by our methodology using the UPPAAL environment, as depicted in Fig. 2. A model of the system is created as a network of timed automata (TA) model using the UPPAAL environment. A network of TA consists of multiple TA templates, each of which is instantiated as a concurrent process. A concurrent process may communicate using 1-to-1 synchronization channels or broadcast channels [5][6]. In UPPAAL, timed automata are enriched with C-syntax like data declarations, expressions, and user defined functions.

We propose to first analyze a TA model by using UPPAAL SMC w.r.t. properties that have been formulated based on the requirements of the system. By simulation, a model is validated to see if it produces correct outputs corresponding to inputs. For this purpose, a SMC query in the form in (5) is used. Also at the initial stage, a number of basic consistency checks should be performed to exclude modeling mistakes, including checking that all edges or locations are in fact reachable, (absence of "dead-code"), and absence of dead- and time-locks.

Second, we statistically verify the model w.r.t. a property. For this purpose, a SMC query in one of the forms in (2), (1), and (3) that requires SMC to estimate a probability that a property is satisfied by a created model. A SMC query in the form of (4) may also be used to find an average of maximum or minimum values of a variable while a model runs up to a specific time limit by a specific number of rounds.

For some properties, we propose to use UPPAAL MC to obtain the 100% certainty of the analysis. Compared to UPPAAL SMC, UPPAAL MC usually consumes much more time and memory for verification, since the underlying state-space grows exponentially in the number system components. Thus, MC should be applied to a model after a considerably high probability regarding a property of the model is obtained by UPPAAL SMC.

Finally, the verified model may be used in UPPAAL Yggdrasil to generate test cases that can be executed on an actual system implementation to check that its behavior conforms to that specified by the model. If faults are found in

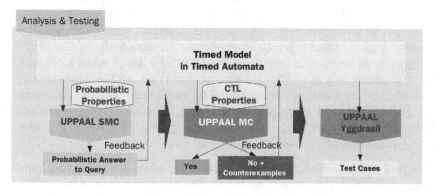

Fig. 2. Analysis adopting UPPAAL environment

the requirements or design which require the models to be updated, test case generation can be re-run automatically to generate new test cases.

3.1   Analysis Properties

Basically, **safety** [17] and **liveness** [16,17] are representative properties for reactive systems in formal analysis. In addition, in terms of timing, this paper divides timing requirements into two classes: function-oriented and non-function-oriented timing requirements. Similarly to functional requirements, a function-oriented timing requirement should be implemented. A non-function-oriented timing requirement should satisfied by the implemented system in actual operation. The following are the TI system properties to be analyzed:

- **Functional Property (FP)** relates to the functionality that the development system implements.
- **Timing Property (TP)** is relevant for timing requirement. A timing property can be either of function-oriented TP (**FTP**) or non-function-oriented TP (**NFTP**). This paper focuses on function-oriented timing property which should be satisfied in terms of functionality.
- **Universal Properties (UP)** refers to a property that the system should satisfy in general, such as absence of deadlocks.

4   Turn Indication Systems

A Turn Indicator (TI) subsystem is an automotive component that signals a car's direction when the driver intends to change the direction. The subsystem is also used to indicate emergency situations and the status of door lock/unlock operations. The TI-Case is an industrial case study raised in the EU Artemis Project MBAT. While it superficially viewed appears to be a basic component, it is a central part of the cars functionality and safety. It furthermore has several timing requirements and interactions that warrants formal analysis.

4.1   Functional Requirements

Fig. 3(a) shows a typical turn indicator system. The TI lamps are divided into two groups: left and right indicator groups. Indication lamps in the same group are supposed to flash synchronously. The commands for turn indications are instantiated by one of three external components: *Steering Column Switch* (SCS), an *Emergency (warning) Control Switch*, and a *Door lock/unlock Control Unit*.

Fig. 3(b) shows a typical SCS generating two types of TI command signals: normal TI and Tip blinking commands. The two commands are distinguished by the position of lever in SCS and by a specific timing requirement within TI control system. Using these external components, TI systems provides the following 4 main and 2 auxiliary functions as follows:

- **Normal turn indication mode** flashes the same group of turn indicator lamps synchronously according to a direction commanded by the driver. Then, the other group of indicator lamps must be silent.

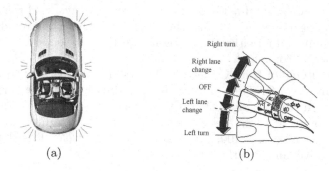

(a)   (b)

Fig. 3. General turn indicator and Steering Column Switch (SCS)

- **Tip blinking mode** differs from the normal turn indication mode in that it has a limited flashing count, e.g. 3 flashes.
- **Emergency mode** is initiated by the driver so that all indicator lamps flash simultaneously as long as the mode is on. Emergency mode prevails the other modes so that any turn indication mode under operation is ignored or delayed when operating in Emergency mode.
- **Door lock/unlock flashing mode** also operates all indicator lamps to indicate the status of door lock/unlock operation status.
- TI system should be able to detect a defect in turn indicator lamps.
- TI system is used to flash indicator lamps by a ON/OFF duty cycle. The duty cycle is the percentage of one period in which a signal is active. A period is the time it takes for a signal to complete one on-and-off cycle.

4.2   Analysis Properties

We identified and categorized the following central properties:

Functional Properties (FP):

- (**FP.001.**) Normal TI Flashing: If a normal TI command is triggered by the driver, the corresponding left or right TI lamp groups shall flash according to a specific On/Off duty cycle, then the other group shall be silent.
- (**FP.002.**) Tip Blinking: If a Tip blinking is commanded for a direction, either left or right, the corresponding TI group lamps exclusively shall flash only 3 times.
- (**FP.003.**) Emergency Flashing: When the emergency command is triggered, all TI lamps shall flash until the emergency command is canceled. If a normal or Tip blinking mode is in operation, it shall be ignored, and when the emergency command is canceled, the previous TI mode which might have operated before the emergency mode may be recovered.

Timing Properties (TP):

- (**FTP.001.**) TI command delay for Tip Blinking: TI requirements specifies that Tip blinking command is distinguished from a normal TI command by a timing requirement. If a TI command is fired by driver and the command signal disappears within 800 ms, then the command is regarded as a Tip blinking command for either left or right direction. Otherwise, it is regarded as a normal TI command.

- **(FTP.002.)** On-Off Duty Cycle: The TI system are operated to flash indication lamps by a ON/OFF duty cycle. The duty cycle is the percentage of one period in which a signal is active. A period is the time it takes for a signal to complete an on-and-off cycle. As a formula, a duty cycle may be expressed as: $D = \frac{T}{P} \times 100$, where D is the duty cycle, T is the time the signal is active, and P is the total period of the signal.

Universal Properties (UP):

- **(UP.001.)** TI system should be free from deadlock, i.e., the TI system should always be responsive to legal TI commands.

Safety Properties (SP):

- **(SP.001.)** TI system that only one group of TI lamps of the commanded direction should flash when a normal and Tip blinking modes are engaged. The opposite group of TI lamps must not flash then as long as the emergency mode is not engaged.

Liveness Properties (LP):

- **(LP.001.)** The TI system must eventually switch on/off one of the indicator lamp groups on the direction designated by the driver's flash command.

5   Formal Modeling of TI system

We capture a functional model of the TI system using UPPAAL TA with user defined functions to do most of the data-manipulations.

5.1   Data and Event Flows of TA Models for TI System

The UPPAAL model consists of nine timed automata (TA) templates which are instantiated as individual processes. In addition, it consists of 10 channels, 11 clocks, 25 global discrete data variables and 5 local ones. We decompose the functionality of the TI system by considering the independence of computation and communication. The processes communicate by processing driver's turn indication commands and signaling control indication lamps.

Figure 4 shows the data and event flow between UPPAAL processes. Solid arrows indicate data flow, and dotted arrows indicate event (channel) signaling. The UPPAAL TI model consists of 3 main parts: **Input**, **Control**, and **Output**, of which each is composed of multiple TA processes.

Figure 5 shows the TA process template and user-defined functions of the TI command handler, which responds to TI commands from SCS and determines which TI mode to activate. The TI system initiates the handler when the

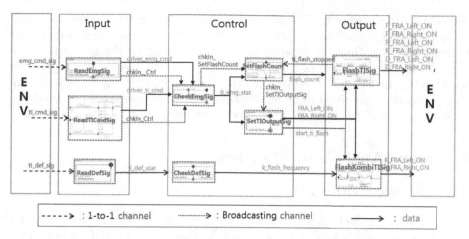

Fig. 4. Overview of the TI-system model: UPPAAL processes, and data and event flows

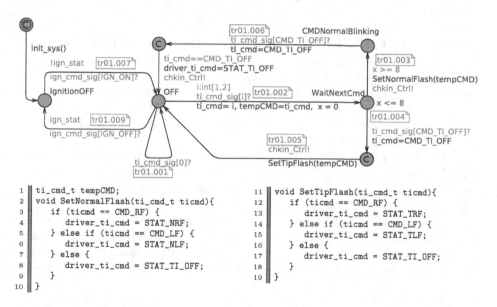

```
 1   ti_cmd_t tempCMD;                        11   void SetTipFlash(ti_cmd_t ticmd){
 2   void SetNormalFlash(ti_cmd_t ticmd){     12      if (ticmd == CMD_RF) {
 3      if (ticmd == CMD_RF) {                13         driver_ti_cmd = STAT_TRF;
 4         driver_ti_cmd = STAT_NRF;          14      } else if (ticmd == CMD_LF) {
 5      } else if (ticmd == CMD_LF) {         15         driver_ti_cmd = STAT_TLF;
 6         driver_ti_cmd = STAT_NLF;          16      } else {
 7      } else {                              17         driver_ti_cmd = STAT_TI_OFF;
 8         driver_ti_cmd = STAT_TI_OFF;       18      }
 9      }                                     19   }
10   }
```

Fig. 5. ReadTICmdSig: TI command handler UPPAAL TA and declarations

event ign_cmd_sig[GIN_ON] is received. Then, the TI command handler is able to respond to three TI commands from SCS, ti_cmd_sig[i], where $0 \leq i \leq 2$ and 0 stands for CMD_TI_OFF, 1 for CMD_TI_RF, and 2 for CMD_TI_LF. If either ti_cmd_sig[CMD_TI_RF] or ti_cmd_sig[CMD_TI_LF] arrive, the TI command handler moves to location WaitNextCmd. At this location, the TI command handler makes the decision whether the TI command is a Tip blinking or a normal blinking for each input direction: If the event ti_cmd_sig[CMD_TI_OFF] arrives within 8 time units (one time unit is 100 ms), the TI system shall operate a Tip blinking according to the input direction. Otherwise, it enters a normal flashing operation. Afterwards, the TI command handler sets the determined operation mode to a shared variable `driver_ti_cmd` using functions `SetNormalFlash()` or `SetTipFlash()`, so that the determined mode is passed to the associated process. Then, the event `chkin_Ctrl` is triggered to call the associated process `CheckEmgSig`. In this TA specification, the timing requirement to initiate Tip blinking mode is supposed to be implemented with the associated functionality, thus it is a typical *function-oriented timing requirement*.

6   Formal Analysis of TI system

6.1   Validation with SMC

Given a model, we apply UPPAAL SMC to validate whether the model is correctly constructed according to given requirements. First, UPPAAL SMC simulates a model for a bounded time by a specific round, and plots the change of values of given variables.

Validation of FP.001, FP.002, FP.003, FTP.001, and FTP.002. In order to check the TI model against functional properties FP.001, FP.002, and FP.003, we formulate a UPPAAL SMC query as follows:

> `simulate 1 [<=1000] { ti_cmd, 3+F_FRA_Left_ON, 5+F_FRA_Right_ON }`

This query asks UPPAAL SMC to generate a trace of the TI system's model and plot the changes of the variables `ti_cmd`, `F_FRA_Left_ON`, and `F_FRA_Right_ON`. The simulation is conducted for 1000 time units by 1 round.

For validation of **FP.001**, a TA environment model which generates TI commands according to a scenario is made as shown in Fig. 6: it ignites the TI system, triggering the event `ign_cmd_sig[IGN_TURN_ON]`. After 200 time units, it triggers one event of `ti_cmd_sig[CMD_TI_LF]` or `ti_cmd_sig[CMD_TI_RF]`. Then, it fires `ti_cmd_sig[CMD_TI_OFF]` to stop TI system after 200 time units. The plot in Fig. 6 displays the triggered TI commands and the corresponding reactions of the TI system. It validates that the correct direction of turn indication lamps flash. Also, it validates the timing property **FTP.002** that is concerning a NO/OFF

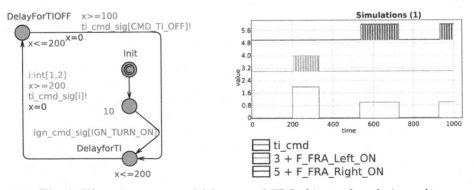

Fig. 6. TA environment model for normal TI flashing and analysis results

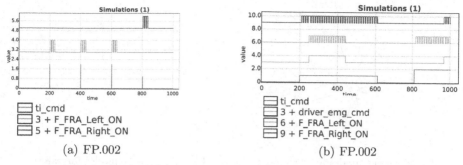

(a) FP.002   (b) FP.002

Fig. 7. Analysis results of Tip and emergency blinking modes

duty cycle, displaying that the duration of `On` and `Off` on the graphs for variables
`F_FRA_Left_ON F_FRA_Right_ON` are varying by a specified NO/OFF cycle.

The graph in Fig. 7(a) validates the property **FTP.002** that states the delay
for the beginning of Tip blinking mode, showing that either one of right or left
direction lamps flashes only 3 times when the duration less than 8 time units
between the TI-OFF command `ti_cmd[CMD_TI_OFF]` and either of TI commands,
`ti_cmd[CMD_TI_RIGHT]` or `ti_cmd[CMD_TI_LEFT]`, leads to TI blinking mode.

The graph in Fig. 7(b) shows that both flashing lamps, right and left directions
(the first and second graph), flash whenever an emergency command (the third
graph) is engaged, validating the property **FP.003**.

6.2 Verification with MC

For the safety and liveness analysis for TI system, we need an environment model
that drives TI model. Fig 8(a) gives an environment model, which triggers any
possible event for TI model at any time. The analysis for safety and liveness
below are conducted together with this environment model.

Safety Analysis for FP.001, FP.002, and UP.001. Before verifying spe-
cific properties it is important to ensure that there are no deadlocks. Property
UP.001 in Table. 1 is formulated for that purpose: it checks that the model of
TI is free from deadlocks under such an extreme environment.

The analysis of properties **FP.001** and **FP.002** impose a specific constraint
on the TI system that only one group of TI lamps of an ordered direction should
flash when normal and Tip blinking modes are engaged. The opposite group
must be silent as long as the emergency mode is not engaged.

For the analysis of the above constraint, the observer TA template in Fig. 8(b)
specifies the following cases on individual transitions: First, the guard on transition leading to location `SReq001_1` specifies that the TI command for the right
direction indication is released, but both directions of TI lamps are operated at
the same time. Second, the guard on the transition going to location `SReq001_3`
specifies the case where the emergency command is released but neither the
right direction lamp nor the left direction lamp operates. The Property IDs
SP.001.01, SP001.02, and SP001.03 in Table. 1 question whether or not those
locations, `SReq001_1`, `SReq001_2`, and `SReq001_3` are reachable.

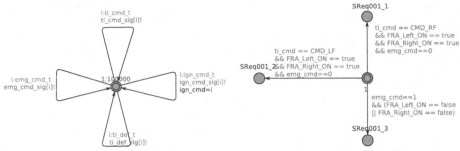

(a) Environment model for TI model   (b) TA property model for safety

Fig. 8. TA templates of property specification

Table. 1 states the verification results using UPPAAL MC. The answer to the first query is satisfied, proving that TI system will never deadlock. The following three queries are proved to be false, showing that no location among SReq001_1, SReq001_2, and SReq001_3 is reachable. Consequently, we obtain proofs that sole group of indication lamps for an ordered direction flash and the other group remains silent when TI system carries out the normal and Tip blinking operations. Table. 1 shows the analysis time for individual analysis. The verification using MC was performed with Intel CPU 2.9 GHz using 8GB memory.

Liveness Analysis. The liveness of TI system is that the system eternally reacts to any TI commands and results in any flashing of indication lamps. For the liveness analysis, we create an observer TA process as shown in Fig. 9. It describes that a group of indication lamps flash corresponding to normal TI commands and the emergency command.

MC is fed with CTL properties, **LP.001.01**, **LP.001.01**, and **LP.001.03**, in Table 1 and the TA process in Fig. 9. The queries question whether the

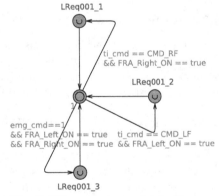

Fig. 9. TA property model for liveness

Table 1. Safety analysis: CTL property checking and results

Property ID	CTL	Results	Analysis Time (Second)
UP.001	`A[] not deadlock`	Satisfied	1.05
SP.001.01	`A[] not FailSafetyReq001.SReq001_1`	Satisfied	0.29
SP.001.02	`A[] not FailSafetyReq001.SReq001_2`	Satisfied	0.30
SP.001.03	`A[] not FailSafetyReq001.SReq001_3`	Satisfied	0.75
LP.001.01	`E<> LivenessReq001.LReq001_1`	Satisfied	0.02
LP.001.02	`E<> LivenessReq001.LReq001_2`	Satisfied	0.01
LP.001.03	`E<> LivenessReq001.LReq001_3`	Satisfied	0.02

locations LReq001_1, LReq001_2, and LReq001_3 are reachable. We could verify that every location is reachable and prove that the system reacts to any TI commands.

6.3   Test-Case Generation with Yggdrasil

Once the model is verified it may be used to generate symbolic test cases. For phase one, the LP queries in Table 1 are used to generate test cases that targets each of these central test purposes. This produces three test cases with length 12, 59, and 203 steps respectively, with a generation time of $89ms$[1].

For phase two, a trace length of 50 was selected. This generated on average three traces with and average generation time of $105ms$. The selected length affects the number of traces generated. While longer traces will get better coverage, they take longer to generate and might affect the execution time of the test case. Too short traces will not generate enough coverage and require too many single trace to be generated in phase three (which is generally slower). A length of 50 showed a good balance between improving coverage and reducing number of tests in this case.

Phase three on average generated three traces with lengths 1278, 3, and 3487, in $1280ms$. This is significantly slower than the other phases since this is often corner-cases which are unlikely to occur in random runs. The short trace is due to a special interaction which has to occur at the beginning of the trace.

7   Related Work

ISO 26262[13], a functional safety standard adopting IEC 61508 [12], classifies the level of integrity of Electric/Electronic control systems. It recommends applying of formal analysis techniques for requirements and designs on ASIL (Automotive Safety Integrity Level) C to D and the use of formal notations for requirements and designs over all integrity levels [13]. For the compliance with such a recommendation, AUTOSAR [1] and AADL [2], a standardized software architecture and methodology, are standardized as open and software architecture supporting specification methods for various level of software systems. However, they do not recommend any analysis and testing methods.

Many formal approaches, such as [4,11,14,8], to automotive software demonstrate the analyze by model-based approaches and formal analysis techniques. Their approaches are limited to some specific properties, and do not collaborate with testing methods.

MATLAB/Simulink is a common tool suite for model-based development of embedded system [8]. Model-validation is primarily achieved using traditional simulation techniques. A main difference to our approach is that our whole methodology is based on models with a formal semantics. In addition we offer integrated SMC, MC, and MBT. For (subsets of) Simulink models, MC and

---

[1] All test case generation experiments are run on a modern i7 laptop. All experiments are run several times and average values are reported.

MBT are available only from third parties[2], and to our knowledge no commercial SMC facility is available.

With respect to model-based test, the study by Tekaya et al. [18] is one of most recent methods for automotive systems. It proposes a tool to generate test cases from Simulink models using SLDV (Simulink Design Verifier) model checker. However, it is limited on relatively small models within the capability of symbolic model checkers.

Compared to the previous work, we approach the analysis of models through multidimensional techniques for multiple analysis purposes, i.e validation, verification, and testing. Thus, we demonstrated gradual use of formal techniques exploiting the same model. In addition, the model beyond the number of states that symbolic model checker can handle may still be subjected to formal statistical analysis to produce quantified analysis proof.

8   Conclusions

This paper demonstrated how to perform model-based analysis and testing of a small but non-trivial and representative industrial case using the UPPAAL tool. By combining statistical and symbolic model-checking we enable fast early validation of system design models prior to e.g., test case generation or performance analysis, allowing the user to control the required level of confidence, including exhaustive model-checking for critical properties.

During collaboration with industrial partners we have experienced that modeling using timed automata in the UPPAAL environment is feasible with an acceptable amount of training, however, many industrial users have difficulty in writing the formal CTL properties to be checked. As future work we therefore investigate how to ease this through e.g., using property-templates or boiler-plates, or graphical specifications like live sequence charts.

References

1. AUTOSAR: Technical Overview. Standard, http://www.autosar.org
2. SAE International Architecture Analysis & Design Language (AADL) Standard, http://www.aadl.info/aadl/currentsite/
3. Alur, R., Dill, D.L.: A theory of timed automata. Theor. Comput. Sci. 126(2), 183–235 (1994)
4. Arun Chakrapani Rao, M.G.D., Sethu, R.: Formal requirements analysis techniques for software-intensive automotive electronic control systems. Technical report (2011)
5. Behrmann, G., David, A., Larsen, K.G.: A tutorial on UPPAAL. In: Bernardo, M., Corradini, F. (eds.) SFM-RT 2004. LNCS, vol. 3185, pp. 200–236. Springer, Heidelberg (2004)
6. Bengtsson, J., Yi, W.: Timed automata: Semantics, algorithms and tools. In: Desel, J., Reisig, W., Rozenberg, G. (eds.) ACPN 2003. LNCS, vol. 3098, pp. 87–124. Springer, Heidelberg (2004)

---

[2] Resp. BTC EmbeddedValidator, and Reactis Tester.

7. Bulychev, P.E., David, A., Larsen, K.G., Mikučionis, M., Poulsen, D.B., Legay, A., Wang, Z.: Uppaal-smc: Statistical model checking for priced timed automata. In: Wiklicky, H., Massink, M. (eds.) QAPL. EPTCS, vol. 85, pp. 1–16 (2012)
8. Cleaveland, R.: Model-based verification of automotive control software. In: Cofer, D., Fantechi, A. (eds.) FMICS 2008. LNCS, vol. 5596, p. 2. Springer, Heidelberg (2009)
9. David, A., Larsen, K.G., Legay, A., Mikučionis, M.: Schedulability of herschel-planck revisited using statistical model checking. In: Margaria, T., Steffen, B. (eds.) ISoLA 2012, Part II. LNCS, vol. 7610, pp. 293–307. Springer, Heidelberg (2012)
10. David, A., Larsen, K.G., Legay, A., Mikučionis, M., Poulsen, D.B.: Uppaal smc tutorial. International Journal on Software Tools for Technology Transfer, 1–19 (2015)
11. Frehse, G., Hamann, A., Quinton, S., Wöhrle, M.: Formal Analysis of Timing Effects on Closed-loop Properties of Control Software. In: 35th IEEE Real-Time Systems Symposium 2014 (RTSS), Rome, Italy (December 2014)
12. IEC 61508: Functional Safety of Electrical/Electronic/Programmable Electronic Safety Related Systems. Standard, International Organization for Standardization, Geneva, CH (2010)
13. ISO 26262-6: Road vehicles – Functional safety – Part 6: Product development at the software level. Standard, International Organization for Standardization, Geneva, CH (2011)
14. Jersak, M., Richter, K., Ernst, R., Braam, J.-C., Jiang, Z.-Y., Wolf, F.: Formal methods for integration of automotive software. In: Design, Automation and Test in Europe Conference and Exhibition, pp. 45–50 (2003)
15. Legay, A., Delahaye, B., Bensalem, S.: Statistical model checking: An overview. In: Barringer, H., Falcone, Y., Finkbeiner, B., Havelund, K., Lee, I., Pace, G., Roşu, G., Sokolsky, O., Tillmann, N. (eds.) RV 2010. LNCS, vol. 6418, pp. 122–135. Springer, Heidelberg (2010)
16. Owicki, S., Lamport, L.: Proving liveness properties of concurrent programs. ACM Trans. Program. Lang. Syst. 4(3), 455–495 (1982)
17. Sistla, A.P.: Safety, liveness and fairness in temporal logic. Formal Asp. Comput. 6(5), 495–512 (1994)
18. Tekaya, M., Bennani, M.T., Youssef, A.: Test case generation for automotive applications. In: 2014 World Symposium on Computer Applications Research (WSCAR), pp. 1–6 (January 2014)

Successful Use of Incremental BMC
in the Automotive Industry

Peter Schrammel[1], Daniel Kroening[1], Martin Brain[1], Ruben Martins[1(✉)],
Tino Teige[2], and Tom Bienmüller[2]

[1] University of Oxford, Oxford, England
[2] BTC Embedded Systems AG, Oldenburg, Germany
ruben.martins@cs.ox.ac.uk, {first.lastname}@cs.ox.ac.uk,
{first.lastname}@btc-es.de

Abstract. Program analysis is on the brink of mainstream usage in embedded systems development. Formal verification of behavioural requirements, finding runtime errors and automated test case generation are some of the most common applications of automated verification tools based on Bounded Model Checking (BMC). Existing industrial tools for embedded software use an off-the-shelf Bounded Model Checker and apply it iteratively to verify the program with an increasing number of unwindings. This approach unnecessarily wastes time repeating work that has already been done and fails to exploit the power of incremental SAT solving. This paper reports on the extension of the software model checker CBMC to support *incremental BMC* and its successful integration with the industrial embedded software verification tool BTC EMBEDDEDTESTER. We present an extensive evaluation over large industrial embedded programs, mainly from automotive industry. We show that incremental BMC cuts runtimes by *one order of magnitude* in comparison to the standard non-incremental approach, enabling the application of formal verification to large and complex embedded software.

1 Introduction

Recent trend estimation [14] in automotive embedded systems revealed ever growing complexity of computer systems, providing increased safety, efficiency and entertainment satisfaction. Hence, automated design tools are vital for managing this complexity and supporting the verification processes in order to satisfy the high safety requirements stipulated by safety standards and regulations. Similar to the developments in hardware verification in the 1990s, verification tools for embedded software are becoming indispensable in industrial practice for hunting runtime bugs, checking functional properties and test suite generation [13]. For example, the automotive safety standard ISO 26262 [22] requires the test suite to satisfy modified condition/decision coverage [18] – a goal that is laborious to achieve without support by a model checker that identifies unreachable test goals and suggests test vectors for difficult-to-reach test goals.

In this paper, we focus on the application of Bounded Model Checking (BMC) to this problem. The technique is highly accurate (no false alarms) and is furthermore able

The research leading to these results has received funding from the ARTEMIS Joint Undertaking under grant agreement number 295311 "VeTeSS" and ERC project 280053 "CPROVER".

© Springer International Publishing Switzerland 2015
M. Núñez and M. Güdemann (Eds.): FMICS 2015, LNCS 9128, pp. 62–77, 2015.
DOI: 10.1007/978-3-319-19458-5_5

to generate counterexamples that aid debugging and serve as test vectors. The spiralling power of SAT solvers has made this technique scale to reasonably large programs and has enabled industrial application.

In BMC, the property of interest is checked for traces that execute loops up to a given number of times k. Since the value of k that is required to find a bug is not known a-priori, one has to try increasingly larger values of k until a bug is found. The analysis is aborted when memory and runtime limits are exceeded.[1]

Industrial verification tools based on BMC, such as BTC EMBEDDEDTESTER, use an off-the-shelf Bounded Model Checker and, without additional information about the program to be checked, apply it in an iterative fashion:

```
k=0
while true do
   if BMC(program,k) fails then
      return counterexample
   fi
   k++
od
```

This basic procedure offers scope for improvement. In particular, note that the Bounded Model Checker has to redo the work of generating and solving the SAT formula for time frames 0 to k when called to check time frame $k + 1$. It is desirable to perform the verification *incrementally* for iteration $k + 1$ by building upon the work done for iteration k.

Incremental BMC has been applied successfully to the verification of hardware designs, and has been reported to yield substantial speedups [33,11]. Fortunately, the typical control-loop structure of embedded software resembles the monolithic transition relation of hardware designs, and thus strongly suggests incremental verification of successive loop unwindings. However – to our knowledge – none of the software model checkers for C programs that have competed in the TACAS 2014 Software Verification Competition implement such a technique that ultimately exploits the full power of incremental SAT solving [35,10].

Contributions. The primary contribution of this paper is *experimental*. We quantify the benefit of incremental BMC in the context of the verification of industrial embedded software. To this end,

(1) we survey the requirements for state-of-the-art embedded software verification tools, briefly summarise the underlying theory of the used techniques, and highlight the challenges faced when applying them to industrial code;
(2) we present the first industrial-strength implementation of incremental BMC in a software model checker for ANSI-C programs combining symbolic execution, slicing and incremental SAT solving;
(3) we report on the successful integration of our incremental Bounded Model Checker in the industrial embedded software verification tools BTC EMBEDDEDTESTER

---

[1] One can stop unwinding when the *completeness threshold* [24] of the system is reached, but this threshold is often impractically large.

and EMBEDDEDVALIDATOR where it is used by several hundred industrial users since version 3.4 and 4.3, respectively; and

(4) we give a comprehensive experimental evaluation over a large set of industrial embedded benchmarks, from mainly automotive origin, that quantify the performance gain due to the incremental approach in a BMC-based tool: incremental BMC outperforms the winner of the TACAS 2014 Software Verification Competition [25] by one order of magnitude.

2   Verification of Model-Based Embedded Software

Recent safety standards, e.g. ISO-26262 [22]), cover model-based development and testing techniques for early simulation, testing and verification, and recommend back-to-back testing for showing simulation equivalence between a high-level model and corresponding production code. In the automotive industry, model-based development including automatic code generation is well-established. In particular, SIMULINK for functional modelling and TARGETLINK[2] for automatic code generation from these models are prominent representatives. SIMULINK DESIGNVERIFIER,[3] BTC EMBEDDEDTESTER,[4] REACTIS,[5] and RT-TESTER[6] are examples of tools that complement the software development tool chain for formal verification of safety requirements against design models. These tools are also used for testing, namely, requirement-based and back-to-back testing, including automatic test vector generation for structural coverage criteria.

2.1   Requirements and Challenges

In the above setting, embedded software verification tools have two main applications: (1) proving/disproving safety properties, and (2) covering test goals or proving their unreachability. BMC-based verification engines are a perfect fit for both applications because they can be used to find counterexamples and prove properties by k-induction.

Embedded C code has to meet many conflicting requirements like real-time constraints, low memory footprint and low energy consumption. Code generators offer options to perform certain optimisations towards these goals, often to the detriment of *code size* (and also readability for humans). The observer instrumentation[7] to encode properties and identify the test goals corresponding to code-coverage criteria such as MC/DC [18] produces a non-negligible overhead in the size of the code but introduces little semantic complexity. When using BMC, the size of the SAT formula built from a program further increases whenever internal loops need to be unwound. File sizes of 10 MB and more are common, which poses difficulties to many tools already when

---

[2] http://www.dspace.com/en/pub/home/products/sw/pcgs/targetli.cfm

[3] http://uk.mathworks.com/products/sldesignverifier

[4] http://www.btc-es.de/index.php?lang=2

[5] http://www.reactive-systems.com

[6] https://www.verified.de/products/rt-tester

[7] The observer instrumentation consists of adding a series of flags to the original source code that enables the analysis tool to determine exactly what parts of the code are exercised.

parsing the source code and encoding the program into a SAT formula, mostly due to inefficient data structures. Incremental BMC helps reducing formula sizes and peak memory consumption (see Sec. 4.2) by incremental formula generation and solving.

In practice, many loop unwindings may be needed to detect errors and reach certain tests goals (more than 100 for some of our industrial benchmarks, see Sec. 4.2). *Non-incremental* bounded model checking repeats work such as file parsing, loop unwinding, SAT formula encoding and discards information learnt in the SAT solver every time it is called and so gives away an enormous amount of performance. This effect exacerbates the cost of large unwinding limits that may be needed.

The main challenge addressed by this paper is to exploit all the benefits of incrementality in BMC and to significantly enhance performance of its integration with an industrial-strength embedded verification and test-vector generation tool, namely BTC EMBEDDEDVALIDATOR and EMBEDDEDTESTER. The impact of this successful technology transfer is demonstrated on original industrial embedded software.

2.2 Case Study: Fault-Tolerant Fuel Control System

In this paper, we focus on the verification of C code generated from SIMULINK models. To this end, we illustrate the characteristics of this verification problem with the help of a well-known case study and explain the workflow and principal techniques that a state-of-the-art embedded software verification tool uses.

The Fault-Tolerant Fuel Control System[8] (FUELSYS) for a gasoline engine is representative of a variety of automotive applications as it combines discrete control logic with continuous signal flow and thus establishes a hybrid discrete-continuous system. More precisely, the control logic of FUELSYS is implemented by six automata with two to five states each, while the signal flow is further subdivided into three subsystems with a rich variety of SIMULINK/TARGETLINK blocks involving arithmetic, lookup tables, integrators, filters and interpolation (Fig. 1). The system is designed to keep the air-fuel ratio nearly constant depending on the inputs given by a throttle sensor, a speed sensor, an oxygen sensor (EGO) and a pressure sensor (MAP). Moreover it is tolerant to individual sensor faults and is designed to be highly robust, i.e. after detection of a sensor fault the system is dynamically reconfigured.

Properties of Interest. The key functional property for FUELSYS is how the air-fuel ratio evolves for each of the four sensor-failure scenarios. Simulation-based approaches show that FUELSYS is indeed fault-tolerant in each case of a single failure: the air-fuel ratio can be regulated after a few seconds to about 80 % of the target ratio. In addition to *functional* testing of industrial embedded software, safety standards call for *structural* testing of the production code before release deployment.

2.3 Structure of Generated Code

Many modelling languages follow the *synchronous programming paradigm* [17], which is well-suited for modelling time-triggered systems, in which tasks (subsystems of the

---

[8] http://www.mathworks.co.uk/help/simulink/examples/modeling-a-fault-tolerant-fuel-control-system.html

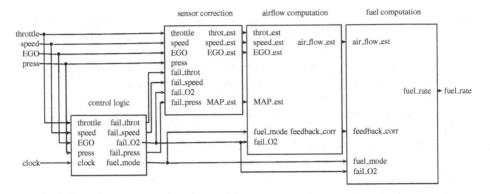

Fig. 1. The SIMULINK Diagram for the Fault-Tolerant Fuel Control System (without the plant model)

model) execute at given rates. Code generation for such languages produces a typical code structure, which corresponds essentially to a non-preemptive operating system task scheduler. Most code generators provide the scheduler for time-triggered execution or code to interface with popular real-time operating systems. In either case, the functionality corresponds to the following pseudo code:

```
1   void main() {
2      state s; inputs i; outputs o;
3      initialize(s);
4      while(true) { //main loop
5         i = read_inputs();
6         (o,s) = compute_step(i,s);
7         write_outputs(o);
8         wait(); // wait for timer interrupt
9      }
10  }
```

The distinguishing characteristic of such a reactive program is its unbounded main loop, which we will analyse incrementally. All other loops contained within that loop, e.g. to iterate over arrays or interpolate values using look-up tables, have a statically bounded number of iterations and can be fully unwound.

2.4   Analysis with BMC and k-Induction

Property Instrumentation. Formal verification requires formalisations of high-level requirements, often using observer Büchi automata with a dedicated 'error state' generated from temporal logic descriptions. Test vector generation is done for code-coverage criteria such as branches, statements, conditions and MC/DC of the production C code. For FUELSYS, for example, MC/DC instrumentation yields 251 test goals. The properties to be verified or tested have in common that they can be reduced to a reachability problem. In formal verification of safety properties, we prove that the error state is unreachable, whereas the aim of test vector generation is to obtain a trace that demonstrates reachability of the goal state.

To validate whether the air-fuel ratio in the FUELSYS controller is regulated after a few seconds to be within some margin of the target ratio, one has to instrument the reactive program, as sketched above, with an observer implementing the asserted property. For instance, consider the requirement "If some sensor fails for the first time then within 10 seconds the air-fuel ratio will keep in between the range of 80 % to 120 % of the target ratio forever." The code fragment for an observer for this requirement may look as follows:

```
1   // detection of first sensor failure
2   if (sensor_fail == 1 && observe_ratio == 0) {
3       // initialize observer variables
4       observe_ratio = 1;
5       counter = 0;
6       violated = 0;
7   }

8   if (observe_ratio == 1) { // observation mode
9       if (counter >= 10 &&
10          (air_fuel_ratio < 0.8*target_ratio ||
11           air_fuel_ratio > 1.2*target_ratio))
12              violated = 1;
13      counter++;
14  }

15  assert(violated == 0); // safety property
```

In order to verify that the above property actually holds, one has to show that the assertion in the observer code is always satisfied. We use BMC for refutation of the assertion, and k-induction for proving it.

Bounded Model Checking. BMC [2] can be used to check the existence of a path $\pi = \langle s_0, s_1, \ldots, s_k \rangle$ of length k between two states s_0 and s_k belonging to sets respectively described by ϕ and ψ. This check is performed by deciding satisfiability of the following formula using a SAT or SMT solver:

$$\phi(s_0) \wedge \bigwedge_{0 \leq j < k} T(s_j, i_j, s_{j+1}) \wedge \psi(s_k) \tag{1}$$

If the solver returns the answer "satisfiable", it also provides a satisfying assignment to the variables $(s_0, i_0, s_1, i_1, \ldots, s_{k-1}, i_{k-1}, s_k)$. The satisfying assignment represents one possible path $\pi = \langle s_0, s_1, \ldots, s_k \rangle$ from ϕ to ψ and identifies the corresponding input sequence $\langle i_0, \ldots, i_{k-1} \rangle$. Hence, BMC is useful for refuting safety properties (where ϕ gives the set of initial states and ψ defines the error states) and generating test vectors (where ψ defines the test goal to be covered).

Unbounded Model Checking by k-Induction. BMC can prove reachability, whereas unreachability can be shown using k-induction [31,11,16,7]. The predicate $\neg\psi$ is an (inductive) invariant, i.e., it holds in all reachable states, if each of the following two formulae, base case (BC) and induction step (SC), are unsatisfiable for a given k (assuming that we have already checked for up to $k - 1$):

$$\begin{aligned}
\text{(BC)} \quad & \phi(s_0) \wedge \bigwedge_{0 \leq j < k} \neg\psi(s_j) \wedge T(s_j, i_j, s_{j+1}) \wedge \psi(s_k) \\
\text{(SC)} \quad & \bigwedge_{0 \leq j \leq k} \neg\psi(s_j) \wedge T(s_j, i_j, s_{j+1}) \wedge \psi(s_{k+1})
\end{aligned} \tag{2}$$

The base case checks if the formula is unsatisfiable, when this occurs we say that $\neg\psi$ holds in the first k steps. The induction step checks if we can conclude from the invariant holding over any k consecutive steps that it holds for the $(k+1)^{st}$ step. If the base step fails, i.e. above formula is satisfiable and a counterexample is given, we have refuted the property. If it holds and the induction step fails, we do not know whether $\neg\psi$ is invariant. Only if both formulae hold we have proved that $\neg\psi$ is invariant.

Both base step and induction step are essentially instances of BMC: starting from the initial state ϕ for the base case, and starting from *any* state for the induction step. Thus, similar to BMC, k-induction can be applied by using a sequence of increasing values for k.

3   Incremental BMC

In this section, we explain the technical background of incremental SAT solving and how it is employed in our implementation of incremental BMC.

3.1   Incremental SAT Solving

The first ideas for incremental SAT solving date back to the 1990s [21,32]. The question is how to solve a sequence of similar SAT problems while reusing effort spent on solving previous instances, i.e. reusing the internal state and learnt information of the solver. Incremental SAT solving is easy as long as formulas are *growing monotonically*, i.e. clauses are added to the formula. Removing clauses is trickier and requires additional solver features like solving *under assumptions* [11], which is the most popular approach to incremental SAT solving: assumptions are temporary assignments to variables that hold solely for one specific invocation of the SAT solver. In Sec. 3.2, we will explain how SAT solving under assumptions allows us to emulate the removal of clauses.

An alternative approach is to use SMT solvers. SMT solvers offer an interface for pushing and popping clauses in a stack-like manner. Pushing adds clauses, popping removes them from the formula. This makes the modification of the formula intuitive to the user, but the efficiency depends on the underlying implementation of the push and pop operations. For example, in [15] it was observed that some SMT solvers (like Z3) are not optimised for incremental usage and hence perform worse incrementally than non-incrementally.

Since CBMC itself implements powerful bitvector decision procedures, we use the SAT solver MINISAT2 [10] as a backend solver, and focus on solving under assumptions in the sequel.

3.2   Incremental BMC

We will now discuss which aspects have to be taken into account when implementing an incremental approach in a software Bounded Model Checker. We will show that symbolic execution and slicing can be performed without interfering with the requirement of monotonic formula construction for incremental SAT solving, whereas incremental unwinding and transition function refinements require solving under assumptions.

Following the construction in [11] for finite state machines, incremental BMC can be formulated as a sequence of SAT problems $\Phi(k)$ that we need to solve:

$$
\begin{aligned}
\Phi(0) \quad &:= \phi(s_0) \wedge (\Psi(0) \vee \alpha_0) \\
\Phi(k+1) &:= \Phi(k) \wedge T(s_k, i_k, s_{k+1}) \wedge \alpha_k \wedge (\Psi(k+1) \vee \alpha_{k+1})
\end{aligned}
\tag{3}
$$

where $\Psi(k)$ is the disjunction $\bigvee_{0 \le j \le k} \psi(s_j)$ of error states ψ to be proved unreachable up to iteration k. This means that the verification fails if *at least one* of the error states is reachable. Since the set of ψ_js grows in each iteration, our problem is not monotonic: one has to *remove* $\Psi(k)$ when adding $\Psi(k+1)$ because $\Psi(k)$ subsumes $\Psi(k+1)$.

Here, solving under assumptions comes to rescue. In iteration k, the α_k is assumed to be false, whereas it is assumed true for iterations $k' > k$. This has the effect that in iteration k' the formula $(\Psi(k) \vee \alpha_k)$ becomes trivially satisfied. Hence, it does not contribute to the (un)satisfiability of $\Phi(k')$, which emulates its deletion.[9]

Symbolic Execution. For software (3) results in large formulae and would be highly inefficient for the purpose of BMC. In practice, software model checkers use *symbolic execution* in order to exploit, for example, constant propagation and pruning branches when conditionals are infeasible, while generating the SAT formula and thus reducing its size. This means that the formula describing T is the result of symbolic execution, and that formulae T and Ψ are actually dependent on k. Fortunately, this does not affect the correctness of above formula construction and we can replace T by T_k in (3) and ψ by ψ_k in the definition of $\Psi(k)$. T_k denotes the transition formula obtained by symbolic execution of the kth time frame (i.e. unwinding), and ψ_k the assertions collected for this time frame.

Slicing. Another feature used by state-of-the-art software model checkers is slicing: The purpose of slicing is, again, reducing the size of the SAT formula by removing (or better: not generating) those parts of the formula that have no influence on its satisfiability. There are many techniques how to implement slicing with the desired trade-off between runtime efficiency and its formula pruning effectiveness [34].

Slicing is performed relative to $\Psi(k)$. We said that the number of disjuncts ψ_j in Ψ is growing monotonically with k. Hence, we will show that, assuming that our slicing operator is monotonic, we obtain a monotonic formula construction:

The transition formula for each time frame T_k obtained by symbolic execution is a conjunction $\bigwedge_{\tau \in M} \tau$ of subrelations τ (e.g., formulae corresponding to program instructions). The slicing operator *slice* selects a subset of M. The operator *slice* is monotonic iff $M \subseteq M' \implies slice(M) \subseteq slice(M')$.

We can then view the conjunction of transition relations for k time frames $\widehat{T}(k) = \bigwedge_{0 \le j \le k} T_j$ as $\bigwedge_{\tau \in M_k} \tau$. A slice $\widehat{T}^{sliced}(k)$ of $\widehat{T}(k)$ is $\bigwedge_{\tau \in M'_k} \tau$ where $M'_k \subseteq M_k$. An incremental slice is then defined as the difference between $\widehat{T}^{sliced}(k+1)$ and $\widehat{T}^{sliced}(k)$: $T^{sliced}_{k+1} = \bigwedge_{\tau \in M'_{k+1} \setminus M'_k} \tau$.

Monotonicity of formula construction follows from $M'_{k+1} \subseteq M_{k+1}$ and the assumed monotonicity $M'_k \subseteq M'_{k+1}$ of the slicing operator. We can thus replace T by T^{sliced}_k in (3). Mind that T^{sliced}_k contains also subrelations τ for time steps $k' < k$.

Our slicing operator computes the (syntactic) variable dependency graph for $\widehat{T}(k+1)$ and obtains M'_{k+1} as the set of all τ which $\Psi(k+1)$ depends on. Then only those τ

---

[9] For a large number of iterations k, such trivially satisfied subformulas might accumulate as "garbage" in the formula and slow down its resolution. Restarting the solver at appropriate moments is the common solution to this issue.

in M'_{k+1} are added to the formula that have not been in the slice for the previous time frame, resulting in T^{sliced}_{k+1}.

Refinements. Incremental SAT solving is also used for incremental refinements of the transition relation T for bitvectors [4,8] and arrays [28], for example. Applying bitvectors and arrays refinements inside an incremental software Bounded Model Checker requires using several incremental formula encodings for (in general, non-monotonic) refinements. These refinements are global over all unwindings, so that in iteration k we have to further refine transition relations $T_{k'}$ from earlier iterations $k' < k$. For details on the formula construction for refinements inside an incremental Bounded Model Checker we refer to the extended version of the paper [30].

4   Experimental Evaluation

We present the results of our experimental evaluation of incremental BMC and incremental k-induction on industrial programs from mainly automotive origin. The goal of this evaluation is to quantify the benefit from an incremental approach in a BMC-based tool infrastructure.[10] The experiments for this study were performed on a 3.5 GHz Intel Xeon machine with 32 GB of physical memory running Windows 7 with a time limit of 3,600 seconds.

4.1   Implementation

We have implemented our extension[11] for incremental BMC in the Bounded Model Checker for ANSI-C programs CBMC [6] using the SAT solver MINISAT2 [10]. Incremental CBMC can be used with specific options that enables extra features, namely: (i) slicing, (ii) preprocessing, and (iii) formula-level refinements. The goal of these techniques is to reduce the size of the SAT formula that is being generated. Slicing reduces the size of the SAT formula by eliminating irrelevant paths of the program. Preprocessing through the MINISAT2 simplifier reduces the size of the SAT formula after it has been generated, and formula-level refinements performs an incremental build of the SAT formula. For information regarding the command line options of incremental CBMC we refer to the CPROVER wiki page.[12]

In the integration of CBMC with BTC EMBEDDEDTESTER and EMBEDDEDVALIDATOR, a master routine selects the next verification/test goal to be analysed starting from instrumented C code. After some preprocessing like source-level slicing and internal-loop unwinding the resulting reachability task is given to CBMC. If CBMC is able to solve the problem within the user-defined time limit, the result, i.e. bounded or unbounded unreachability, or a counterexample in case of reachability, is reported back

---

[10] For a comparison with alternative verification approaches, we kindly refer to the results of the Software Verification Competition (http://sv-comp.sosy-lab.org), where BMC-based tools rank in the top 3 every year.

[11] Source code available from http://www.cprover.org/svn/cbmc/branches/peter-incremental-un winding

[12] http://www.cprover.org/wiki/doku.php?id=how_to_use_incremental_unwinding

Table 1. Benchmark characteristics from industrial programs

		LOC	operators			input variables			state variables			observer	unwindings
			cond	mul	div/rem	bool	int	float	bool	int	float	bool	
SAT	max	31222	17103	669	75	688	477	189	3876	750	107	22	106
	average	7572	4306	188	9	103	79	19	583	136	15	9	22
UNSAT	max	23014	49530	567	37467	212	282	188	708	663	32	22	10
	average	4854	6014	160	1257	30	51	9	163	73	3	7	10

to the master process. Otherwise, i.e. in case of a timeout, CBMC is killed but information about the solved unwindings of the reactive main loop is given back, which frequently is a useful result for the user since it may indicate the absence of shallow bugs.

To prove unreachability of verification/test goals (properties), k-induction is performed (see Sec. 2.4). For this purpose BTC EMBEDDEDTESTER generates two source files, one containing the base case, which is a normal BMC problem with the property given as assertion (cf. Equ. (2) (BC)); the file for the step case havocs variables modified in the loop and the invariant property is assumed at the beginning of the loop and asserted at the end of the loop (cf. Equ. (2) (SC)). To check the step case, we require a reversed termination behaviour of CBMC, i.e. it continues unwinding as long as the problem is SAT and stops as soon as it is UNSAT.

4.2   Incremental BMC for Embedded Software

We report results on industrial programs for the integration of CBMC with BTC EMBEDDEDTESTER and EMBEDDEDVALIDATOR. For these experiments, we used 60 industrial benchmarks, which are original, unmodified code from BTC customers, mainly from automotive applications. Unfortunately, software in the automotive domain is closed source, and hence, being subject to NDAs, these benchmarks cannot be made public.[13] These benchmarks have the property of having only one unbounded loop. Half of the benchmarks are bug-free (UNSAT instances), half contain a bug (SAT instances). This benchmark suite is an indicator for performance of model checking tools in an industrial setting as it covers a representative spectrum of embedded software.

A summary of the benchmark characteristics is listed in Table 1. Besides the number of lines of code, we give the number of conditional operators, multiplications and divisions or remainder operations, which are a good indicator for the difficulty of the benchmark, because they generate large formulae — recall that for each "/" occurring in the program, CBMC has to generate a divider circuit. The surprisingly high number of conditional operators in most of the benchmarks is due to the preprocessing of conditional assignments by BTC EMBEDDEDTESTER and hints at the amount of branching in these benchmarks. Moreover, we list the number of input and state variables, and the variables introduced by the observer instrumentation.

Runtimes. We compared the incremental (i) with the non-incremental (ni) approach and evaluated the impact of slicing (s), SAT preprocessing (p) and bitvector refinement (r).[14] The incremental and non-incremental approaches were compared by activating

---

[13] To mitigate this problem, we present a detailed summary of the benchmark characteristics in the extended version of the paper [30].

[14] Array refinement is not used because the benchmarks do not contain arrays.

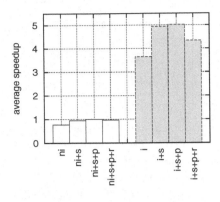 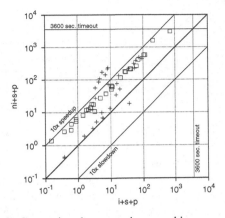

(a) Effect of slicing, SAT formula prepro-   (b) Comparison between ni+s+p and i+s+p
cessing and bitvector refinement   (+ SAT instances; □ UNSAT instances)

Fig. 2. Incremental vs. non-incremental BMC

none of the three techniques, with slicing only (+s), with slicing and preprocessing (+s+p), and with all three options activated (+s+p+r). The maximum number of loop unwindings was fixed to 10 for the UNSAT instances in order to balance a significant exploration depth with reasonable analysis runtimes. For SAT instances, a maximum number of loop unwindings was not fixed since the incremental and non-incremental approaches are bound to terminate when the unwinding depth reaches the depth of the bug. The number of unwindings are listed in the last column in Table 1.

Fig. 2 shows the comparison between the incremental and non-incremental approaches and the impact of each tool option on their performance. Fig. 2a shows the average geometric mean [12] speedup of instances that were solved by all approaches. We consider as baseline the (ni+s+p) approach since it was the best non-incremental approach. Each bar shows the average geometric mean speedup of each approach when compared to (ni+s+p). For example, (ni) has a speedup of 0.77, i.e. (ni) is on average 0.77× slower than (ni+s+p). On the other hand, all incremental versions are much faster than the non-incremental versions. For example, (i) is on average over 3.5× faster than (ni+s+p) and (i+s+p) is on average over 5× faster than (ni+s+p). We observe the following effects of the tool options: (i) slicing shows significant benefits overall (also on peak memory consumption); (ii) not using formula preprocessing is a bad idea in general; and (iii) bitvector refinement shows benefits for UNSAT instances, but produces overhead for SAT instances which deteriorates the overall performance of the tool (see the extended version of the paper [30] for more details). Even though the tool options have some positive effects, they are rather minor in comparison to the performance gains from using an incremental approach.

Since the best incremental and non-incremental approaches were obtained with the configuration (+s+p), we will use this configuration for both approaches on the results described in the remainder of the paper.

Fig. 2b shows a scatter plot with runtimes of the best non-incremental (ni+s+p) and incremental (i+s+p) approaches. Each point in the plot corresponds to an instance, where the x-axis corresponds to the runtime required by the incremental approach and the y-axis corresponds to the runtime required by the non-incremental approach. If an instance is above the diagonal, then it means that the incremental approach is faster than the non-incremental approach, otherwise it means that the non-incremental approach is faster. SAT instances are plotted as crosses, whereas UNSAT instances are plotted as squares. Incremental BMC significantly outperforms non-incremental BMC. For SAT instances, the advantage of incremental BMC is negligible for the easy instances, whereas speedups are around a factor of 10 for the medium and hard instances. For UNSAT instances, speedups are also significant and most instances have a speedup of more than a factor of 5.

Solving vs. Overall Runtime. Since CBMC is used as a black-box with BTC EMBEDDEDTESTER and EMBEDDEDVALIDATOR, the non-incremental approach has to re-parse files in each iteration. One might argue that removing this overhead is the main reason for the speedup observed. However, the overhead for parsing files, symbolic execution and slicing when compared to generating and solving SAT formula is similar for the incremental and non-incremental approach. The incremental approach spends 27% of its time solving the SAT formula (582 out of 2,151 seconds), whereas the non-incremental approach spends 28% of its time (3,317 out of 11,811 seconds). Unsurprisingly, solving the instance for the largest k in the non-incremental approach takes a considerable amount of time (around 24%), when compared to the total time for solving the SAT formulae for iterations 1 to k (784 out of 3,317 seconds).

An explanation for these speedups might be the size of the queries issued in both approaches. The average number of clauses per solver call is halved from 1,367k clauses for the non-incremental approach to 709k clauses for the incremental approach. Similarly, the average number of variables is less than a third in the incremental approach when compared to the non-incremental approach, being 217k and 746k respectively.

Smaller query sizes also have an effect on peak memory consumption which is reduced by 30% for UNSAT benchmarks; for SAT benchmarks, however, we observed a 10% increase.

4.3   Code Coverage on FUELSYS Using BTC EMBEDDEDTESTER

As reported in the previous section, enabling CBMC to work incrementally led to tremendous performance gains. In order to assess whether these improvements have practical impact in the *integration* of CBMC with an industrial-strength test-vector generation tool, we compared the performance of BTC EMBEDDEDTESTER with the incremental feature of CBMC being disabled and enabled. The time limit per subtask was 10 minutes and the unwinding depth for all internal loops was 50. For unwinding depth 10 of the main loop, the incremental feature improves the overall runtime from 152.3 to 70.4 minutes, i.e. more than 2× faster, and for unwinding depth 50 from 377.4 to 108.5 minutes, i.e. more than 3× faster.

4.4   Incremental k-Induction for Embedded Software

To compare the performance of incremental and non-incremental approaches for k-induction, we considered the subset of UNSAT benchmarks for which k-induction required more than 1 iteration (see the extended version of the paper [30] for more details). Note that when k-induction requires only 1 iteration, the performance of both approaches is similar.

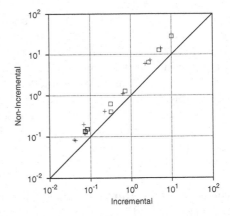

Fig. 3 shows a scatter plot with the runtimes of incremental and non-incremental k-induction using the tool options (+s+p). Instances that correspond to the base case are plotted as crosses, whereas instances that correspond to the step case are plotted as squares. The runtimes for

Fig. 3. Incremental k-induction (+ BC instances; □ SC instances)

both incremental and non-incremental checking are relatively small. These are due to the small number of iterations required by k-induction to prove the unreachability of the properties present on these benchmarks (between 2 and 4 iterations with an average of 2.4 iterations per instance). Incremental checking is on average $2\times$ faster than non-incremental checking, on both base and step cases.

5   Related Work

Most related is recent work on a prototype tool NBIS [15] implementing incremental BMC using SMT solvers. They show the advantages of incremental software BMC. However, they do not consider industrial embedded software and have evaluated their tool only on small benchmarks that are very easy for both, incremental and non-incremental, approaches (runtimes <1s).[15]

Bit-precise formal verification techniques are indispensable for embedded system models and implementations, that have low-level, i.e. C language, semantics like discrete-time SIMULINK models. The importance of this topic has recently attracted attention as shown by publications on verification using SMT Solving [19,26], test case generation [27], symbolic analysis for improving simulation coverage [1], and directed random testing [29]. Yet, all these works have not exploited incremental BMC.

The test vector generation tool FSHELL [20] uses incremental SAT solving to check the reachability of a set of test goals. However, it assumes a fixed unwinding of the loops. There is no reason why incremental BMC should not boost its performance when increasing loop unwindings need to be considered. Test vector generation tools like KLEE [5] use incremental SAT solving to extend the paths to be explored. However, they consider only single paths at a time, whereas BMC explores all paths simultaneously.

---

[15] Unfortunately, a working version of the tool was not available at time of submission.

Incremental SAT solving has important applications in other verification techniques like the IC3 algorithm [3,9] and incremental BMC is standard for hardware verification [23,36]. We show that the speedups of incremental SAT solving reported in [11] regarding k-induction on small HW circuits carry over to industrial embedded software.

6 Conclusions

We claim that incremental BMC is an indispensable technique for industrial embedded software verification based on BMC. To underpin this claim, we report on the successful integration of our incremental extension of CBMC into an industrial embedded software verification tool. Our experiments demonstrate one-order-of-magnitude speedups from incremental approaches on industrial embedded software benchmarks for BMC and k-induction. These performance gains result in faster property verification and higher test coverage, and thus, a productivity increase in embedded software verification.

Incremental BMC is effective on embedded software because of its specific properties (one big unbounded loop, whereas other loops are bounded). Nonetheless, we can also expect benefits for general software where loops and control structures are more irregular. A preliminary report on incremental BMC for programs with *multiple loops* is presented in the extended version of the paper [30]. Even though the current approach for multiple loops can still be improved, we already observe significant speedups that show the applicability of incremental BMC beyond embedded software.

References

1. Alur, R., Kanade, A., Ramesh, S., Shashidhar, K.C.: Symbolic analysis for improving simulation coverage of Simulink/Stateflow models. In: EMSOFT, pp. 89–98 (2008)
2. Biere, A., Cimatti, A., Clarke, E., Zhu, Y.: Symbolic model checking without BDDs. In: Cleaveland, W.R. (ed.) TACAS 1999. LNCS, vol. 1579, pp. 193–207. Springer, Heidelberg (1999)
3. Bradley, A.R.: IC3 and beyond: Incremental, Inductive Verification. In: Madhusudan, P., Seshia, S.A. (eds.) CAV 2012. LNCS, vol. 7358, p. 4. Springer, Heidelberg (2012)
4. Bryant, R.E., Kroening, D., Ouaknine, J., Seshia, S.A., Strichman, O., Brady, B.A.: Deciding Bit-Vector Arithmetic with Abstraction. In: Grumberg, O., Huth, M. (eds.) TACAS 2007. LNCS, vol. 4424, pp. 358–372. Springer, Heidelberg (2007)
5. Cadar, C., Dunbar, D., Engler, D.: KLEE: Unassisted and Automatic Generation of High-Coverage Tests for Complex Systems Programs. In: OSDI, pp. 209–224 (2008)
6. Clarke, E., Kroning, D., Lerda, F.: A tool for checking ANSI-C programs. In: Jensen, K., Podelski, A. (eds.) TACAS 2004. LNCS, vol. 2988, pp. 168–176. Springer, Heidelberg (2004)
7. Donaldson, A.F., Haller, L., Kroening, D., Rümmer, P.: Software Verification Using k-Induction. In: Yahav, E. (ed.) Static Analysis. LNCS, vol. 6887, pp. 351–368. Springer, Heidelberg (2011)
8. Eén, N., Mishchenko, A., Amla, N.: A single-instance incremental SAT formulation of proof- and counterexample-based abstraction. In: FMCAD, pp. 181–188 (2010)
9. Eén, N., Mishchenko, A., Brayton, R.K.: Efficient implementation of property directed reachability. In: FMCAD, pp. 125–134 (2011)

10. Eén, N., Sörensson, N.: An Extensible SAT-solver. In: Giunchiglia, E., Tacchella, A. (eds.) SAT 2003. LNCS, vol. 2919, pp. 502–518. Springer, Heidelberg (2004)
11. Eén, N., Sörensson, N.: Temporal induction by incremental SAT solving. ENTCS 89(4), 543–560 (2003)
12. Fleming, P., Wallace, J.: How Not To Lie With Statistics: The Correct Way To Summarize Benchmark Results. CACM 29(3), 218–221 (1986)
13. Fraser, G., Wotawa, F., Ammann, P.: Testing with model checkers: a survey. STVR 19(3), 215–261 (2009)
14. Gunnarsson, D., Kuntz, S., Farrall, G., Iwai, A., Ernst, R.: Trends in automotive embedded systems. In: CODES+ISSS, pp. 9–10 (2012)
15. Günther, H., Weissenbacher, G.: Incremental bounded software model checking. In: SPIN, pp. 40–47 (2014)
16. Hagen, G., Tinelli, C.: Scaling up the formal verification of Lustre programs with SMT-based techniques. In: FMCAD, pp. 1–9 (2008)
17. Halbwachs, N.: Synchronous programming of reactive systems. Kluwer (1993)
18. Hayhurst, K.J., Veerhusen, D.S., Chilenski, J.J., Rierson, L.K.: A practical tutorial on modified condition/decision coverage. Tech. rep., NASA (May 2001)
19. Herber, P., Reicherdt, R., Bittner, P.: Bit-precise formal verification of discrete-time MATLAB/Simulink models using SMT solving. In: EMSOFT, pp. 1–10 (2013)
20. Holzer, A., Schallhart, C., Tautschnig, M., Veith, H.: Query-driven program testing. In: Jones, N.D., Müller-Olm, M. (eds.) VMCAI 2009. LNCS, vol. 5403, pp. 151–166. Springer, Heidelberg (2009)
21. Hooker, J.N.: Solving the incremental satisfiability problem. JLP 15(1&2), 177–186 (1993)
22. ISO 26262: Road vehicles – Functional safety (2011)
23. Jin, H., Somenzi, F.: An incremental algorithm to check satisfiability for bounded model checking. ENTCS 119(2), 51–65 (2005)
24. Kroning, D., Strichman, O.: Efficient computation of recurrence diameters. In: Zuck, L.D., Attie, P.C., Cortesi, A., Mukhopadhyay, S. (eds.) VMCAI 2003. LNCS, vol. 2575, pp. 298–309. Springer, Heidelberg (2002)
25. Kroening, D., Tautschnig, M.: CBMC – C bounded model checker – (competition contribution). In: Ábrahám, E., Havelund, K. (eds.) TACAS 2014. LNCS, vol. 8413, pp. 389–391. Springer, Heidelberg (2014)
26. Manamcheri, K., Mitra, S., Bak, S., Caccamo, M.: A step towards verification and synthesis from Simulink/Stateflow models. In: HSCC, pp. 317–318 (2011)
27. Peranandam, P., Raviram, S., Satpathy, M., Yeolekar, A., Gadkari, A.A., Ramesh, S.: An integrated test generation tool for enhanced coverage of Simulink/Stateflow models. In: DATE, pp. 308–311 (2012)
28. Pnueli, A., Strichman, O.: Reduced functional consistency of uninterpreted functions. ENTCS 144(2), 53–65 (2006)
29. Satpathy, M., Yeolekar, A., Ramesh, S.: Randomized directed testing (REDIRECT) for Simulink/Stateflow models. In: EMSOFT, pp. 217–226 (2008)
30. Schrammel, P., Kroening, D., Brain, M., Martins, R., Teige, T., Bienmüller, T.: Incremental bounded model checking for embedded software (extended version). CoRR abs/1409.5872 (2014), http://arxiv.org/abs/1409.5872
31. Sheeran, M., Singh, S., Stålmarck, G.: Checking safety properties using induction and a SAT-solver. In: Johnson, S.D., Hunt Jr., W.A. (eds.) FMCAD 2000. LNCS, vol. 1954, pp. 108–125. Springer, Heidelberg (2000)

32. Silva, J.M., Sakallah, K.A.: Robust search algorithms for test pattern generation. In: FTCS, pp. 152–161 (1997)
33. Shtrichman, O.: Pruning techniques for the SAT-based bounded model checking problem. In: Margaria, T., Melham, T.F. (eds.) CHARME 2001. LNCS, vol. 2144, pp. 58–70. Springer, Heidelberg (2001)
34. Tip, F.: A survey of program slicing techniques. Tech. rep., CWI-Amsterdam (1994)
35. Whittemore, J., Kim, J., Sakallah, K.A.: SATIRE: A new incremental satisfiability engine. In: DAC, pp. 542–545 (2001)
36. Wieringa, S.: On incremental satisfiability and bounded model checking. In: Design & Impl. of Formal Tools & Sys., pp. 46–54 (2011)

Protocols

Colored Petri Net Modeling of the Publish/Subscribe Paradigm in the Context of Web Services Resources

Valentin Valero, Hermenegilda Macià$^{(\boxtimes)}$, Gregorio Díaz, and M. Emilia Cambronero

School of Computer Science, University of Castilla-La Mancha, 02071 Albacete, Spain
{Valentin.Valero,Hermenegilda.Macia,Gregorio.Diaz, MEmilia.Cambronero}@uclm.es

Abstract. In this paper a Prioritized-Timed Colored Petri Net model for the Publish/Subscribe paradigm in the context of Web services distributed resources is considered. We present a generic CPN model for publishing and managing WS-resources, which includes operations for clients to subscribe to these resources, with the intention of being notified when the resource property values fulfill certain conditions. We use CPN Tools to check and validate the model, and a case study is presented to illustrate how this CPN model works.

Keywords: Publish/Subscribe · Distributed systems · Formal modeling · Petri nets

1 Introduction

The publish/subscribe paradigm has received considerable attention in the last years. It provides a loosely coupled form of interaction in large scale settings, where subscribers register their interest in a topic or a pattern of events and then receive asynchronously the notification messages corresponding to the events that match their interest. A taxonomy of Publish/Subscribe systems, with a comparison between the different alternatives has been made by Eugster et al. [6] and also by Lin and Plade [11]. The most popular division of these systems considers two categories, the subject-based vision, and the content-based systems. In the subject-based systems the clients join to groups of interest, and all of them are notified of the events related to that group. In content-based systems, in contrast, the subscriber indicates a query or predicate related to the resource contents, and she is only notified when this predicate becomes true. In this paper we consider the contents-based approach, so that subscriptions will have a predicate associated, related to the WS-resource property values, and

This work has received financial support from the Spanish Government (cofinanced by FEDER funds) through the TIN2012-36812-C02-02 Project.

© Springer International Publishing Switzerland 2015
M. Núñez and M. Güdemann (Eds.): FMICS 2015, LNCS 9128, pp. 81–95, 2015.
DOI: 10.1007/978-3-319-19458-5_6

notifications will immediately be sent when the resource state makes true this predicate.

Some formalizations have been made of the Publish/Subscribe paradigm, but most of them focus on subject-based systems. Baldoni et al. [2] have defined a formalization based on the following process operations: *publish*, *notify*, *subscribe* and *unsubscribe*. They establish several information availability models, proving completeness and minimality for the computations they produce. They consider the subject-based approach, so no predicates are considered for notifications, which occur when items are published. The subject-based approach is also considered by Zanolin et al. [16]. In this case, the application-specific components are modeled as UML statechart diagrams and the middleware in charge of publication and notification of events is supplied as a configurable predefined component. The SPIN model-checker is then used to verify the properties of interest. This work was later extended [3], by including some additional features, such as message reliability, message ordering, message priorities, etc.

Garlan et al. [7] have also applied model-checking techniques for the analysis of a generic Publish/Subscribe framework. They have built a tool that works on a parameterized state machine model, which accepts as input a set of component descriptions together with a set of properties, thus producing a model that can be checked with the Cadence SMV model checker.

More related to our work, L. Abidi et al. [1] have developed a CPN model for the Publish/Subscribe paradigm, in this case in the context of a specific Grid protocol (BonjourGrid middleware), which supports resource discovery and coordination in a desktop Grid computing environment. However, they do not use Web Services, Web Service Publishing or Web Service Discovery standards in their work, since it is focused on a specific application. Our work in this paper, in contrast, is focused on providing a rigorous CPN model capturing the main elements for the publishing, discovery and management of WS-resources on the basis of Web Services standards, such as UDDI (Universal Description Discovery and Integration) [14], WSRF (Web Services Resource Framework) [15] and WSN (Web Services Notifications) [13]. There is another standard for Web services notifications from the W3C, namely WS-Eventing [4], which has many similarities with WSN, so any of them could be considered as reference for the subscribe/notify operations. Another Colored Petri Net representation of the basic operators of WS-BPEL and WS-RF standards has been presented by Mateo et al. in [12], where the main focus was to study the WS-BPEL operations together with some of the WS-RF operators, but excluding the publish/discovery process.

Another Petri net representation of the subject-based Publish/Subscribe systems was made by Hens et al. [8]. In this case time restrictions are not included in the model, and thus an ordinary Petri net model establishes the connection between the publishers and subscribers, in order to send the corresponding notifications when the events are published.

From all these works it becomes obvious that the way in which the publish/subscribe systems are modeled varies considerably depending on the specific model goals. In this paper, a mechanism to publish distributed resources identified by a textual name is introduced, as well as a mechanism to allow clients to discover these resources, by using these names. We omit a discussion about rules or policies to resolve the discovery problem, since for our purposes any resource whose identifier matches the given name will be valid.

Discovery of resources provides the clients with the required EPRs (End Point References) to access and manipulate these resources. They can read or modify the resource property values, as well as the resource expiration time (lifetime). Clients can also subscribe to resources, indicating a predicate that depends on the resource property values, with the purpose of being notified when the predicate becomes true. These subscriptions have also a lifetime associated, which means that once this time has elapsed, the corresponding subscription is canceled if it has not been notified before.

The rest of the paper is organized as follows. A background about WSRF, the Publish/Subscribe paradigm and Prioritized-Timed Colored Petri Nets is shown in Section 2. The Publish/Subscribe CPN-model is introduced by parts in Section 3, and a case study showing the complete PTCPN in Section 4. Section 5 finishes the paper, giving some conclusions and the possible lines of future work.

2   Background

In this section we establish the required background for both the WS-resource contents-based Publish/Subscribe paradigm and the prioritized-timed colored Petri net formalism that we use for the modeling of these systems.

2.1   WSRF and the Publish/Subscribe Paradigm

The Web Services Resource Framework (WSRF) [15] is an OASIS standard (Organization for the Advancement of Structured Information Standards), which defines a framework for modeling and accessing persistent resources using Web services. This approach consists of a set of specifications that define the representation of WS-resources manipulated by Web services. WS-resources are described by the so-called *Resource Properties Documents*, which are XML specifications that contain all the relevant resource information, such as the resource properties and the way the requestors can query or update its property values. This document is a projection of the actual state of the WS-resource and serves to define the structure upon which query and update messages are directed. Thus, any operation that manipulates a resource property via the WS-resource properties document must be reflected in the actual implementation of the WS-resource's state.

The WSRF standard provides us with operations to read or modify the resource properties (*getProp* and *setProp*, respectively), as well as to obtain or modify the resource lifetime (*getTime* and *setTime*, respectively), but no indication is made about the way in which resources are created and made visible. It is assumed that WS-resources are created by some external mechanism or through the use of a WS-resource factory, which creates the resource and establishes an association with a Web service, returning an endpoint reference (EPR), which can thereafter be used to direct requests to the WS-resource.

We then enrich our model with publish/discovery registry-based mechanisms. We consider two operations, *Publish* and *Discover* which resemble the *save_service* and *find_service* operations of UDDI [14]. A *Publish* operation is then provided to publish a WS-resource, indicating its EPR, tag (textual resource type identifier), initial value and initial lifetime. Notice that there can be several distinct implementations of a WS-resource (e.g., a printing service may be offered using different printers), so the discovery mechanism will only return the EPR of one of them. Thus, a *Discover* operation is also provided, which allows us to obtain a WS-resource from the *Registry*, according to a given *tag*.

Resources can be destroyed either by invoking the operation *Destroy* or because their lifetime has expired. The *Destroy* operation is equivalent to reassigning the resource lifetime to zero, so we can use this operation as a way to destroy resources.

WSRF can be complemented with WSN (Web Services Notifications) [13], which defines a set of specifications to standardize the *Subscription/Notification* mechanism, with the purpose of allowing clients to subscribe to WS-resources and be notified about specific changes in the resource state. A *Subscribe* operation is therefore provided, in which the client indicates the EPR of the resource and the *TopicExpression* that indicates the condition upon which the notification must be sent. In addition, subscriptions may have a finite duration, after which the subscription is canceled.

There are some other features of WSRF that will not be considered in this paper, such as the insertion and deletion of properties for existing WS-resources, the aggregation of multiple WS-resources or Web services into *ServiceGroups*, or the fault handling mechanisms.

2.2 Prioritized-Timed Colored Petri Nets

We use prioritized-timed colored Petri nets (PTCPNs), which are a prioritized-timed extension of colored Petri nets [9,10], the well-known formalism supported by CPN Tools [5], developed by the CPN group at the University of Aarhus. We specifically use a discrete time model, with a direct control of time elapsing, which is required for the correct reevaluation of the transition guards as time elapses. The technical problem here becomes from the fact that CPN Tools only reevaluates the guards when new tokens are produced.

A Petri Net (PN) is a directed graph, which consists of places (circles), transitions (rectangles) and arcs connecting places and transitions and viceversa. In colored PN (CPN) places have an associated *color set* (a data type), which specifies the set of allowed token colors at this place. Each token then has an attached data value, a *color*, which belongs to the corresponding place *color set*. The set of all tokens in a place specifies the multiset of colors associated to this place, that is, its marking. Furthermore in timed CPN (TCPN), tokens have a timestamp associated, which is a non-negative integer number, indicating the time at which they will be available for the firing of transitions. There is a discrete global clock that represents the total time elapsed in the system model.

Arcs can have inscriptions (*arc expressions*), constructed using variables, constants, operators and functions. The arc expressions must evaluate to a color or multiset of colors in the *color set* of the attached place. A transition is *binding enabled* if there is a **binding** such that each input arc expression is associated to one or more colors in the corresponding input place.

Transitions can also have guards that can restrict their firing, as well as priorities. Guards are predicates constructed by using the variables, constants, operators and functions of the model, and they must evaluate to true with the selected binding for the transition to be *fireable*. We also use priorities to establish an order of firing, and specifically we use 4 levels of priority, from $P1$ to $P4$ where the highest priority corresponds to $P1$.

In TCPN we can also include delays associated to output arcs (or to transitions, as a shorthand notation, when all the output arcs have the same delay inscription), which are used to age the timestamps of the tokens produced at the output places with respect to the current time. Hence, in a TCPN model an enabled transition must be binding, enabled, its guard must evaluate to true with the selected binding, the timestamp of the selected tokens in its preconditions must be less than or equal to the global clock value and there is no other transition with a greater priority fulfilling these conditions.

When an enabled transition is fired, new tokens are generated at the output places, with colors according to the corresponding output arc expressions, and the selected tokens for its firing (from the binding) are removed from its input places. Notice that in TCPN tokens are only available at the time they have attached. This time will therefore determine the instant at which a transition will be able to use this token for its firing. When there is no enabled transitions at the current instant, the global clock is aged to the earliest time at which a transition is enabled.

We have presented an informal description of PTCPNs, a complete and formal definition of the formalism can be found in [10].

Example 1. Let us consider the marked PTCPN depicted in Figure 1, obtained from CPN Tools.

Tokens in CPN Tools are drawn using the notation $n'v@s$, meaning that we have n instances of a token with color value v and *timestamp* s. Besides, the symbol '++' is used to represent the union of timed multisets in CPN Tools.

All places in the example have as color set $INTT$ (int timed), and the variables x, y, z, w are integers. Transitions are labeled with their associated guard, time delay and priority information, and arcs are labeled with the corresponding expressions. Empty guards are always evaluated to true and empty delays are considered as $@ + 0$ to specify instantaneous transitions.

From the initial marking shown in Figure 1 we can see that only transition $t1$ can be fired (at instant 0), and any token of those in $p1$ can be used for its firing (the binding can be either $x = 3$ or $x = 5$). Taking the binding $x = 5$, which fulfills the transition guard ($x < 7$), we get 5@0 on $p1$. The firing of $t1$ with this

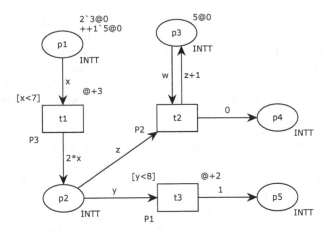

Fig. 1. Graphical view of a PTCPN

binding removes the token 5@0 from $p1$, and produces a new token on $p2$ with a timestamp 3. Thus, considering the output arc inscription, we get a token 10@3 on $p2$. The transition $t1$ must fire again twice (until $p1$ becomes empty), because the new token on $p2$ will not be available until instant 3. As a result we obtain in $p2$ the following marking $\{1'10@3, 2'6@3\}$, and the global clock value is 3, so that no more transitions can be fired until instant 3.

At instant 3, there are two enabled transitions $t2$ and $t3$, since for both transitions we have bindings allowing its firing ($\{y = 6\}$ for $t3$ and $\{z = 10, w = 5\}$ or $\{z = 6, w = 5\}$ for $t2$) and the guards are satisfied ($y < 8$ and *True (empty)* for $t3$ and $t2$ respectively). Since $t3$ has a higher priority ($P1$ vs. $P2$), this transition must be fired, producing a new token 1@5 on $p5$. Next, the only transition that can be fired is $t3$ again, and the other instance of the token 6@3 on $p2$ is used to produce another instance of 1@5 on $p5$. Then, the next fired transition is $t2$, since it is the only binding enabled transition and its guard is empty, despite its lower priority. The firing of $t2$ produces the tokens 11@3 at $p3$ and 0@3 at $p5$. Token 5@0 is replaced by 11@3 at $p3$ with this firing.

Finally, $p1$ and $p2$ are both empty after the firing of all the enabled transitions, $p3$ has one token 11@3, $p4$ one token 0@3 and $p5$ two instances of 1@5. The final value for the global clock is 3.   □

3   PTCPN Modeling of Publish/Subscribe

In this section, we describe the PTCPN model for the WS-resources and the Publish/Subscribe mechanism. We present and validate the model by parts. Thus, we first present the PTCPN for the publishment and basic management of WS-resources, after which the discovery and subscription mechanisms are modeled, and finally, notifications are included in the model. The analysis of

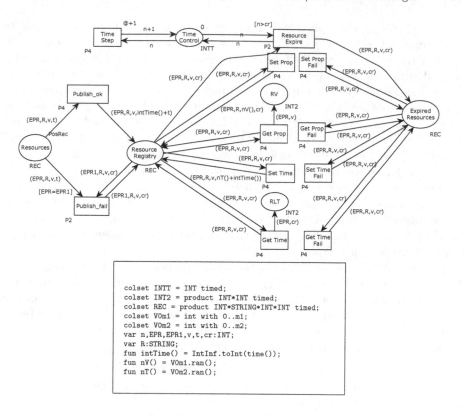

```
colset INTT = INT timed;
colset INT2 = product INT*INT timed;
colset REC = product INT*STRING*INT*INT timed;
colset VOm1 = int with 0..m1;
colset VOm2 = int with 0..m2;
var n,EPR,EPR1,v,t,cr:INT;
var R:STRING;
fun intTime() = IntInf.toInt(time());
fun nV() = VOm1.ran();
fun nT() = VOm2.ran();
```

Fig. 2. WS-resource Modeling

the complete model is accomplished in the next section, by using a specific case study.

3.1   WS-resource Modeling

Figure 2 shows the basic WS-resource modeling. The place *Resources* initially contains all the colored tokens representing potential resources in the system (PosRec), which will eventually be published. The information attached to each one of these tokens is a tuple (EPR, R, v, t), where EPR is the End Point Reference of the WS-resource [1], R is a textual tag identifying the resource type, v is the initial value, and t its initial lifetime.

Resources are published by firing the transition *Publish_ok*, but notice that in the event that there exists an already published resource in the *Registry* with the same EPR, the transition *Publish_fail* will instead be fired (it has greater priority), indicating a failure in the resource publishment. We use the CPNTools function *intTime()*, which provides us with the current clock value, so the tokens

---

[1] We use non-negative integer numbers as EPRs, and also as WS-resource values.

produced in the *Registry* place will only be available until the time indicated in its last component: $intTime() + t$. Time elapsing is modeled by transition *TimeStep*, which updates the value of the token on the place *TimeControl*, which is initially marked with one token with value 0, and represents the current model time. Transition *TimeStep* is required for technical reasons, for the reevaluation of the guards, because otherwise CPN Tools do not reevaluate the guards as time elapses. Thus, we can check if a resource has expired, represented by the guard $[n > cr]$, where n is the current model time and cr the resource expiration time. This transition has the lower priority, since we only allow time elapsing when there is no transition that can be fired at the current model time.

Transition *ResourceExpire* will be fired when some token on the *Registry* has a lifetime value (cr) smaller than the token value on the place *TimeControl*, i.e., resources are unpublished when their lifetime has expired. The firing of *ResourceExpire* is enforced by its priority, and the corresponding resource token is moved to the place *ExpiredResources*.

The remaining transitions model the basic operations on WS-resources: *SetProp, GetProp, SetTime* and *getTime*. We use in this generic model a function $nV()$ for *SetProp* (resp. $nT()$ for *SetTime*) in order to assign a new value [2] for the resource (resp. for its lifetime). Notice also that we have included *Fail*-labeled versions of these transitions, in order to capture what happens when a client invokes one of these operations over an expired WS-resource.

Validation: This part has been validated with CPNTools, by assigning an initial marking to the place *Resources* and the initial token on the place *TimeControl*, but we have needed to restrict the possible infinite behaviors by including a control place that feeds the transitions for the WS-resource operations *GetProp, SetProp, GetTime, SetTime* and their Fail-versions, thus limiting their maximum number of firings. We have also included a guard in *TimeStep* to limit the maximum model time, otherwise *TimeStep* will continue to fire indefinitely. This maximum time must be big enough to allow the resources to be published and expire.

The analysis with CPNTools allows us to conclude that resources were published in their correct times, they also expired according to their lifetimes, and any attempt to republish a resource fails. The operations *Getprop, SetProp, SetTime, GetTime* and their Fail-versions were also performed. The state space analysis with a big enough maximum model time allows us to conclude that all the obtained dead (terminating) markings correspond to a situation in which all the resources have expired.

3.2 Discovery and Subscription Modeling

The WS-resource discovery and subscription part is modeled as indicated in Figure 3. The potential subscribers and the resources they intend to subscribe are represented by the tokens on the place[3] *Roles* (marking *PosCli* in Figure

---

[2] This value is randomly selected in this generic framework.

[3] This initial marking can be updated to adapt the model to a specific case study.

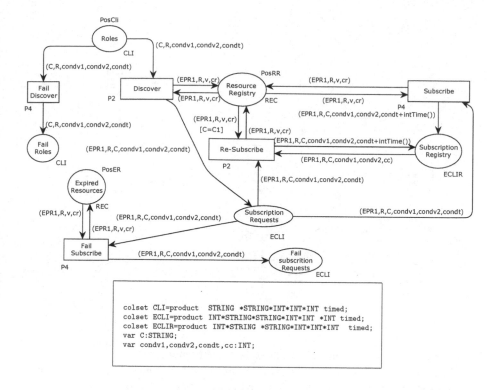

Fig. 3. Discovery and Subscription Modeling

3). These tokens have as colors tuples indicating the client name (C), a resource tag (R), two integer values ($condv1, condv2$) defining an interval and a subscription lifetime ($condt$). They have as timestamp the time instant at which the corresponding client intends to perform the discovery and subsequently the subscription at the obtained WS-resource.

The transition *Discover* obtains one of the tokens in the place *Resource Registry* (already introduced in Figure 2) that matches with the indicated *tag*, producing a token in the place *SubscriptionRequests*, labeled with the corresponding *EPR*, in order to activate the subscription (transition *Subscribe*). Clients are also allowed to resubscribe to a resource, in this case, the transition *Re-Subscribe* is fired, which replaces the old interval and subscription lifetime with new values.

A WS-resource discovery fails when there is no published resource with the indicated tag. The transition *FailDiscover* has been therefore included for this purpose, but notice that it has less priority than *Discover*, in order to enforce the firing of *Discover* when there is some published resource with the indicated tag. Furthermore, a subscription can fail when the corresponding resource has expired, so we have included a *FailSubscribe* transition that will be fired in that case (the place *Expired Resources* connected with this transition was already introduced in Figure 2).

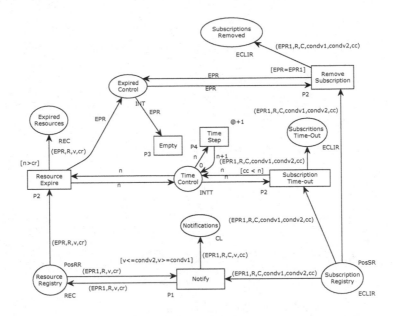

Fig. 4. Notification and Subscription Time-Out Modeling

<u>Validation</u>: The validation of this part has been made by assigning an initial marking to the places *Roles*, *ExpiredResources* and *ResourceRegistry*. We have checked the discovery of resources, subscriptions, resubscriptions, failed subscriptions and that a discover on a non-published tag produces a failure (transition *FailDiscover*).

The state space analysis has also been made for this part of the model by assigning an initial marking capturing the different actions related to this part. Thus, the places *Roles*, *ResourceRegistry* and *ExpiredResources* are initially marked and we have concluded that the final markings include the published and expired resources indicated in the initial marking, and also the failing discovery actions and the registered subscriptions.

3.3   Notification and Subscription Time-Out Modeling

Figure 4 shows the notification and subscription time-out modeling parts. Transition *Notify* must be be fired when a subscription condition is satisfied for some published WS-resource, which is actually enforced by assigning the maximum priority to this transition ($P1$). Notification conditions are here represented by intervals, i.e., the resource value must be in the interval defined by *condv1*, *condv2* in order to send the notification. From the generic modeling viewpoint, notifications are saved into the place *Notifications*, and the corresponding subscriptions are removed from the place *SubscriptionRegistry*.

In the left-hand side of Figure 4 we can see again the transition *Resource-Expire* and its associated places and transitions for the time control as explained above, whose firing produces one token on the place *ExpiredControl*, whose color is the EPR of the expired resource. This token is used to remove all the pending subscriptions to this resource in the place *SubscriptionRegistry*, by firing the transition *RemoveSubscription* until no more tokens with this EPR are available on this place. Transition *Empty* can then be fired (it has less priority than *RemoveSubscription*) to remove this token on *ExpiredControl*. The priority assigned to *Empty* guarantees us that this transition must be fired before a new publication is made, to avoid that this same resource be published again without this token being previously removed from this place.

Finally, the transition *SubscriptionTimeOut* must be fired when a subscription expires, removing the corresponding subscription token from the place *SubscriptionRegistry* and putting it on the place *SubscriptionsRemoved*. This firing is enforced by its high priority ($P2$), but notice that in the event that several of these transitions, *Notify, SubscriptionTimeOut* and *RemoveSubscription* are simultaneously enabled, *Notify* will always win (if enabled) to any of them, so we are giving more importance to notifications than subscription time-outs or resource lifetime expiration.

Validation: This part has been validated by assigning an initial marking to the places *ResourceRegistry, SubscriptionRegistry* and *TimeControl*, respectively indicating the published resources, current subscriptions and current model control time. We have checked that resources expire according to their remaining lifetimes, and that in this case all the pending subscriptions to these expired resources are canceled. We have also checked that notifications occur if the corresponding conditions hold, and that subscriptions expire according to their indicated lifetimes.

In order to obtain the state space of this part of the model we consider again a guard on the transition *TimeStep*, which restricts the maximum model time. The places that must be initially marked for this part of the model are *ResourceRegistry, SubscriptionRegistry* and *TimeControl*. Thus, we have obtained that for all the final markings the only marked places correspond to the expired resources and subscriptions, notifications, removed subscriptions and the token on the place *TimeControl*.

4   Case Study

The complete PTCPN for the Publish/Subscribe paradigm is shown in Figure 5, where we have introduced a place named *OpControl* in order to restrict the instants at which the operations *SetTime, SetProp, GetTime* or *GetProp* can be performed, thus avoiding infinite behaviors. We could even introduce colors in this place and guards in these operations.in order to establish which operation is specifically performed at each of these instants, and over which WS-resource. However, we have decided just to introduce the place *OpControl* to avoid the infinite behaviors, and keep this non-determinism in the specific operation performed, as well as about the value or time assigned in the case of a *SetProp* or *GetProp* operation.

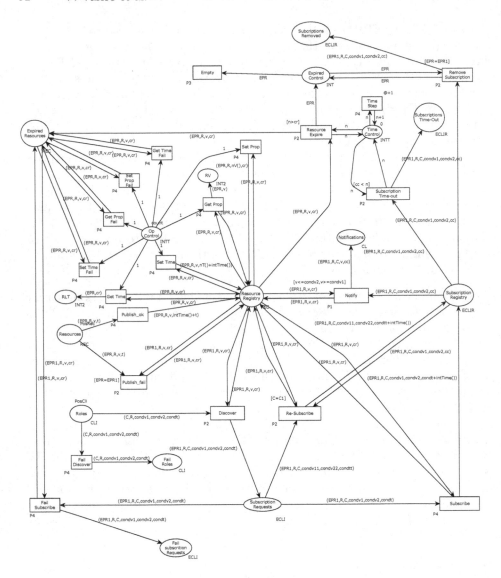

Fig. 5. PTCPN for the Publish/Subscribe Paradigm

In table 1 we show the initial marking for the scenario that we have considered, which illustrates the complete PTCPN functionality. Two printers and one tablet are published, their respective values could be for instance their prices, so the potential clients can be interested in them according to their current prices. Two tokens corresponding to a printer with EPR 1 are available at time 0, which means that only one of them will be published, and the other one produces a failure when attempting to publish the printer twice. The potential clients are Alice, Bob and Carla. For instance, Alice intends to discover and subscribe to a printer at instants 0 and 1. According to our model, subscriptions are performed immediately after the resource discovery, but this model could be easily modified in order to include an additional time in the tokens on the place *Roles*, indicating the time at which the subscription must be requested. Notice that it is possible for a resource to expire between the discovery and the subscription (in time zero), in particular due to the higher priority (P2) of transition *ResourceExpire* with respect to *Subscribe*, which has a lower priority (P4). For instance, this scenario occurs when Alice discovers at time 1 the printer with EPR 1, whose initial lifetime was 2, but as a consequence of a SetTime operation with argument 0 it is unpublished at time 1, causing the failure of the subscribe operation.

Table 1. Initial Marking for the PTCPN

PLACE	INITIAL MARKING
Resources	2'(1,"PRINTER",2,2)@0++1'(2,"PRINTER",2,1)@2++ 1'(3,"TABLET",3,1)@2
Roles	1'("Alice","PRINTER",0,1,2)@0++1'("Alice","PRINTER",0,2,1)@1++ 1'("Bob","PRINTER",2,3,1)@2++1'("Carla","TABLET",1,2,1)@1
OpControl	2'1@0++1'1@1++1'1@2
TimeControl	0

For this initial marking we have obtained a state space consisting of 49103 nodes, 102857 arcs and 2224 dead (final) markings. These terminating markings correspond to all the possible terminating executions of the system, once the maximum model time was reached. Notice that this number of final markings is also a consequence of the way we generate the values and lifetimes for the resources, which are randomly generated.

We can still check that these dead markings are really the expected, just by including some transitions in order to remove the tokens on the places *Fail-SubscriptionsRequests, FailRoles, Notifications, SubscriptionTimeOut, Subscrip-tionsRemoved*, and another transition (with the lowest priority) for removing the final tokens of the place *ExpiredResources*. With these changes we have obtained that there is only one *dead marking*, in which only the place *TimeControl* is marked with one token, which means that all resources were either published or their publishment failed, and those but were published were finally unpublished when their lifetime expired. Furthermore, the client's requests were all processed, some subscriptions were notified, and those that were active when the corresponding resource was unpublished were removed.

5   Conclusions and Future Work

In this paper we have presented a generic Colored Petri Net modeling of the WS-resource contents-based Publish-Subscribe paradigm. We have therefore established a generic framework for the modeling of WS-resource interactions, providing a set of operations that match with the standards related to WS-resource management (WSRF), publish and discovery of services (UDDI), and Web Services Notifications (WSN). The main benefit from this Publish/Subscribe PTCPN model is that we can use CPNTools in order to simulate and analyze the specific systems modeled, so we can predict their behavior, and we can discover potential problems before the implementation.

This generic model can be easily modified to introduce the specific behavior of clients, who may change their behavior in accordance with the values obtained from the resources, or as response to the received notifications. However, our goal has been to provide a generic model that can be easily applied to a great variety of systems.

The validation of the Publish/Subscribe model presented in this paper has been made by considering several specific initial markings that capture samples of all the possible behaviors. We intend to extend this work by defining a formal set of properties that a Publish/Subscribe model must fulfill, and then use the CTL-like temporal logic model-checker provided by CPN Tools in order to check if these properties are satisfied in our framework.

As another future work in this area, we are planning to define a complete formalism to manage WS-resources in the framework of composite Web services. Thus, we plan to integrate this generic model into a more general formalism, with the purpose to capture the broader interrelations among the different parties involved in a Web service composition using WS-resources.

References

1. Abidi, L., Cérin, C., Evangelista, S.: A Petri-Net Model for the Publish-Subscribe Paradigm and its Application for the Verification of the BonjourGrid Middleware. In: Proc. 2011 IEEE International Conference on Services Computing, pp. 496–503 (2011)
2. Baldoni, R., Contenti, M., Tucci, S., Virgilio, A.: Modelling Publish/Subscribe Communication Systems: Towards a Formal Approach. In: Proc. 8th IEEE International Workshop on Object-Oriented Real-Time Dependable Systems, pp. 304–311 (2003)
3. Baresi, L., Ghezzi, C., Mottola, L.: On Accurate Automatic Verification of Publish/Subscribe Architectures. In: Proc. 29th International Conference on Software Engineering (ICSE 2007), pp. 199–208 (2007)
4. Box, D., et al.: Web Services Eventing (WS-Eventing). W3C Member Submission (March 2006), http://www.w3c.org/submission/ws-eventing
5. CPN Tools homepage, http://www.cs.au.dk/CPNTools
6. Eugster, P.T., Felber, P.A., Guerraoui, R., Kermarrec, A.M.: The Many Faces of Publish/Subscribe. ACM Computing Surveys 35(2) (2003)
7. Garlan, D., Khersonsky, S., Kim, I.: Model Checking Publish-Subscribe Systems. In: Ball, T., Rajamani, S.K. (eds.) SPIN 2003. LNCS, vol. 2648, pp. 166–180. Springer, Heidelberg (2003)
8. Hens, P., Snoeck, M., Poels, G., Backer, M.: A Petri Net Formalization of a Publish-Subscribe System. Int. report, Faculty of Business and Economics, Katholieke Univ. Leuven, http://dx.doi.org/10.2139/ssrn.1886198
9. Jensen, K.: Coloured Petri Nets. Basic Concepts, Analysis Methods and Practical Use. Monographs in Theoretical Computer Science. Springer (1997)

10. Jensen, K., Kristensen, L.M.: Coloured Petri Nets. Modelling and Validation of Concurrent Systems. Springer (2009)
11. Lin, Y., Plade, B.: Survey of Publish-Subscribe Event Systems. Computer Science Department, Indiana University. Technical Report, vol. 16 (2003)
12. Mateo, J.A., Valero, V., Macià, H., Díaz, G.: A Coloured Petri Net Approach to Model and Analyse Stateful Workflows Based on WS-BPEL and WSRF. In: Canal, C., Idani, A. (eds.) SEFM 2014 Workshops. LNCS, vol. 8938, pp. 389–404. Springer, Heidelberg (2015)
13. Niblett, P., Graham, S.: Events and Service-Oriented Architecture: The OASIS Web Services Notification Specifications. IBM Systems Journal 44(4), 869–886 (2005)
14. OASIS. UDDI Version 3.02 API Specification (2005), https://www.oasis-open.org/committees/uddi-spec/doc/tcspecs.htm#uddiv3
15. OASIS. OASIS Web Services Resource Framework (WSRF), v1.2 (2006), https://www.oasis-open.org/committees/tc_home.php?wg_abbrev=wsrf
16. Zanolin, L., Ghezzi, C., Baresi, L.: An Approach to Model and Validate Publish/Subscribe Architectures. In: Proc. of the SAVBS 2003 Workshop, pp. 35–41 (2003)

Model Checking a Server-Side Micro Payment Protocol

Kaylash Chaudhary[✉] and Ansgar Fehnker

School of Computing, Information and Mathematical Sciences,
University of the South Pacific, Suva, Fiji
kaylash.chaudhary@usp.ac.fj

Abstract. Many virtual payment systems are available on the world
wide web for micropayment, and as they deal with money, correctness
is important. One such payment system is Netpay. This paper examines
the server-side version of the Netpay protocol and provides its formalization as a CSP model. The PAT model checker is used to prove three
properties essential for correctness: impossibility of double spending, validity of an ecoin during the execution and the absence of deadlock. We
prove that the protocol is executing according to its description based on
the assumption that the customers and vendors are cooperative. This is
a very strong assumption for system built to prevent abuse, but further
analysis suggests that without it the protocol does no longer guarantee
all correctness properties.

Keywords: Model checking · Verification · CSP · Micropayment
protocols · Virtual payment systems · PAT

1 Introduction

The Internet has grown into a virtual market where the exchange of a wide range
of goods is everyday practice. For many payments users have to use their credit
cards, even though the transaction costs are significant for small transactions.
To facilitate payment of smaller amounts micro-payment technologies emerged
[7]. With the increase of paid services and content on the Internet, these online
payment system promise the ease of using cash. There are many micro-payment
systems available for users to buy goods online such as Netpay [7], Millicent
[8], Micro-mint [12], Payword [12], MiniPay [10], Micro-iKP [9] and POPCORN
[11]. There are also many micro-payment systems proposed for content sharing
in peer to peer networks [1] [2], [14], [15] and [16].

Every payment protocol should guarantee certain essential properties of correctness. In this paper we will model one such system, Netpay, formally, and
show that it satisfies essential properties. This paper considers a variant called
server-side Netpay in which the e-coins are kept by trusted brokers and vendors,
while the customer will only have access to the e-coin ID. This is in contrast
to the so-called client-side Netpay protocol in which e-coins are kept by the
customers. Previous work considered the correctness of client-side Netpay [3].

© Springer International Publishing Switzerland 2015
M. Núñez and M. Güdemann (Eds.): FMICS 2015, LNCS 9128, pp. 96–110, 2015.
DOI: 10.1007/978-3-319-19458-5_7

This paper models the server-side Netpay using CSP [13]. The model in this paper covers the handling of e-coins, and omits the parts of the protocol that are concerned with redeeming e-coins, and digital signatures of e-coins. It is assumed that the correctness of these are guaranteed independently, especially the correctness of the used cryptographic hash functions. Instead, we prove that the protocol can guarantee that a trusted broker will correctly track an e-coin, even though it will be passed from vendor to vendor, that at any time only one vendor will have a copy of the e-coin, that the customer can not spend more than the e-coin is worth. Finally, we considered whether the system was deadlock free and discovered that some arguably strong assumptions are necessary to ensure correctness. If customers do not cooperate they can get the system into a state where deadlock is possible. We also analysed a design alternative that does not have this problem.

Section 2 introduces the server-side Netpay protocol. Section 3 shows the description of the Netpay protocol using the CSP language. Correctness of this protocol is discussed in Section 4. This paper concludes with discussion for future research in section 5.

2   The Netpay Protocol

The Netpay protocol with server-side e-wallet was proposed by Dai et.al. [5]. It has three types of e-wallets: client side, server-side and cookie-based e-wallet [6]. There are three parties involved in this protocol; customer, vendor and broker. It is assumed that the broker and vendors are honest and are trusted by the customers who may not be honest. To use the protocol, the customers and vendors need to register by opening an account and depositing funds with the broker. The broker is responsible for registration, e-coin generation, debiting and crediting accounts for customers and vendors respectively. The payment is between customers and vendors. Previous work has modeled and verified some properties of client-side Netpay [3]

Netpay uses a number of cryptography and micro-payment terminologies such as:

- **One-way Hash Function:** Netpay uses this function to generate and verify e-coins. In [6] MD5 was used, but it could be replaced by more secure SHA-1.
- **E-coin:** The one-way hash function is applied repeatedly to a seed to generate a series of paywords called e-coin. The paywords are represented in reverse order with the seed at the end. The length of the e-coin determines its value.
- **E-wallet:** An e-wallet is a database to store e-coins.
- **Seed:** It is a randomly selected value used for e-coin generation.
- **Touchstone:** This is the first payword of the e-coin. It is used to verify e-coins.

Using the one way hash function h, an e-coin $W_1, ..., W_n$ is constructed by applying the hash function $n + 1$ times to a seed i.e. $W_0 = h(W_1), W_1 = h(W_2), ..., W_n = h(W_{n+1})$ where W_{n+1} is the seed, and W_0 the touchstone.

The remainder of this section will describe the four basic types of transactions in this protocol. It is assumed that each customer and vendor have a unique ID.

Customer-Broker Transaction. The customer sends an e-coin request with parameter n to the broker, who generates e-coins of length n. Each chain has a unique e-coin ID. The broker stores this information in its database, and sends the e-coin ID to the customer.

Customer-Vendor Transaction. If a customer wishes to buy something from the vendor, the customer sends an e-coin ID. The vendor checks if it has the e-coin and verifies it. If the verification is successful, the customer is notified. If the vendor does not have the e-coin, it requests the location from the broker. The broker will reply with the location of the e-coin, the vendor requests this e-coin from that vendor or broker. Initially, the broker will have the e-coin and after that it will be transferred from one vendor to another.

Vendor-Vendor Transaction. This transaction occurs when one vendor requests an e-coin from another vendor.

Vendor-Broker Transaction. Vendors need to redeem the e-coins spent by customers. The vendor sends the e-coin IDs, touchstones, customer IDs, vendor ID, e-coins and amount to the broker. The broker will verify e-coins and credit the corresponding amount to the vendors account if the spent e-coins are valid. This paper focuses on the spending of e-coins, and omits redemption of e-coins from the model.

Properties of the Netpay Protocol. This paper considers three important properties. The first is on the validity of e-coins. Since there will be transfer of an e-coin from one vendor to another, an e-coin should remain valid in this chain of transfer. The second is on preventing double spending. This protocol prohibits a customer to double spend an e-coin at a different or same vendor. The last property is to show absence of deadlocks.

3   Description of Netpay Protocol Using CSP

This section provides models and description for the Server-Side Netpay protocol. The three parties of the protocol: customer, vendor and broker have been modeled as one process each. For simplicity we assume that there is only one broker, while there can be many customers and vendors.

3.1   Customer Process

Table 1 shows the *Customer*(CID) process for the customer CID. This process has three possible statuses: IDLE, BUYCOIN or SPENDING. Variable STATUS_C keeps track of the status of a customer.

The customer database is stored in variable DB_C. It contains e-coin ID's and amounts. Recall, that an e-coin is constructed by applying hash function to a seed. Each payword in Netpay is accompanied by an index to record number of

Table 1. Customer Process

```
    Customer(CID) =
    [STATUS_C[CID] == IDLE && (||y:{0..(MAXCOINS-1)}@(DB_C[CID][y][0] == -1))]
        BuyCoin!CID
5           {STATUS_C[CID] = BUYCOIN;} ->Customer(CID)
    [] [STATUS_C[CID] == BUYCOIN ]
        SellCoin[CID]?id
            {
            var index = 0;
10          while(index < MAXCOINS)
            {
                if (DB_C[CID][index][0] == -1)
                {
                    DB_C[CID][index][0] = id ;
15                  DB_C[CID][index][1] = ISPOSITIVE;
                    index = MAXCOINS;//break the loop
                }
                index = index + 1;
            }
20
            STATUS_C[CID] = IDLE} -> Customer(CID)
    [] ([]x:{0..(VENDORS-1)};y:{0..(MAXCOINS-1)}@([STATUS_C[CID] == IDLE
    && DB_C[CID][y][0] != -1 ]
        Spend[x]!CID.DB_C[CID][y][0].DB_C[CID][y][1]
25          {STATUS_C[CID] = SPENDING;} ->Customer(CID)))
    [] [STATUS_C[CID] == SPENDING]
        Approval[CID]?eid1.amt
            {
            if (amt == ISZERO)
30          {
                var index = 0;
                while(index < MAXCOINS)
                {
                    if(DB_C[CID][index][0]==eid1)
35                  {
                        DB_C[CID][index][0] = -1;
                        DB_C[CID][index][1] = -1;
                    }
                    index = index + 1;
40              }
            }
            STATUS_C[CID] = IDLE;} ->Customer(CID)
    [] [STATUS_C[CID] == SPENDING]
        Disapproval[CID]?vid
45          {STATUS_C[CID] = IDLE;} ->Customer(CID)
```

unspent paywords; the amount. The amount will be abstracted in this paper as either IsPositive or IsZero. This is because the properties shown in this paper are independent of hash function and the exact amount.

Initially, the customer will have no e-coin ID stored in DB_C. The only enabled event is to buy e-coins on the *BuyCoin* channel with parameter CID, which is the customer ID. Events that use the *BuyCoin* channel have precondition STATUS_C[CID] == IDLE i.e. the customer should be IDLE in order to send a message on this channel. After sending the message to the broker, the customer will change to the BUYCOIN state. The broker can reply on the *SellCoin* channel, since the condition STATUS_C[CID] == BUYCOIN for the customer is met. The customer adds the e-coin ID and the amount to DB_C, and changes to IDLE.

If customer has e-coins and is in the IDLE state, it can buy goods from a vendor on channel *Spend*, which will synchronize with one of the vendors. The channel has two parameters: e-coin ID and amount. After this event, the customer will change the state to SPENDING. The vendor will reply on channel *Approval* or *Disapproval*, depending on whether the payment was accepted or not. In either case, the customer's state will change to IDLE.

There is not much processing done by the customer side compared to the Client-Side Netpay protocol [3]. Most processing is done by the vendor. Note, that the customer can try spending an e-coin as often as it wants. It is up to the vendors and brokers to prevent double spending.

3.2 Broker Process

The process *Broker*(BID) in Table 2 and Table 3 models the broker with unique broker ID BID. The broker has a database DB_B to store all generated e-coins. In addition it has a database LOOKUP that maps an e-coin ID to a vendor or broker. The broker can have status IDLE, BUYCOIN, REQLOC or REQCOIN. Variable STATUS_B is used for tracking the status. Variables *vid_B*, *eloc_B*, *cid_B*, *eid_B* and *amount_B* are used to store intermediate results while generating e-coins or replying to request from customers or vendors.

This process models three tasks for the broker. The first task is the generation of new e-coins, lines 6 - 15 of Table 2. A customer requests a new e-coin on channel *BuyCoin* with parameter *cid*, the ID of the requesting customer. This event is guarded by the expression STATUS_B == IDLE. The event changes the status to BUYCOIN. The broker replies to the customer on channel *SellCoin* with two parameters, an e-coin id and the amount of coins. The broker then updates the two databases (Table 2, lines 26 - 29). The status of the process changes to IDLE.

The next task is to pass new e-coins to vendors upon request. The request by a vendor is modeled by the channel *ReqCoin*[BID]. The model uses an array of channel *ReqCoin*, one channel for each vendor. The vendor *vid* is requesting the broker BID to send the e-coin *eid1* on channel *ReqCoin*[BID] with parameters *vid* and *eid1*. It is enabled if the status is IDLE. This event will change the status to REQCOIN and the variables *eid_B*, *amount_B* and *vid_B* will store the e-coin ID, the amount, and the ID of the requesting vendor respectively. These will be used by the broker to send the e-coin to the requesting vendor BVID on channel *SendCoin*[BVID]. This event is enabled, if the status is REQCOIN. The status will then change to IDLE.

The final task keeps track of the e-coin location and responds to the location request by vendors. The channel *ReqLoc* is used for requests from vendors *vid*

Table 2. Broker Process

```
   Broker(BID) =
   [STATUS_B == IDLE && (||x:{0..(BROKER_SIZE-1)}@(DB_B[x][0]==-1))]
      BuyCoin?cid
 5       {
          cid_B = cid;
          var index = 0;
          while(index < BROKER_SIZE)
          {
10            if (DB_B[index][0] == eid)
              {
                  eid = (eid+1)%MAXEID;
                  index = BROKER_SIZE;
              }
15            index = index + 1;
          }
          STATUS_B = BUYCOIN;} -> Broker(BID)
   [][STATUS_B == BUYCOIN ]
      SellCoin[cid_B]!eid
20       {
          var index = 0;
          while(index < BROKER_SIZE)
          {
              if (DB_B[index][0] == -1 && DB_B[index][1] == -1)
25            {
                  DB_B[index][0] = eid;
                  DB_B[index][1] = ISPOSITIVE;
                  LOOKUP[index][0] = eid;
                  LOOKUP[index][1] = BID;
30                index = BROKER_SIZE;
              }
              index = index + 1;
          }
          cid_B = 0;
35        eid = (eid+1)%MAXEID;
          STATUS_B = IDLE;} -> Broker(BID)
   [][STATUS_B == IDLE]
      ReqLoc?vid.eid1
          {
40        vid_B = vid;
          var index = 0;
          while(index < BROKER_SIZE)
          {
              if (LOOKUP[index][0] == eid1)
45            {
                  eloc_B = LOOKUP[index][1];
                  LOOKUP[index][1] = vid;
                  index = BROKER_SIZE;//break the loop
              }
50            index = index + 1;
          }
          STATUS_B = REQLOC;} -> Broker(BID)
```

Table 3. Broker Process (continued)

```
     [] [STATUS_B == REQLOC]
          SendLoc[vid_B]!eloc_B
               {
5             vid_B = 0;
               eloc_B = -1;
               STATUS_B = IDLE;} -> Broker(BID)
     [] [STATUS_B == REQCOIN]
          SendCoin[vid_B]!eid_B.amount_B
10            { STATUS_B = IDLE;} -> Broker(BID)
     [] [STATUS_B == IDLE]
          ReqCoin[BID]?eid1.vid
               {
               STATUS_B = REQCOIN;
15            var index = 0;   .
               vid_B = vid;
               while (index < BROKER_SIZE)
               {
                    if (DB_B[index][0] == eid1 && DB_B[index][0] != -1)
20                  {
                         eid_B = DB_B[index][0];
                         amount_B = DB_B[index][1];
                         index = BROKER_SIZE; //end loop
                    }
25                  index = index + 1;
               }
               } -> Broker(BID);
```

for the location of the e-coin *eid1*. This event is enabled if the status is IDLE. The broker will look up the entry for the e-coin ID *eid1* in the LOOKUP database, and save it in variable *Beloc*, and also update the location of the e-coin in the LOOKUP database to that of the requesting vendor *vid*. The state will change to REQLOC, which enables the channel *SendLoc*. This channel is used for the reply to the vendor request. The status of the process changes to IDLE.

3.3 Vendor Process

The process $Vendor(\text{VID})$ shown in Tables 4 and 5 models a vendor with ID VID. Each vendor maintains an e-wallet EWALLET which contains e-coins of the various customers. A vendor can have status IDLE, SPENDING, HAVECOIN, HAVELOC, NOCOIN, REQLOC, RECVREQ and REQCOIN. The status is stored in variable STATUS_V. Other variables used to store intermediate results are *vid_V*, *eloc_V*, *cid_V*, *amount_V* and *eid_V*.

The vendor performs two major task: verifying e-coins received from a customer and transferring an e-coin to a requesting vendor. The verification of the e-coins has two cases; either the current vendor has the e-coin in its e-wallet,

Table 4. Vendor Process

```
    Vendor(VID) =
    [STATUS_V[VID] == IDLE &&
    (||x:{0..(EWALLET_SIZE-1)}@(Ewallet[VID][x][0]==-1))]
 5      Spend[VID]?cid.Eid.amount
            {
            cid_V[VID]=cid;
            var index = 0;
            var flag = false;
10          while(index < EWALLET_SIZE)
            {
                if (Ewallet[VID][index][0] == Eid )
                {
                    flag = true;
15                  index_V[VID] = index;
                    index = EWALLET_SIZE;//break the loop
                }
                index = index + 1;
            }
20          if (flag == true)
                STATUS_V[VID] = HAVECOIN;
            else{
                eid_V[VID] = Eid;
                STATUS_V[VID] = NOCOIN;
25              }
            } ->Vendor(VID)

    [] [STATUS_V[VID] == HAVECOIN && Ewallet[VID][index_V[VID]][1] == ISPOSITIVE]
        Approval[cid_V[VID]]!Ewallet[VID][index_V[VID]][0].ISPOSITIVE
30          {
            Ewallet[VID][index_V[VID]][1] = ISPOSITIVE;
            index_V[VID] = 0;
            cid_V[VID] =-1;
            STATUS_V[VID] = IDLE;} ->Vendor(VID)
35  [] [STATUS_V[VID] == HAVECOIN && Ewallet[VID][index_V[VID]][1] == ISPOSITIVE]
        Approval[cid_V[VID]]!Ewallet[VID][index_V[VID]][0].ISZERO
            {
            Ewallet[VID][index_V[VID]][1] = ISZERO;
            index_V[VID] = 0;
40          cid_V[VID] = -1;
            STATUS_V[VID] = IDLE;} ->Vendor(VID)
    [] [STATUS_V[VID] == HAVECOIN ]
        Disapproval[cid_V[VID]]!VID
            {STATUS_V[VID] = IDLE;} ->Vendor(VID)
45  [] [STATUS_V[VID] == NOCOIN]
        ReqLoc!VID.eid_V[VID]
            {STATUS_V[VID] = REQLOC;} ->Vendor(VID)
```

or it is with another vendor or broker. In this case it has to first lookup the
location, and then request the e-coin at that location.

The first task is initiated by the customer process on channel *Spend*. The
customer, *cid*, sends an e-coin ID, *Eid*, and the amount, *amount*, to a vendor.

Table 5. Vendor Process (continued)

```
   [] [STATUS_V[VID] == REQLOC]
        SendLoc[VID]?loc
            {
 5          eloc_V[VID] = loc;
            STATUS_V[VID] = HAVELOC;
            } ->Vendor(VID)

   [] [STATUS_V[VID] == REQCOIN]
10      SendCoin[VID]?eid1.amt
            {
            var index = 0;
            while(index < EWALLET_SIZE)
            {
15              if (Ewallet[VID][index][0] == -1 && Ewallet[VID][index][1] == -1)
                {
                    Ewallet[VID][index][0] = eid1;
                    Ewallet[VID][index][1] = amt;
                    index_V[VID] = index;
20                  index = EWALLET_SIZE;//break the loop
                }
                index = index + 1;
            }
            STATUS_V[VID] = HAVECOIN
25          } ->Vendor(VID)
   [] [STATUS_V[VID] == RECVREQ]
        SendCoin[vid_V[VID]]!eid_V[VID].amount_V[VID]
            {
            vid_V[VID] = -1;
30          amount_V[VID]=0;
            eid_V[VID] = -1;
            STATUS_V[VID] = IDLE;} ->Vendor(VID)
   [] [STATUS_V[VID] == IDLE]
        ReqCoin[VID]?eid1.vid
35          {
            var index = 0; vid_V[VID] = vid;
            while (index < EWALLET_SIZE)
            {
                if (Ewallet[VID][index][0] == eid1)
40              {
                    eid_V[VID] = Ewallet[VID][index][0];
                    amount_V[VID] = Ewallet[VID][index][1];
                    Ewallet[VID][index][0] = -1;
                    Ewallet[VID][index][1] = -1;
45                  index = EWALLET_SIZE; //end loop
                }
                index = index + 1;
            }
            STATUS_V[VID] = RECVREQ;} ->Vendor(VID)
50 [] [STATUS_V[VID] == HAVELOC]
        ReqCoin[eloc_V[VID]]!eid_V[VID].VID
            {
            eloc_V[VID]= -1;
            eid_V[VID]=-1;
55          STATUS_V[VID] = REQCOIN;} ->Vendor(VID);
```

This event is enabled, if the vendor status is IDLE. If the vendor has an e-coin with a matching ID (line 12 of Table 4) it will enter status HAVECOIN. If not it will store the e-coin ID and change the status to NOCOIN.

If the vendor does not have the e-coin and the status is NOCOIN, it will first request the e-coin location from the broker and then, wait for the broker to reply with the e-coin location, and then request the e-coin from that vendor or broker. This three step process is modeled as follows:

- The model uses channel *RecLoc* for the request of the location. It is enabled when the process is in the status NOCOIN (Table 4, line 45)
- After this request the vendor changes its status to REQLOC. The vendor then waits for the broker to reply on channel *SendLoc* with the e-coin location *loc* (Table 5, line 5). The vendor then stores the location, $Veloc[\text{VID}]$, and changes the status to HAVELOC.
- The request of the vendor VID from the vendor/broker $Veloc[\text{VID}]$ to send e-coin EID[VID] uses channel *ReqCoin*. The reply uses the *SendCoin* channel, upon which the vendor VID changes the status to HAVECOIN.

In status HAVECOIN, the vendor approves on channel *Approval* if the amount is positive (lines 28 and 35 of Table 4). Otherwise, it will disapprove the transaction on channel *Disapproval*. If the payment is approved, the vendor saves the remaining e-coins (line numbers 31 and 37 of Table 4).

The second task for the vendor is to send an e-coin to requesting vendor. A request for an e-coin *eid1*, from another vendor, *vid*, is modeled using channel *ReqCoin*. This is a message from vendor *vid* to vendor *VID*. The event is enabled in status IDLE. This event stores the details of the e-coins and changes the status to RECVREQ. This enables the reply to the requesting vendor on channel *SendCoin*. The status will change to IDLE and the e-coin will be removed from the e-wallet.

The Netpay process is composed of customer, vendor and broker process. There are three vendors, two customers and one broker in this model as shown in [4]. The next section will look at the correctness of this protocol to prove three different properties namely chain of trust, preventing double spending and non-blocking behavior.

4   Correctness of the Netpay Protocol

This section assumes that vendors are cooperative and trusted, which seems consistent with the fact that in the server-side protocol the customer e-coins are stored by vendors. Since the touchstone and payword are always stored together at a trusted party there is no need to prove that the payword remains valid. In contrast, that was an important property to prove for the client-side Netpay protocol [3], in which e-coins were stored by the customers, while the broker and vendors kept the touchstones to verify the e-coins.

For the server-side model we will show three properties. The first is that the e-coin will not be lost by the vendors, which means that the location of the e-coin as recorded by the broker will be correct at the end of a transaction. While a payment is ongoing, it might be temporarily incorrect.

Furthermore, we show that at most one vendor can have a copy of an e-coin. The length of an e-coin, and thus its amount, is abstracted, and we assume that subtracting from the amount is dealt correctly by the trusted vendor. The only remaining way to double spend would be to have two coins. We show that an e-coin cannot be spent twice at different vendors. Finally, we show that there is a deadlock in the protocol and we will present a solution for this.

4.1   Chain of Trust

E-coins are transferred from broker to vendor and from one vendor to another vendor, and the customer should be sure that the location of the e-coin will be tracked in this process. For the server-side Netpay protocol, the following two properties can be shown to hold:

1. If the customer is in the IDLE or BUYCOIN state, then the broker will have the location of the e-coin pointing to the vendor with the e-coin.
2. If the customer is in the SPENDING state, then the broker will have the location of the e-coin, or it will point to the vendor which will receive the e-coin after the next exchange of e-coins.

The following lists the goals defined in the PAT model checker:

- Property 1 shows for each e-coin ID held by a customer, that there exists a corresponding e-coin in the broker database.
- Property 2 shows for each e-coin ID in the LOOKUP database, that there exists a corresponding e-coin in the broker database, if the location LOOKUP$[y][1]$ is the broker ID.
- Property 3 shows for each e-coin ID held by the customer, that if the location of the e-coin is not the broker ID and the customer status is IDLE or BUYCOIN, then there exists a corresponding e-coin at that location.
- Property 4 shows for each e-coin ID held by the customer, that if the location of the e-coin is not equal to the broker ID and the customer status is SPENDING, then there exists a corresponding e-coin at that location or at a location stored in variable eloc_V. This means that while the broker may have information that is temporarily not valid, the correct location is stored in an auxiliary variable.

The properties 1 - 4 were verified using the PAT model checker.

4.2   Double Spending

The main goal of this property is to prevent customers from spending an e-coin more than once. Note, that because we abstract the exact amount of an e-coin it can be spent as long as the amount is IsPOSITIVE. This assumes that the vendor updates the amount correctly. However, double spending could still

Property 1. Chain of Trust - Comparison of customer and broker databases

```
#define Chain_of_Trust_1(&&y:{0..(MAXCOINS-1)};x:{0..(CUSTOMERS-1)}
        @(DB_C[x][y][0]==-1 ||(||z:{0..(BROKER_SIZE-1)}
        @(DB_C[x][y][0] == DB_B[z][0]))));

#assert Netpay |=[] Chain_of_Trust_1 ;
```

Property 2. Chain of Trust - Comparison of broker and lookup databases

```
#define Chain_of_Trust_2(&&y:{0..BROKER_SIZE-1}@(LOOKUP[y][1]!= BROKERID
        ||(||z:{0..BROKER_SIZE-1}@(DB_B[z][0] == LOOKUP[y][0]))));

#assert Netpay |=[] Chain_of_Trust_2 ;
```

Property 3. Chain of Trust - Comparison of vendor, customer and lookup databases

```
#define Chain_of_Trust_3(&&y:{0..(MAXCOINS-1)};a:{0..(CUSTOMERS-1)}
        @(||z:{0..(BROKER_SIZE-1)}@(!(DB_C[a][y][0] == LOOKUP[z][0]
        && LOOKUP[z][1]!= BROKERID &&(STATUS_C[a] == IDLE ||
        STATUS_C[a] == BUYCOIN))) || (||x:{0..(VENDORS-1)}
        @(||b:{0..(EWALLET_SIZE-1)}@(DB_C[a][y][0]==Ewallet[x][b][0])))));

#assert Netpay |=[] Chain_of_Trust_3;
```

Property 4. Chain of Trust - Comparison of customer, lookup and different vendor databases

```
#define Chain_of_Trust_4(&&y:{0..(MAXCOINS-1)};a:{0..(CUSTOMERS-1)}
        @(||z:{0..(BROKER_SIZE-1)}@(DB_C[a][y][0] != LOOKUP[z][0]
        || STATUS_C[a] != SPENDING || (&&x:{0..(VENDORS-1)}
        @(LOOKUP[z][1]!= x || eloc_V[x]==-1 || eloc_V[x]==BROKERID)
        ||(||b:{0..(EWALLET_SIZE-1)}@(DB_C[a][y][0] == Ewallet[eloc_V[x]][b][0]
        || DB_C[a][y][0] == Ewallet[x][b][0]))))) )  ;

#assert Netpay |=[] Chain_of_Trust_4;
```

occur, if there would be e-wallets with same e-coin ID and a positive amount. In that case the customer could spend the same e-coin at two different vendors. We prove that all e-coins exists only once in one e-wallet at any time. This is expressed in Property 5: No two e-wallets have the same e-coin ID whose amount is ISPOSITIVE. This means that the coin cannot be spent twice. A Windows 7, i5 processor, 3.2 GHz and 6 GB RAM machine took about eleven minutes to verify all 5 properties.

4.3 Non-Blocking Behavior

The CSP model described in Section 3 uses channels for communication between different processes. A sender process will be blocked on an output channel if no

Property 5. Double Spending

```
#define DoubleSpending(&&x:{0..VENDORS-1};a:{0..VENDORS-1}
        @(&&y:{0..EWALLET_SIZE-1};z:{0..EWALLET_SIZE-1}
        @((Ewallet[x][y][0]==-1||Ewallet[a][z][0]==-1
        ||Ewallet[x][y][1]==ISZERO||Ewallet[a][z][1]==ISZERO || a==x)
        ||(Ewallet[x][y][0]!=Ewallet[a][z][0])))));
```

```
#assert Netpay |=[] DoubleSpending;
```

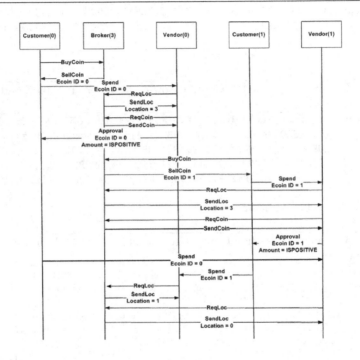

Fig. 1. Deadlock in Netpay protocol

other process has a matching input channel that is enabled. If a channel is blocked indefinitely, then there is a deadlock in the protocol. We use PAT to check for absence of deadlocks.

PAT did identify a deadlock in the protocol. Figure 1 depicts the trace that was generated by PAT model checker. The deadlock occurs as follows: Customer(0) buys an e-coin with Broker(3) and spends e-coins at vendor(0). Vendor(0) requests the e-coin location from the broker. The broker provides its own ID as e-coin location and updates the location for this e-coin to 0. Vendor(0) requests and receives the e-coin from the broker. Vendor(0) approves payment for Customer(0), but the amount remains positive. Likewise, Customer(1) buys an e-coin and spends it at Vendor(1), with a positive amount remaining. Now Customer(0) spends e-coins with ID 0 at vendor(1) while Customer(1) spends e-coins with ID 1 at Vendor(0). Vendor(1) requests and receives e-coin location as

0 from broker. Vendor(1) requests for e-coin location and receives 1 from broker. Now they ask request the e-coin from each other, and enter a circular wait.

This model of the protocol has been corrected by adding a separate process for the vendor side to handle reply for e-coins request. This process can be found in [4]. With these changes PAT can verify deadlock freedom. The description of the protocol does not specify how many processes a vendor should have [7], although it is presented as if it were a single process. A prototype implementation also used a single process. Our results suggest that the vendor should be split instead into two parts to avoid a deadlock.

4.4   Non-Cooperative Customers and Vendors

A system is not only composed of cooperative parties but there will be some parties who will try to cheat the protocol. In such a case, the protocol may not be correct anymore. The current protocol does deal with customers who try to spend e-coins that have zero amount, and also with customers who want to spend the same e-coin twice. However, if we would enable a customer to send e-coin IDs that do not exists in the broker or vendor databases, it will cause currently a deadlock. The current protocol provides no way for a broker to communicate back to vendor that an e-coin does not exist. This problem is, however, easily addressed by adding one more case for a declined payment.

We also considered cheating vendors in models that do not abstract from the exact amount an e-coin is worth. Since vendors in the Server-side Netpay protocol handle the e-wallet they can cheat by deducting or redeeming the wrong amount. It will be very difficult for the customer (or broker) to detect such behavior. In the client-side protocol the customer owned the payword, and could use this to verify correct behavior of the vendor.

5   Conclusions and Future Research

This paper modeled the server-side Netpay protocol used for micro-payment using CSP, and verified three important properties using the PAT model checker. The first is that the broker keeps track of e-coins throughout, even if it is transferred from vendor to vendor. The second is that a customer cannot spend more than an e-coin is worth. The protocol prevents double spending. The last is that the protocol has deadlock when two vendors request e-coins from each other. This has been rectified by adding a separate process to deal with transfer of e-coins from one to another.

The verification was done based under the assumption that the broker, vendors, and customers adhere to the protocol. There have been few restrictions on the behavior of the customer though, who is able use the same e-coin again and again. Future research involves working on proving validity of e-coins and double spending when the customer and vendors are not cooperative, and when the vendors cannot be fully trusted.

References

1. Cai, Y., Grundy, J., Hosking, J., Dai, X.: Software Architecture Modeling and Performance Analysis with Argo/MTE. In: SEKE 2004 (1990)
2. Chaudhary, K., Dai, X.: P2P-NetPay: An off-line Micro-payment System for Content Sharing in P2P-Networks. JETWI 1(1), 46–54 (2009)
3. Chaudhary, K., Fehnker, A.: Modeling and Verification for the Micropayment Protocol Netpay. In: WASET 2012, vol. 72 (2012)
4. Chaudhary, K., Fehnker, A.: Server-Side Netpay Protocol Models (2015), http://repository.usp.ac.fj/id/eprint/8165
5. Dai, X., Grundy, J.: Architecture for a Component-Based, Plug-In Micro-payment System. In: Zhou, X., Zhang, Y., Orlowska, M.E. (eds.) APWeb 2003. LNCS, vol. 2642, pp. 251–262. Springer, Heidelberg (2003)
6. Dai, X., Grundy, J.: Three Kinds of E-wallets for a NetPay Micro-Payment System. In: Zhou, X., Su, S., Papazoglou, M.P., Orlowska, M.E., Jeffery, K. (eds.) WISE 2004. LNCS, vol. 3306, pp. 66–77. Springer, Heidelberg (2004)
7. Dai, X., Lo, B.: NetPay - An Efficient Protocol for Micropayments on the WWW. In: AusWeb 1999, Australia (1999)
8. Glassman, S., Manasse, M., Abadi, M., Gauthier, P., Sobalvarro, P.: The Millicent Protocol for Inexpensive Electronic Commerce. In: WWW 1995 (December 1995)
9. Hauser, R., Steiner, M., Waidner, M.: Micro-payments Based on ikp. In: SECURICOM 1996. LNCS (1996)
10. Herzberg, A., Yochai, H.: Mini-pay: Charging Per Click on the Web (1996)
11. Nisan, N., London, S., Regev, O., Camiel, N.: Globally Distributed Computation Over the Internet. The POPCORN project. In: ICDCS 1998. IEEE (1998)
12. Rivest, R., Shamir, A.: PayWord and MicroMint: Two Simple Micropayment Schemes. In: Crispo, B. (ed.) Security Protocols 1996. LNCS, vol. 1189, pp. 69–87. Springer, Heidelberg (1997)
13. Sun, J., Liu, Y., Dong, J.: Protocol Analysis Toolkit, http://www.comp.nus.edu.sg/~pat/
14. Wei, K., Smith, A., Chen, Y., Vo, B.: WhoPay: A Scalable and Anonymous Payment System for Peer-to-Peer Environments. In: Distributed Computing Systems. IEEE (2006)
15. Yang, B., Garcia-Molina, H.: PPay: Micro-payments for Peer-to-Peer Systems. In: CSS 2003, pp. 300–310 (2003)
16. Zou, E., Si, T., Huang, L., Dai, Y.: A New Micro-payment Protocol Based on P2P Networks. In: ICEBE 2005 (2005)

Specification and Analysis

Require, Test and Trace IT

Bernhard K. Aichernig[1], Klaus Hörmaier[2], Florian Lorber[1(✉)],
Dejan Ničković[3], and Stefan Tiran[1,3]

[1] Graz University of Technology, Graz, Austria
aichernig@ist.tugraz.at
[2] Infineon Technologies Austria AG, Villach, Austria
[3] AIT Austrian Institute of Technology, Vienna, Austria

Abstract. We propose a framework for requirement-driven test generation that combines contract-based interface theories with model-based
testing. We design a specification language, *requirement interfaces*, for
formalizing different views (aspects) of synchronous data-flow systems
from informal requirements. Multiple views of a system, modeled as requirement interfaces, are naturally combined by conjunction.

We develop an incremental test generation procedure with several advantages. The test generation is driven by a single requirement interface
at a time. It follows that each test assesses a specific aspect or feature of
the system, specified by its associated requirement interface. Since we do
not explicitly compute the conjunction of all requirement interfaces of
the system, we avoid state space explosion while generating tests. However, we incrementally complete a test for a specific feature with the
constraints defined by other requirement interfaces. This allows catching violations of any other requirement during test execution, and not
only of the one used to generate the test. Finally, this framework defines a natural association between informal requirements, their formal
specifications and the generated tests, thus facilitating traceability. We
implemented a prototype test generation tool and we demonstrate its
applicability on an industrial use case.

Keywords: Model-based testing · Test-case generation · Requirements
engineering · Traceability · Requirement interfaces · Formal specification · Synchronous systems · Consistency checking · Incremental test-case
generation

1 Introduction

Modern software and hardware systems are becoming increasingly complex, resulting in new design challenges. For safety-critical applications, correctness evidence for designed systems must be presented to the regulatory bodies (see for
example the automotive standard ISO 26262 [16]). It follows that verification
and validation techniques must be used to provide evidence that the designed
system meets its requirements. *Testing* remains the preferred practice in industry for gaining confidence in the design correctness. In classical testing, an
engineer designs a test experiment, i.e. an input vector that is executed on the

© Springer International Publishing Switzerland 2015
M. Núñez and M. Güdemann (Eds.): FMICS 2015, LNCS 9128, pp. 113–127, 2015.
DOI: 10.1007/978-3-319-19458-5_8

system-under-test (SUT) in order to check whether it satisfies its requirements. Due to the finite number of experiments, testing cannot prove the absence of errors. However, it is an effective technique for catching bugs. Testing remains a predominantly manual and ad-hoc activity that is prone to human errors. As a result, it is often a bottleneck in the complex system design.

Model-based testing (MBT) is a technology that enables systematic and automatic test case generation (TCG) and execution, thus reducing system design time and cost. In MBT, the SUT is tested for conformance against its *specification*, a mathematical model of the SUT. In contrast to the specification, that is a formal object, the SUT is a physical implementation with often unknown internal structure, also called a "black-box". The SUT can be accessed by the tester only through its external interface. In order to reason about the conformance of the SUT to its specification, one needs to use the *testing assumption* [24], stating that the SUT can react at all times to all inputs and can be modeled in the same language as its specification.

The formal model of the SUT is derived from its *informal requirements*. The process of formulating, documenting and maintaining system requirements is called *requirement engineering*. Requirements are typically written in a textual form, using possibly constrained English, and are gathered in a *requirements document*. The requirements document is structured into chapters describing various (behavioural, safety, timing, etc.) *views* of the system. Intuitively, a system must correctly implement the *conjunction* of all its requirements. Sometimes, requirements can be *inconsistent*, resulting in a specification that does not admit any correct implementation.

In this paper, we propose a *requirement-driven* framework for MBT of *synchronous data-flow* reactive systems. In contrast to classical MBT, in which the requirements document is usually formalized into one monolithic specification, we exploit the structure of the requirements and adopt a *multiple viewpoint* approach.

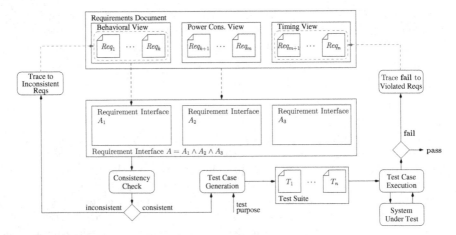

Fig. 1. Overview of using requirement interfaces for testing, analysis and tracing

We first introduce *requirement interfaces* as the formalism for modeling system views as subsets of requirements. It is a state-transition formalism that supports compositional specification of synchronous data-flow systems by means of assume/guarantee rules, that we call contracts. We associate subsets of contracts to requirement identifiers, to facilitate their tracing to the informal requirements from which the specification is derived. These associations can later on be used to generate links between the work products [2], connecting severals tools.

A requirement interface is intended to model a specific view of the SUT. We define the *conjunction* operation that enables combining different views of the SUT. Intuitively, a conjunction of two requirement interfaces is another requirement interface that requires contracts of both interfaces to hold. We assume that the overall specification of the SUT is given as a conjunction of requirement interfaces modeling its different views.

Next, we develop a requirement-driven TCG and execution procedure from requirement interfaces, with *language inclusion* as the conformance relation. We present a procedure for TCG from a specific SUT view, modeled as a requirement interface, and a *test purpose*. Such a test case can be used directly to detect if the implementation by the SUT violates a given requirement, but cannot detect violation of other requirements in the conjunction. Next, we extend this procedure by completing such a partial test case with additional constraints from other view models that enable detection of violations of any other requirement.

Finally, we develop a tracing procedure that exploits the natural mapping between informal requirements and our formal model. Thus, inconsistent contracts or failing test cases can be traced back to the violated requirements. We believe that such tracing information provides precious maintenance and debugging information to the engineers. We illustrate the entire workflow of using requirement interfaces for consistency checking, testing and tracing in Figure 1.

2   Requirement Interfaces

We introduce *requirement interfaces*, a formalism for specification of synchronous data-flow systems. Their semantics is given in the form of labeled transition systems (LTS). We define *consistent* interfaces as the ones that admit at least one correct implementation. The *refinement* relation between interfaces is given as *language inclusion*. Finally, we define the *conjunction* of requirement interfaces as another interface that subsumes all behaviors of both interfaces.

2.1   Syntax

Let X be a set of typed variables. A valuation v over X is a function that assigns to each $x \in X$ a value $v(x)$ of the appropriate type. We denote by $V(X)$ the set of all valuations over X. We denote by $X' = \{x' \mid x \in X\}$ the set obtained by priming each variable in X. Given a valuation $v \in V(X)$ and a predicate φ on X, we denote by $v \models \varphi$ the fact that φ is satisfied under the variable valuation v. Given two valuations $v, v' \in V(X)$ and a predicate φ on $X \cup X'$, we denote by $(v, v') \models \varphi$ the fact that φ is satisfied by the valuation that assigns to $x \in X$ the value $v(x)$, and to $x' \in X'$ the value $v'(x')$.

Given a subset $Y \subseteq X$ of variables and a valuation $v \in V(X)$, we denote by $\pi(v)[Y]$, the projection of v to Y. We will commonly use the symbol w_Y to denote a valuation projected to the subset $Y \subseteq X$. Given the sets X, $Y_1 \subseteq X$, $Y_2 \subseteq X$, $w_1 \in V(Y_1)$ and $w_2 \in V(Y_2)$, we denote by $w = w_1 \cup w_2$ the valuation $w \in V(Y_1 \cup Y_2)$ such that $\pi(w)[Y_1] = w_1$ and $\pi(w)[Y_2] = w_2$.

Given a set X of variables, we denote by X_I, X_O and X_H three disjoint partitions of X denoting sets of *input*, *output* and *hidden* variables, such that $X = X_I \cup X_O \cup X_H$. We denote by $X_{obs} = X_I \cup X_O$ the set of *observable* variables and by $X_{ctr} = X_H \cup X_O$ the set of *controllable* variables[1]. A *contract c* on $X \cup X'$, denoted by (φ, ψ), is a pair consisting of an *assumption* predicate φ on $X_I' \cup X$ and a *guarantee* predicate ψ on $X_{ctr}' \cup X$. A contract $\hat{c} = (\hat{\varphi}, \hat{\psi})$ is said to be an *initial* contract if $\hat{\varphi}$ and $\hat{\psi}$ are predicates on X_I' and X_{ctr}', respectively, and an *update* contract otherwise. Given two valuations $v, v' \in V(X)$ and a contract $c = (\varphi, \psi)$ over $X \cup X'$, we say that (v, v') satisfies c, denoted by $(v, v') \models c$, if $(v, \pi(v')[X_I]) \models \varphi \rightarrow (v, \pi(v')[X_{ctr}]) \models \psi$. In addition, we say that (v, v') satisfies the assumption of c, denoted by $(v, v') \models_A c$ if $(v, \pi(v')[X_I]) \models \varphi$. The valuation pair (v, v') satisfies the guarantee of c, denoted by $(v, v') \models_G c$, if $(v, \pi(v')[X_{ctr}]) \models \psi)$[2].

Definition 1. *A requirement interface A is a tuple $\langle X_I, X_O, X_H, \hat{C}, C, \mathcal{R}, \rho \rangle$, where*

- X_I, X_O *and X_H are disjoint finite sets of* input, output *and* hidden *variables, respectively, and $X = X_I \cup X_O \cup X_H$ denotes the set of all variables;*
- $\hat{C}$ *and C are finite non-empty sets of* initial *and* update *contracts;*
- $\mathcal{R}$ *is a finite set of* requirement identifiers;
- $\rho : \mathcal{R} \rightarrow \mathcal{P}(C \cup \hat{C})$ *is a function mapping requirement identifiers to subsets of contracts, such that $\bigcup_{r \in \mathcal{R}} \rho(r) = C \cup \hat{C}$.*

We say that a requirement interface is *receptive* if in any state it has defined behaviors for all inputs, that is $\bigvee_{(\hat{\varphi}, \hat{\psi}) \in \hat{C}} \hat{\varphi}$ and $\bigvee_{(\varphi, \psi) \in C} \varphi$ are both valid. A requirement interface is *fully-observable* if $X_H = \emptyset$. A requirement interface is *deterministic* if for all $(\hat{\varphi}, \hat{\psi}) \in \hat{C}$, $\hat{\psi}$ has the form $\bigwedge_{x \in X_O} x' = c$, where c is a constant of the appropriate type, and for all $(\varphi, \psi) \in C$, ψ has the form $\bigwedge_{x \in X_{ctr}} x' = f(X)$, where f is a function over X that has the same type as x.

Example 1. We use the N-bounded FIFO buffer example to illustrate all the concepts introduced in the paper. Let A^{beh} be the behavioral model of the buffer. The buffer has two Boolean input variables enq, deq, i.e. $X_I^{beh} = \{enq, deq\}$, two Boolean output variables E, F, i.e. $X_O^{beh} = \{E, F\}$ and a bounded integer internal variable $k \in [0 : N]$ for some $N \in \mathbb{N}$, i.e. $X_H^{beh} = \{k\}$. The textual requirements are listed below:

r_0: The buffer is empty and the inputs are ignored in the initial state.

---

[1] We adopt SUT-centric conventions to naming the roles of variable.
[2] We sometimes use the direct notation $(v, w_I') \models_A c$ and $(v, w_{ctr}') \models_G c$, where $w_I \in V(X_I)$ and $w_{ctr} \in V(X_{ctr})$.

r_1: enq triggers an enqueue operation when the buffer is not full.
r_2: deq triggers a dequeue operation when the buffer is not empty.
r_3: E signals that the buffer is empty.
r_4: F signals that the buffer is full.
r_5: Simultaneous enq and deq (or their simultaneous absence), an enq on the full buffer or a deq on the empty buffer have no effect.

We formally define[3] A^{beh} as $\hat{C}^{beh} = \{c_0\}$, $C^{beh} = \{c_i \mid i \in [1,5]\}$, $\mathcal{R}^{beh} = \{r_i \mid i \in [0,5]\}$ and $\rho^{beh}(r_i) = \{c_i\}$, where

$$c_0 : \textbf{true} \vdash (k' = 0) \wedge \textsf{E}' \wedge \neg \textsf{F}'$$
$$c_1 : \textsf{enq}' \wedge \neg\textsf{deq}' \wedge k < N \vdash k' = k + 1$$
$$c_2 : \neg\textsf{enq}' \wedge \textsf{deq}' \wedge k > 0 \vdash k' = k - 1$$
$$c_3 : \textbf{true} \vdash k' = 0 \Leftrightarrow \textsf{E}'$$
$$c_4 : \textbf{true} \vdash k' = N \Leftrightarrow \textsf{F}'$$
$$c_5 : (\textsf{enq}' = \textsf{deq}') \vee (\textsf{enq}' \wedge \textsf{F}) \vee (\textsf{deq}' \wedge \textsf{E}) \vdash k' = k$$

2.2   Semantics

Given a requirement interface A defined over X, let $V = V(X) \cup \{\hat{v}\}$ denote the set of states in A, where a *state* v is a valuation $v \in V(X)$ or the *initial* state $\hat{v} \notin V(X)$. The latter is not a valuation, as the initial contracts do not specify unprimed and input variables. There is a transition between two states v and v' if (v, v') satisfies all its contracts. The transitions are labeled by the (possibly empty) set of requirement identifiers corresponding to contracts for which (v, v') satisfies their assumptions. The semantics $[[A]]$ of A is the following LTS.

Definition 2. *The semantics of the requirement interface A is the LTS $[[A]] = \langle V, \hat{v}, L, T \rangle$, where V is the set of states, $\hat{v}$ is the initial state, $L = \mathcal{P}(\mathcal{R})$ is the set of labels and $T \subseteq V \times L \times V$ is the transition relation, such that:*

- *$(\hat{v}, R, v) \in T$ if $v \in V(X)$, $\bigwedge_{\hat{c} \in \hat{C}}(\hat{v}, v) \models \hat{c}$ and $R = \{r \mid (\hat{v}, v) \models_A \hat{c}$ for some $\hat{c} \in \hat{C}$ and $\hat{c} \in \rho(r)\}$;*
- *$(v, R, v') \in T$ if $v, v' \in V(X)$, $\bigwedge_{c \in C}(v, v') \models c$ and $R = \{r \mid (v, v') \models_A c$ for some $c \in C$ and $c \in \rho(r)\}$.*

We say that $\tau = v_0 \xrightarrow{R_1} v_1 \xrightarrow{R_2} \cdots \xrightarrow{R_n} v_n$ is an *execution* of the requirements interface A if $v_0 = \hat{v}$ and for all $1 \leq i \leq n - 1$, $(v_i, R_{i+1}, v_{i+1}) \in T$. In addition, we use the following notation: (1) $v \xrightarrow{R}$ iff $\exists v' \in V(X)$ s.t. $v \xrightarrow{R} v'$; (2) $v \rightarrow v'$ iff $\exists R \in L$ s.t. $v \xrightarrow{R} v'$; (3) $v \rightarrow$ iff $\exists v' \in V(X)$ s.t. $v \rightarrow v'$; (4) $v \xrightarrow{\epsilon} v'$ iff $v = v'$; (5) $v \xrightarrow{w} v'$ iff $\exists Y \subseteq X$ s.t. $\pi(v')[Y] = w$ and $v \rightarrow v'$; (6) $v \xrightarrow{w}$ iff $\exists v', Y \subseteq X$ s.t. $\pi(v')[Y] = w$ and $v \rightarrow v'$; (7) $v \xrightarrow{w_1 \cdot w_2 \cdots w_n} v'$ iff $\exists v_1, \ldots, v_{n-1}, v_n$ s.t. $v \xrightarrow{w_1} v_1 \xrightarrow{w_2} \cdots v_n \xrightarrow{w_n} v'$; and (8) $v \xrightarrow{w_1 \cdot w_2 \cdots w_n}$ iff $\exists v'$ s.t. $v \xrightarrow{w_1 \cdot w_2 \cdots w_n} v'$.

We say that a sequence $\sigma \in V(X_{\text{obs}})^*$ is a *trace* of A if $\hat{v} \xrightarrow{\sigma}$. We denote by $\mathcal{L}(A)$ the set of all traces of A. Given a trace σ of A, let A after $\sigma = \{v \mid \hat{v} \xrightarrow{\sigma} v\}$. Given a state $v \in V$, let $\text{succ}(v) = \{v' \mid v \rightarrow v'\}$ be the set of successors of v.

[3] For readability we use the concrete syntax $\varphi \vdash \psi$ to denote (φ, ψ) in our examples.

2.3   Consistency, Refinement and Conjunction

A requirement interface consists of a set of contracts, that can be conflicting. Such an interface does not allow any correct implementation. We say that a requirement interface is *consistent* if it allows at least one correct implementation.

Definition 3. *Let A be a requirement interface, $[[A]]$ its associated LTS, $v \in V$ a state and $\mathcal{C} = \hat{C}$ if v is initial, and C otherwise. We say that a state $v \in V$ is consistent, denoted by $cons(v)$, if for all $w_I \in V(X_I)$, there exists v' such that $w_I = \pi(v')[X_I]$, $\bigwedge_{c \in \mathcal{C}}(v, v') \models c$ and $cons(v')$. We say that A is consistent if $cons(\hat{v})$.*

Example 2. A^{beh} is consistent – every reachable state accepts every input valuation and generates an output valuation satisfying all contracts. Consider now replacing c_2 in A^{beh} with the contract $c'_2 : \neg \mathsf{enq}' \wedge \mathsf{deq}' \wedge k \geq 0 \vdash k' = k - 1$, that incorrectly models r_2 and decreases the counter k upon deq even when the buffer is empty, setting it to the value minus one. This causes an inconsistency with the contracts c_3 and c_5, that state that if k equals zero the buffer is empty, and that dequeue on an empty buffer has no effect on k.

We define the *refinement* relation between two requirement interfaces A^1 and A^2, denoted by $A^2 \preceq A^1$, as *trace inclusion*.

Definition 4. *Let A^1 and A^2 be two requirement interfaces. We say that A^2 refines A^1, denoted by $A^2 \preceq A^1$, if (1) A^1 and A^2 have the same sets X_I, X_O and X_H of variables; and (2) $\mathcal{L}(A^1) \subseteq \mathcal{L}(A^2)$.*

We use a requirement interface to model a view of a system. Multiple views are combined by *conjunction*. The conjunction of two requirement interfaces is another requirement interface that is either inconsistent due to a conflict between views, or is the greatest lower bound with respect to the refinement relation. The conjunction of A^1 and A^2, denoted by $A^1 \wedge A^2$, is defined if the two interfaces share the same sets X_I, X_O and X_H of variables.

Definition 5. *Let $A^1 = \langle X_I, X_H, X_O, \hat{C}^1, C^1, \mathcal{R}^1, \rho^1 \rangle$ and $A^2 = \langle X_I, X_H, X_O, \hat{C}^2, C^2, \mathcal{R}^2, \rho^2 \rangle$ be two requirement interfaces. Their conjunction $A = A^1 \wedge A^2$ is the requirement interface $\langle X_I, X_H, X_O, \hat{C}, C, \mathcal{R}, \rho \rangle$, where*

- $\hat{C} = \hat{C}^1 \cup \hat{C}^2$ *and* $C = C^1 \cup C^2$;
- $\mathcal{R} = \mathcal{R}^1 \cup \mathcal{R}^2$; *and*
- $\rho(r) = \rho^1(r)$ *if* $r \in \rho^1$ *and* $\rho(r) = \rho^2(r)$ *otherwise.*

Remark: For refinement and conjunction, we require the two interfaces to share the same alphabet. This additional condition is used to simplify definitions. It does not restrict the modeling – arbitrary interfaces can have their alphabets *equalized* without changing their properties by taking union of respective input, output and hidden variables. Contracts in the transformed interfaces do not constrain newly introduced variables. For requirement interfaces A^1 and A^2, alphabet equalization is defined if $(X_I^1 \cup X_I^2) \cap (X_{ctr}^1 \cup X_{ctr}^2) = (X_O^1 \cup X_O^2) \cap (X_H^1 \cup X_H^2) = \emptyset$. Otherwise, $A_1 \not\preceq A_2$ and vice versa, and $A^1 \wedge A^2$ is not defined.

Example 3. We now consider a *power consumption* view of the bounded FIFO buffer. Its model A^{pc} has the Boolean input variables enq and deq and a bounded integer output variable pc. The following textual requirements specify A^{pc}:

r_a: The power consumption equals zero when no enq/deq is requested.
r_b: The power consumption is bounded to 2 units otherwise.

The interface A^{pc} consists of $\hat{C}^{pc} = C^{pc} = \{c_a, c_b\}$,
$\mathcal{R}^{pc} = \{r_i \mid i \in \{a, b\}\}$ and $\rho(r_i) = \{c_i\}$, where:

$$c_a : \quad \neg\text{enq} \wedge \neg\text{deq} \vdash \text{pc}' = 0$$
$$c_b : \quad \text{enq} \vee \text{deq} \quad \vdash \text{pc}' \leq 2$$

The conjunction $A^{buf} = A^{beh} \wedge A^{pc}$ is the requirement interface such that $X_I^{buf} = \{\text{enq}, \text{deq}\}$, $X_O^{buf} = \{\text{E}, \text{F}, \text{pc}\}$, $X_H^{buf} = \{k\}$, $\hat{C}^{buf} = \{c_0, c_a, c_b\}$, $C^{buf} = \{c_1, c_2, c_3, c_4, c_5, c_a, c_b\}$, $\mathcal{R}^{pc} = \{r_i \mid i \in \{a, b, 0, 1, 2, 3, 4, 5\}\}$, and $\rho(r_i) = \{c_i\}$.

The conjunction of two requirement interfaces with the same alphabet is the intersection of their traces.

Theorem 1. *Let A^1 and A^2 be two consistent requirement interfaces defined over the same alphabet. Then either $A^1 \wedge A^2$ is inconsistent, or $\mathcal{L}(A^1 \wedge A^2) = \mathcal{L}(A^1) \cap \mathcal{L}(A^2)$.*

We now show some properties of requirement interfaces.
The conjunction of two requirement interfaces with the same alphabet is either inconsistent, or it is the greatest lower bound with respect to refinement.

Theorem 2. *Let A^1 and A^2 be two consistent requirement interfaces defined over the same alphabet such that $A^1 \wedge A^2$ is consistent. Then $A^1 \wedge A^2 \preceq A^1$ and $A^1 \wedge A^2 \preceq A^2$, and for all consistent requirement interfaces A, if $A \preceq A^1$ and $A \preceq A^2$, then $A \preceq A^1 \wedge A^2$.*

The following theorem states that the conjunction of an inconsistent requirement interface with any other interface remains inconsistent. This result enables incremental detection of inconsistent specifications.

Theorem 3. *Let A be an inconsistent requirement interface. Then for all consistent requirement interfaces A' with the same alphabet as A, $A \wedge A'$ is also inconsistent.*

For proofs we refer to our technical report [4].

3   Testing and Tracing

In this section, we present our test-case generation and execution framework and instantiate it with bounded model checking techniques. For now, we assume that all variables range over finite domains. This restriction can be lifted by considering richer data domains in addition to theories that have decidable quantifier elimination, such as linear arithmetic over reals. Note that before executing the test-case generation, we can apply a consistency check on the requirement interface. For details, we refer to our technical report [4].

3.1   Test Case Generation

A *test case* is an experiment executed on the SUT I by the *tester*. We assume that I is a black-box that is only accessed via its observable interface. We assume that I can be modeled as an input-enabled, deterministic[4] requirement interface. Without loss of generality, we can represent I as a total sequential function $I : V(X_I) \times V(X_{\mathrm{obs}})^* \to V(X_O)$. A test case T_A for a requirement interface A over X takes a history of actual input/output observations $\sigma \in \mathcal{L}(A)$ and returns either the next input value to be executed or a verdict. Hence, a test case can be represented as a *partial* function $T_A : \mathcal{L}(A) \to V(X_I) \cup \{\mathbf{pass}, \mathbf{fail}\}$.

We first consider the problem of generating a test case from A. The test case generation procedure is driven by a *test purpose*. Here, a test purpose is a condition specifying the target set of states that a test execution should reach. Hence, it is a formula Π defined over X_{obs}.

Given a requirement interface A, let $\hat{\phi} = \bigvee_{(\hat{\varphi},\hat{\psi})\in\hat{C}} \hat{\varphi} \wedge \bigwedge_{(\hat{\varphi},\hat{\psi})\in\hat{C}} \hat{\varphi} \to \hat{\psi}$ and $\phi = \bigvee_{(\varphi,\psi)\in C} \varphi \wedge \bigwedge_{(\varphi,\psi)\in C} \varphi \to \psi$. The predicates $\hat{\phi}$ and ϕ encode the transition relation of A, with the additional requirement that at least one assumption must be satisfied, thus avoiding input vectors for which the test purpose can be trivially reached due to under-specification. A test case for A that can reach Π is defined iff there exists a trace $\sigma = \sigma' \cdot w_{obs}$ in $\mathcal{L}(A)$ such that $w_{obs} \models \Pi$. The test purpose Π can be reached in A in at most k steps if

$$\exists i, X^0, \ldots, X^k . \, i \leq n \wedge \phi^0 \wedge \ldots \wedge \phi^k \wedge \bigvee_{i\leq k} \Pi[X_{\mathrm{obs}}\backslash X_{\mathrm{obs}}^i],$$

where $\phi^0 = \hat{\phi}[X'\backslash X^0]$ and $\phi^i = \phi[X'\backslash X^i, X\backslash X^{i-1}]$ represent the transition relation of A unfolded in i steps.

Given A and Π, assume that there exists a trace σ in $\mathcal{L}(A)$ that reaches Π. Let σ_I be a projection to inputs. $\pi(\sigma)[X_I] = w_I^0 \cdot w_I^1 \cdots w_I^n$. We first compute $\omega_{\sigma_I,A}$ (see Algorithm 1), a formula[5] characterizing the set of output sequences that A allows on input σ_I.

Algorithm 1. OutMonitor

Input: $\sigma_I = w_I^0 \cdot w_I^1 \cdots w_I^n$, A
Output: $\omega_{\sigma_I,A}$
1: $\omega_{\sigma_I,A}^0 \leftarrow \hat{\theta}[X_I'\backslash w_I^0, X_{\mathrm{ctr}}'\backslash X_{\mathrm{ctr}}^0]$
2: **for** $i = 1$ to n **do**
3:    $\omega_{\sigma_I,A}^i \leftarrow \theta[X_I\backslash w_I^{i-1}, X_I'\backslash w_I^i, X_{\mathrm{ctr}}\backslash X_{\mathrm{ctr}}^{i-1}, X_{\mathrm{ctr}}'\backslash X_{\mathrm{ctr}}^i]$
4: **end for**
5: $\omega_{\sigma_I,A}^* \leftarrow \omega_{\sigma_I,A}^0 \wedge \ldots \wedge \omega_{\sigma_I,A}^n$
6: $\omega_{\sigma_I,A} \leftarrow \mathbf{qe}(\exists X_H^0, X_H^1, \ldots, X_H^n . \omega_{\sigma_I,A}^*)$
7: **return** $\omega_{\sigma_I,A}$

Let $\hat{\theta} = \bigwedge_{(\hat{\varphi},\hat{\psi})\in\hat{C}} \hat{\varphi} \to \hat{\psi}$ and $\theta = \bigwedge_{(\varphi,\psi)} \varphi \to \psi$. For every step i, we represent by $\omega_{\sigma_I,A}^i$ the allowed behavior of A constrained by σ_I (Lines $1-4$). The formula $\omega_{\sigma_I,A}^*$ (Line 5) describes the transition relation of A, unfolded to n steps and constrained by σ_I. However, this formula refers to the hidden variables of A and cannot be directly used to characterize

---

[4] The restriction to deterministic implementations is for presentation purposes only, the technique is general and can also be applied to non-deterministic systems.
[5] The formula $\omega_{\sigma_I,A}$ can be seen as a monitor for A under input σ_I.

the set of output sequences allowed by A under σ_I. Since any implementation of hidden variables that preserves correctness of the outputs is acceptable, it suffices to existentially quantify over hidden variables in $\omega^*_{\sigma_I,A}$. After eliminating the existential quantifiers with strategy **qe**, we obtain a simplified formula $\omega_{\sigma_I,A}$ over output variables only (Line 6).

Algorithm 2. $T_{\sigma_I,A}$

Input: $\sigma_I = w_I^0 \cdots w_I^n$, A, $\sigma = w_{obs}^0 \cdots w_{obs}^k$
Output: $V(X_I^I) \cup \{\textbf{pass}, \textbf{fail}\}$
1: $\omega_{\sigma_I,A} \leftarrow \text{OutMonitor}(\sigma_I, A)$
2: **for** $i = 0$ to k **do**
3:    $w_O^i \leftarrow \pi(w_{obs}^i)[X_O]$
4: **end for**
5: $\omega_{\sigma_I,A}^{0,k} \leftarrow \omega_{\sigma_I,A}[X_O^0 \backslash w_O^0, \ldots, X_O^k \backslash w_O^k]$
6: **if** $\omega_{\sigma_I,A}^{0,k} = \textbf{true}$ **then**
7:    **return pass**
8: **else if** $\omega_{\sigma_I,A}^{0,k} = \textbf{false}$ **then**
9:    **return fail**
10: **else**
11:    **return** w_I^{k+1}
12: **end if**

Let $T_{\sigma_I,A}$ be a test case, parameterized by the input sequence σ_I and the requirement interface A from which it was generated. It is a partial function, where $T_{\sigma_I,A}(\sigma)$ is defined if $|\sigma| \leq |\sigma_I|$ and for all $0 \leq i \leq |\sigma|$, $w_I^i = \pi(w_{obs}^i)[X_I]$, where $\sigma_I = w_I^0 \cdots w_I^n$ and $\sigma = w_{obs}^0 \cdots w_{obs}^k$. Algorithm 2 gives a constructive definition of the test case $T_{\sigma_I,A}$. *Incremental test-case generation:* So far, we considered test case generation for a flat requirement interface A. We now describe how test cases can be *incrementally* generated when the interface A consists of multiple views[6], i.e. $A = A^1 \wedge A^2$. Let Π be a test purpose for the view modeled with A_1. We first check whether Π can be reached in A^1, which is a simpler check than doing it on the conjunction $A^1 \wedge A^2$. If Π can be reached, we fix the input sequence σ_I that drives A^1 to Π. Instead of creating the test case T_{σ_I,A^1}, we generate $T_{\sigma_I,A^1 \wedge A^2}$, which keeps σ_I as the input sequence, but collects output guarantees of A^1 and A^2. Such a test case drives the SUT towards the test purpose in the view modeled by A^1, but is able to detect possible violations of both A^1 and A^2.

We note that test case generation for fully observable interfaces is simpler than the general case, because there is no need for the quantifier elimination, due to the absence of hidden variables in the model. A test case from a deterministic interface is even simpler as it is a direct mapping from the observable trace that reaches the test purpose – there is no need to collect constraints on the output since the deterministic interface does not admit any freedom to the implementation on the choice of output valuations.

Example 4. Consider the requirement interface A_{beh} for the behavioral view of the 2-bounded buffer, and the test purpose F. Our test case generation procedure gives the input vector σ_I of size 3 such that $\sigma_I[0] = (\textsf{enq}, \textsf{deq})$, $\sigma_I[1] = (\textsf{enq}, \neg\textsf{deq})$ and $\sigma_I[2] = (\textsf{enq}, \neg\textsf{deq})$. The observable output constraints for σ_I (encoded in OutMonitor) are $E \wedge \neg F$ in step 0, $\neg E \wedge \neg F$ in step 1 and $\neg E \wedge F$ in step 2. Together, the input vector σ_I and the associated output constraints form the test case $T_{\sigma_I,beh}$. By using the incremental test case generation procedure,

---

[6] We consider two views for the sake of simplicity.

we can extend $T_{\sigma I, beh}$ to a test case $T_{\sigma I, buf}$ that also takes into account the power consumption view of the buffer, resulting in output constraints $E \wedge \neg F \wedge pc \leq 2$ in step 0, $\neg E \wedge \neg F \wedge pc \leq 2$ in step 1 and $\neg E \wedge F \wedge pc \leq 2$ in step 2.

3.2 Test Case Execution

Algorithm 3. TestExec

Input: $I, T_{\sigma I, A}$
Output: {**pass, fail**}
1: in : $V(X_I) \cup \{\textbf{pass}, \textbf{fail}\}$
2: out : $V(X_O)$
3: $\sigma \leftarrow \epsilon$
4: in $\leftarrow T_{\sigma I, A}(A, \sigma)$
5: **while** in $\notin \{\textbf{pass}, \textbf{fail}\}$ **do**
6:     out $\leftarrow I(\text{in}, \sigma)$
7:     $\sigma \leftarrow \sigma \cdot (\text{in} \cup \text{out})$
8:     in $\leftarrow T_{\sigma I, A}(A, \sigma)$
9: **end while**
10: **return** in

Let A be a requirement interface, I a SUT with the same set of variables as A, and $T_{\sigma I, A}$ a test case generated from A. Algorithm 3 defines the test case execution procedure TestExec that takes as input I and $T_{\sigma I, A}$ and outputs a verdict **pass** or **fail**. TestExec gets the next test input *in* from the given test case $T_{\sigma I, A}$ (Lines 4, 8), stimulates at every step the SUT I with this input and waits for an output *out* (Line 6). The new inputs/outputs observed are stored in σ (Line 7), which is given as input to $T_{\sigma I, A}$. The test case monitors if the observed output is correct with respect to A. The procedure continues until a **pass** or **fail** verdict is reached (Line 5). Finally, the verdict is returned (Line 10).

Proposition 1. *Let A, $T_{\sigma I, A}$ and I be arbitrary requirement interface, test case generated from A and implementation, respectively. Then, we have that:*

1. *if $I \preceq A$, then $TestExec(I, T_{\sigma I, A}) = \textbf{pass}$; and*
2. *if $TestExec(I, T_{\sigma I, A}) = \textbf{fail}$, then $I \npreceq A$.*

Proposition 1 immediately holds for test cases generated incrementally from a requirement interface of the form $A = A^1 \wedge A^2$. In addition, we notice that a test case $T_{\sigma I, A^1}$, generated from a single view A^1 of A does not need to be extended to be useful, and can be used to incrementally show that a SUT does not conform to its specification. We state the property in the following corollary, that follows directly from Proposition 1 and Theorem 2.

Corollary 1. *Let $A = A^1 \wedge A^2$ be an arbitrary requirement interface composed of A^1 and A^2, I an arbitrary implementation and $T_{\sigma I, A^1}$ an arbitrary test case generated from A^1. Then, if $TestExec(I, T_{\sigma I, A^1}) = \textbf{fail}$, then $I \npreceq A^1 \wedge A^2$.*

3.3 Traceability

Requirement identifiers as first-class elements in requirement interfaces facilitate traceability between informal requirements, views and test cases. A test case generated from a view A^i of an interface $A = A^1 \wedge \ldots \wedge A^n$ is naturally mapped to the set $\mathcal{R}^i$ of requirements. In addition, requirement identifiers enable tracing violations caught during consistency checking and test case execution back to the conflicting/violated requirements.

Tracing inconsistent interfaces to conflicting requirements: When we detect an inconsistency in a requirement interface A defining a set of contracts C, we use QuickXPlain, a standard conflict set detection algorithm [17], in order to compute a minimal set of contracts $C' \subseteq C$ such that C' is inconsistent. Once we compute C', we use the requirement mapping function ρ defined in A, to trace back the set $\mathcal{R}' \subseteq \mathcal{R}$ of conflicting requirements.

Tracing **fail** *verdicts to violated requirements:* In fully observable interfaces, every trace induces at most one execution. In that case, a test case resulting in **fail** can be traced to a unique set of violated requirements. This is not the case in general for interfaces with hidden variables. A trace that violates such an interface may induce multiple executions resulting in **fail** with different valuations of hidden variables, and thus different sets of violated requirements. In this case, we report all sets to the user, but ignore internal valuations that would introduce an internal requirement violation before inducing the visible violation. Again, more details can be found in our technical report [4].

4   Implementation and Experimental Results

Implementation and experimental setup: We present a prototype that implements our test case generation framework introduced in Section 3. The prototype was integrated in our model-based testing toolchain MoMuT[7] and named MoMuT::REQs. The implementation uses Scala 2.10 and the SMT solver Z3. The tool implements both *monolithic* and *incremental* approaches to test case generation. All experiments were run on a MacBook Pro with a 2.53 GHz Intel Core 2 Duo Processor and 4 GB RAM.

Demonstrating example: In order to experiment with our implementation, we model three variants of the buffer behavioral interface. All three variants model buffers of size 150, with different internal structure. *Buffer 1* models a simple buffer with a single counter variable k. *Buffer 2* models a buffer that is composed of two internal buffers of size 75 each and *Buffer 3* models a buffer that is composed of three internal buffers of size 50 each. We also remodel a variant of the power consumption interface that created a dependency between the power used and the state of the internal buffers (idle/used).

We compare the monolithic and incremental approach to test case generation, by generating tests for the conjunction of the buffer interfaces and the power consumption interface, and incrementally, by generating tests only for the buffer interfaces, and completing them with the power consumption interface. Table 1 summarizes the results. The three examples diverge in complexity, expressed in the number of contracts and variables. Our results show that the incremental approach outperforms the monolithic one, resulting in speed-ups from 33% to 68%. Results on the consistency check can be found in our technical report [4].

Industrial application: We present an automotive use case from the European ARTEMIS project[8], that partially motivated our work on requirement interfaces. The use case was initiated by our industrial partner Infineon and evolves around building a formal model for analysis and test case generation for the

---

[7] http://www.momut.org
[8] https://mbat-artemis.eu

Table 1. Run-time in seconds for incremental and monolithic test case generation

	# Contracts	# Variables	t_{inc}	t_{mon}	speed-up
Buffer 1	6	6	10	16.8	68 %
Buffer 2	15	12	36.7	48.8	33 %
Buffer 3	20	15	69	115.6	68 %

safing engine of an airbag chip. The requirements document, developed by a customer of Infineon, is written in natural (English) language. We identified 39 requirements that represent the core of the system's functionality and iteratively formalized them in collaboration with the designers of Infineon. The resulting formal requirement interface is deterministic and consists of 36 contracts.

The formalization process revealed several under-specifications in the informal requirements that were causing some ambiguities. These ambiguities were resolved in collaboration with the designers. The consistency check revealed two inconsistencies between the requirements. Tracing the conflicts back to the informal requirements allowed their fixing in the customer requirements document.

We generated 21 test cases from the formalized requirements, that were designed to ensure that every boolean internal and output variable is at least activated once and that every possible state of the underlying finite state machine is reached at least once. The average length of the test cases was 3.4, but since the test cases are synchronous, each of the steps is able to trigger several inputs and outputs at once. The test cases were used to test the Simulink model of the system, developed by Infineon as the part of their design process. The Simulink model of the safing engine consists of a state machine with seven states, ten smaller blocks transforming the input signals and a Matlab function calculating the final outputs according to the current state and the input signals. In order to execute the test cases, Infineons engineers developed a test adapter that transforms abstract input values from the test cases to actual inputs passed to the Simulink model. We illustrate a part of the use case with three customer requirements that give the flavor of the underlying system's functionality:

r_1: There shall be seven operating states for the safing engine: RESET state, INITIAL state, DIAGNOSTIC state, TEST state, NORMAL state, SAFE state and DESTRUCTION state.

r_2: The safing engine shall change per default from RESET state to INIT state.

r_3: On a reset signal, the safing engine shall enter RESET state and stay while the reset signal is active.

These informal requirements were formalized with the following contracts with a one to one relationship between requirements and contracts:

c_1: true $\vdash$ state' = RESET $\vee$ state' = INIT $\vee$ state' = DIAG $\vee$ state' = TEST $\vee$ state' = NORM $\vee$ state' = SAFE $\vee$ state' = DESTR

c_2 : state = RESET $\vdash$ state' = INIT

c_3 : reset' $\vdash$ state' = RESET

This case study extends an earlier one [2] with test-case execution and a detailed mutation analysis evaluating the quality of the generated test cases.

We created 66 mutants (six turned out to be equivalent), by flipping every boolean signal (also internal ones) involved in the Matlab function calculating the final output signals. Our 21 test cases were able to detect 31 of the 60 non-equivalent mutants, giving a mutation score of 51.6%. These numbers show that state and signal coverage is not enough to find all faults and confirm the need to incorporate a more sophisticated test case generation methodology. Therefore, we manually added 10 test purposes generating 10 additional test cases. The combined 31 test cases finally reached a 100% mutation score. This means that all injected faults were detected. In order to achieve this high mutation score fully automatically, we will add support for fault-based test-case generation to our tool, like we recently did for UML [1] and timed automata [3].

5   Related Work

The main inspiration for this work was the introduction of the conjunction operation and the investigation of its properties [11] in the context of synchronous interface theories [9]. While the mathematical properties of the conjunction in different interface theories were further studied in [6,21,15], we are not aware of any similar work related to model-based testing.

Synchronous data-flow modeling [7] has been an active area of research in the past. The most important synchronous data-flow programming languages are Lustre [8] and SIGNAL [13]. These languages are implementation languages, while requirement interfaces enable specifying high-level properties of such programs. Testing of Lustre-like programs was studied by Raymond et al. [20] and Papailiopoulou [19]. Compositional properties of specifications in the context of testing were studied before [25,18,22,5,10]. None of these workes consider synchronous data-flow specifications, and the compositional properties are investigated with respect to the parallel composition and hiding operations, but not conjunction. A different notion of conjunction is introduced for the test case generation with SAL [14]. In that work, the authors encode test purposes as trap variables, and conjunct them in order to drive the test case generation process towards reaching all the test purposes with a single test case. Consistency checking of contracts has been studied in [12], yet for a weaker notion of consistency.

Our specifications using constraints share similarities with the Z specification language [23], that also follows a multiple-viewpoint approach to structuring a specification into pieces called schemas. However, a Z schema defines the dynamics of a system in terms of operations. In contrast, our requirement interfaces follow the style of synchronous languages.

Finally, the application of the TCG and consistency checking tool for requirement interfaces and its integration into a set of software engineering tools was presented in [2]. That work focuses on the requirement-driven testing methodology, workflow and tool integration and gives no technical details about requirement interfaces. In contrast, this paper provides a sound mathematical theory for requirements interfaces and their associated incremental TCG, consistency checking and tracing procedures.

6   Conclusions and Future Work

We presented a framework for requirement-driven modeling and testing of complex systems that naturally enables multiple-view incremental modeling of synchronous data-flow systems. The formalism enables conformance testing of complex systems to their requirements and combining partial models via conjunction.

Our requirement-driven framework opens many future directions. We will extend our procedure to allow generation of adaptive test cases. We will investigate in the future other compositional operations in the context of testing synchronous systems such as the parallel composition and quotient. We also plan to study whether partitioning the requirements into views is feasible via (semi) automation, based on static analysis of input/output dependencies between requirements. We will consider additional coverage criteria and test purposes and will use our implementation to generate test cases for other industrial-size systems from our automotive, avionics and railways partners.

Acknowledgment. We are grateful to the anonymous reviewers for their valuable and detailled feedback. The research leading to these results has received funding from the ARTEMIS Joint Undertaking under grant agreements N° 269335 and N° 332830 and from the Austrian Research Promotion Agency (FFG) under grant agreements N° 829817 and N° 838498 for the implementation of the projects MBAT, Combined Model-based Analysis and Testing of Embedded Systems and CRYSTAL, Critical System Engineering Acceleration.

References

1. Aichernig, B.K., Auer, J., Jöbstl, E., Korošec, R., Krenn, W., Schlick, R., Schmidt, B.V.: Model-based mutation testing of an industrial measurement device. In: Seidl, M., Tillmann, N. (eds.) TAP 2014. LNCS, vol. 8570, pp. 1–19. Springer, Heidelberg (2014)
2. Bernhard, K.A., Hörmaier, K., Lorber, F., Ničković, D., Schlick, R., Simoneau, D., Tiran, S.: Integration of Requirements Engineering and Test-Case Generation via OSLC. In: QSIC, pp. 117–126 (2014)
3. Aichernig, B.K., Lorber, F., Ničković, D.: Time for mutants — model-based mutation testing with timed automata. In: Veanes, M., Viganò, L. (eds.) TAP 2013. LNCS, vol. 7942, pp. 20–38. Springer, Heidelberg (2013)
4. Aichernig, B.K., Lorber, F., Ničković, D., Tiran, S.: Require, test and trace it. Technical Report IST-MBT-2014-03, Graz University of Technology, Institute for Software Technology (2014), https://online.tugraz.at/tug_online/voe_main2.getVollText?pDocumentNr=637834&pCurrPk=77579
5. Aiguier, M., Boulanger, F., Kanso, B.: A formal abstract framework for modelling and testing complex software systems. Theor. Comput. Sci. 455, 66–97 (2012)
6. Benveniste, A., Caillaud, B., Ferrari, A., Mangeruca, L., Passerone, R., Sofronis, C.: Multiple viewpoint contract-based specification and design. In: de Boer, F.S., Bonsangue, M.M., Graf, S., de Roever, W.-P. (eds.) FMCO 2007. LNCS, vol. 5382, pp. 200–225. Springer, Heidelberg (2008)
7. Benveniste, A., Caspi, P., Le Guernic, P., Halbwachs, N.: Data-flow synchronous languages. In: de Bakker, J.W., de Roever, W.-P., Rozenberg, G. (eds.) REX 1993. LNCS, vol. 803, pp. 1–45. Springer, Heidelberg (1994)

8. Caspi, P., Pilaud, D., Halbwachs, N., Plaice, J.: Lustre: A declarative language for programming synchronous systems. In: POPL, pp. 178–188. ACM Press (1987)
9. Chakrabarti, A., de Alfaro, L., Henzinger, T.A., Mang, F.Y.C.: Synchronous and bidirectional component interfaces. In: Brinksma, E., Larsen, K.G. (eds.) CAV 2002. LNCS, vol. 2404, pp. 414–427. Springer, Heidelberg (2002)
10. Daca, P., Henzinger, T.A., Krenn, W., Ničković, D.: Compositional specifications for ioco testing: Technical report. Technical report, IST Austria (2014), http://repository.ist.ac.at/152/
11. Doyen, L., Henzinger, T.A., Jobstmann, B., Petrov, T.: Interface theories with component reuse. In: EMSOFT, pp. 79–88. ACM (2008)
12. Ellen, C., Sieverding, S., Hungar, H.: Detecting consistencies and inconsistencies of pattern-based functional requirements. In: Lang, F., Flammini, F. (eds.) FMICS 2014. LNCS, vol. 8718, pp. 155–169. Springer, Heidelberg (2014)
13. Gautier, T., Le Guernic, P.: Signal: A declarative language for synchronous programming of real-time systems. In: Kahn, G. (ed.) FPCA 1987. LNCS, vol. 274, pp. 257–277. Springer, Heidelberg (1987)
14. Hamon, G., De Moura, L., Rushby, J.: Automated test generation with sal. CSL Technical Note (2005)
15. Henzinger, T.A., Ničković, D.: Independent implementability of viewpoints. In: Calinescu, R., Garlan, D. (eds.) Monterey Workshop 2012. LNCS, vol. 7539, pp. 380–395. Springer, Heidelberg (2012)
16. ISO. ISO/DIS 26262-1 - Road vehicles - Functional safety - Part 1 Glossary. Technical report, International Organization for Standardization / Technical Committee 22 (ISO/TC 22), Geneva, Switzerland (July 2009)
17. Junker, U.: Quickxplain: Preferred explanations and relaxations for over-constrained problems. In: AAAI, pp. 167–172. AAAI Press (2004)
18. Krichen, M., Tripakis, S.: Conformance testing for real-time systems. Formal Methods in System Design 34(3), 238–304 (2009)
19. Papailiopoulou, V.: Automatic test generation for lustre/scade programs. In: ASE, pp. 517–520. IEEE Computer Society, Washington, DC (2008)
20. Raymond, P., Nicollin, X., Halbwachs, N., Weber, D.: Automatic testing of reactive systems. In: RTSS, pp. 200–209. IEEE Computer Society (1998)
21. Reineke, J., Tripakis, S.: Basic problems in multi-view modeling. Technical Report UCB/EECS-2014-4, EECS Department, University of California, Berkeley (January 2014)
22. Sampaio, A., Nogueira, S., Mota, A.: Compositional verification of input-output conformance via csp refinement checking. In: Breitman, K., Cavalcanti, A. (eds.) ICFEM 2009. LNCS, vol. 5885, pp. 20–48. Springer, Heidelberg (2009)
23. Michael Spivey, J.: Z Notation - a reference manual, 2nd edn. Prentice Hall International Series in Computer Science. Prentice Hall (1992)
24. Tretmans, J.: Test generation with inputs, outputs and repetitive quiescence. Software - Concepts and Tools 17(3), 103–120 (1996)
25. van der Bijl, M., Rensink, A., Tretmans, J.: Compositional testing with ioco. In: Petrenko, A., Ulrich, A. (eds.) FATES 2003. LNCS, vol. 2931, pp. 86–100. Springer, Heidelberg (2004)

Applying Finite State Process Algebra to Formally Specify a Computational Model of Security Requirements in the Key2phone-Mobile Access Solution

Sunil Chaudhary[1(✉)], Linfeng Li[2(✉)], Eleni Berki[1,3], Marko Helenius[4], Juha Kela[5], and Markku Turunen[1]

[1] School of Information Sciences, University of Tampere,
Kanslerinrinne 1, Pinni B, 30014, Tampere, Finland
chaudhary.sunil.x@student.uta.fi, eleni.berki@uta.fi,
markku.turunen@sis.uta.fi
[2] Information Engineering College, Beijing Institute of Petrochemical Technology,
19 Qingyuan North Rd, Daxing, Beijing, China
lilinfeng@bipt.edu.cn
[3] Department of Computer Science and Information Systems, University of Jyväskylä,
P.O. Box 35 (Agora), 40014, Jyväskylä, Finland
[4] Department of Pervasive Computing, Tampere University of Technology,
P.O. Box 553, 33101, Tampere, Finland
marko.t.helenius@tut.fi
[5] Finwe Ltd., Elektroniikkatie 8, 90590, Oulu, Finland
juha.kela@finwe.fi

Abstract. *Key2phone* is a mobile access solution which turns mobile phone into a key for electronic locks, doors and gates. In this paper, we elicit and analyse the essential and necessary safety and security requirements that need to be considered for the Key2phone interaction system. The paper elaborates on suggestions/solutions for the realisation of safety and security concerns considering the Internet of Things (IoT) infrastructure. The authors structure these requirements and illustrate particular computational solutions by deploying the Labelled Transition System Analyser (LTSA), a modelling tool that supports a process algebra notation called Finite State Process (FSP). While determining an integrated solution for this research study, the authors point to key quality factors for successful system functionality.

1 Introduction

People carry their mobile phone most of the time, and this is the main reason that the mobile phone could be deployed as an alternative of a door-key. There exist many mobile applications that are available using communication technologies like Near Field Communication (NFC), Bluetooth, and other. A mobile phone could be used to unlock e.g. a hotel room, work office, house door; even to open garage and car doors.

Although, the use of a mobile phone as an integrated door-key has several advantages, it also has various safety and security vulnerabilities and threats. What will

© Springer International Publishing Switzerland 2015
M. Núñez and M. Güdemann (Eds.): FMICS 2015, LNCS 9128, pp. 128–145, 2015.
DOI: 10.1007/978-3-319-19458-5_9

possibly happen when a mobile phone is stolen, lost or misplaced? How will the whole communication system behave during some severe disasters? For example, work premises are on fire and people are trapped inside. Will the trapped people have to dial the door number and enter the Personal Identification Number (PIN) code to open the door? This can be a time-consuming and in this situation unreliable process, which may prove fatal when time runs out. Even the slightest vulnerability or threat in this system can severely hinder the safety and security of the owners, their family, and valuables. Hence, it is essential to have a comprehensive analysis of personal safety and system security requirements. Further, there is a need for a resulting formal specification and verification model of the mobile phone based door access-control system in order to determine safety and security considerations and integrate them within the system's design. The resulted model could help the designers to articulate what they must include and avoid in order to improve the safety and security of the system.

In this paper, we consider the case study of Key2phone mobile access solution [1]. We provided safety and security suggestions and measures that can be purposeful, applicable and realisable through implementation in the Key2phone system.

For writing the *applicable* formal specifications, we utilised the Finite State Process (FSP) formal specification method, which is a formal process algebra notation used to *generate finite Labelled Transition System* (LTS) [2, 3]. By *applicable* specifications, we mean only those specifications which can be a part of the Key2phone interaction system. The formal specifications demonstrate and verify different safety and security interactions in the Key2phone system. In order to verify the previous in FSP notation, we used a model checking tool called Labelled Transition System Analyser (LTSA) [4], which is a verification tool for concurrent systems and supports FSP for the concise description of components' behaviour.

This paper is organised as follows: section 2 discusses related work. Section 3 and 4 include brief introductions of the Key2phone system, and FSP and LTSA respectively. Section 5 further investigates and scrutinises the security vulnerabilities and threats, and presents their management control; these are exhibited in tabular representation. Section 6 analyses the safety and security requirements, demonstrating the interaction support for various security levels in the Key2phone system, utilising FSP specification models. Section 7 briefly revisits the need for this approach and concludes on its strengths and limitations

2   Related Work

In general, formal specification models have been employed to present the system specification in an unambiguous way and discover errors early, already in requirements specification. This constitutes a significant effort, especially for safety critical and real-time systems development, where emergent properties such as safety, reliability and security are very important in practice [5]. Magee and Maibaum [6] employed FSP to write the formal requirements specification of a fault tolerance system and LTSA to model and analyse fault tolerance mechanisms in self managed or self-healing systems. Likewise, the work of Kaisar et al. [7] utilised LTSA to define narrow passageway system operations in terms of a finite state machine and, thus, verify and validate its architecture-level behaviour.

To our knowledge, there is no other research study that has formalised the safety and security requirements of a mobile-phone-based door access-control system. However, there are a few studies, mentioned next, which have analysed the design and deployment of similar systems and have also considered some security aspects.

Ogri et al. [8] have described their design for a door-locking security system, which can be operated and controlled by a mobile phone. Regarding security, they have considered only *authentication* mechanism(s) in their design. The latter design overlooks other crucial properties for achieving a level of sound security: *authorization* mechanism(s) suited to different users; confirmation of *accountability*; *integrity* of transmitted data; *availability* of service to authorized users, to mention just a few of the limitations. Further, they have failed to address emergency cases: even during an emergency case, a user has to go through all the procedures, i.e. dial the door number and enter suitable PIN... in order to open the door.

Another study is that of Bauer et al. [9], in which the authors investigated the usability challenges in building a Smartphone-based access-control system and the users' expectations when the system is deployed. Their claim '*security properties are unimportant for the user*' is rather controversial and misleading. The degree of security is contextual and varies according to the needs of individuals [10, 11]. It cannot, therefore, be generalized for every type of user, merely by conducting studies on a single type of user, which in their case is university staff. Nevertheless, we understand the issue 'failure to open the door' which is mentioned in [9] as a usability issue, pertained to security as well, since failure to open the door during a normal situation can only be a cause of frustration. Naturally and while prioritising properties the level of significance will be different during any emergency situations e.g. the building is on fire or there is an earthquake and the door cannot be opened.

3   Key2phone-Mobile Access Solution

Key2phone is a mobile access solution that turns mobile phone into a key for electronic locks at e.g. industrial and office gates, and generally supports door automation procedures in an enhanced way. By deploying this solution, a door can be opened simply by dialing the number assigned to it or with Bluetooth connection. When the number assigned to a door is dialed, the *door control module* checks whether the calling mobile number belongs to a valid user (group) or not. In case of a valid number, it rejects the call and opens the gate; otherwise, it simply ignores the call, which means the call is always free of charge. Likewise, when any mobile phone with authorised Bluetooth address and *Key2phone Bluetooth application* installed enters into the Bluetooth range of the door, the door detects it and opens automatically. The access rights are managed online with a *web-based configuration management system* and access policies are transmitted wirelessly to the Key2phone control module. This mobile access solution is available in two products:

A. Key2phone Easy. This product is suitable for single and multiple electronic locks, doors, gates or barriers. It supports up to 1000 users per door.

B. Key2phone Access Control. This product can be tailored to communicate with the most common access control systems. In this product, management of access rights can be performed via the system interface or with a web configuration tool.

This mobile access solution can be suitable for different usages environments, e.g. in industry, logistics, harbours, airports, offices, and for resident. Currently, it is available for Nokia N-Series, Nokia E-Series, and many other Nokia models.

4   LTSA Tool and FSP Notation

LTSA is a verification tool used to specify behaviour modelling or generate LTS. This tool helps in modeling various processes of a system as a Finite State Machine (FSM) with well defined mathematical properties, and thus facilitates formal analysis and mechanical checking and control of the system. It obeys easy to grasp formal syntax and semantics, and displays the result in an intuitive manner, i.e., simple graphical representations. Further, a user can animate the LTS by stepping through the sequences of the actions it models, and model-check the LTS for various properties, including deadlock freedom, safety and progress properties.

In LTS, the basic building block of a specification is FSP. The major component of FSP is *process*, defined by one or more local processes separated by commas. To write the specification, we have employed the following process operators: action represented by an *action prefix* ("->"), *choice* represented by a bar ("|"), conditional ("*if* boolean_condition *then* expression1 *else* expression2"), *guarded action* (*when* (boolean_condition) expression), and a *primitive local process* "STOP". The process names start with uppercase and the action names with lowercase. For example,

```
KEY= (primaryKey->ADMINISTRATOR
     |nonPrimaryKey->GENERAL_USER),
```

In the above code snippet, `primaryKey` and `nonPrimaryKey` are the actions while `KEY`, `ADMINISTRATOR`, and `GENERAL_USER` are the processes. Moreover, the choice ("|") states that after the first action has occurred, the subsequent behaviour is described by `ADMINISTRATOR` if the first action was `primaryKey`, and `GENERAL_USER` if the first action was `nonPrimaryKey`. The meaning of this code is that when the key is primary, the key bearer is an administrator otherwise a general user.

The components conditional and guarded action are used as condition checking statements, and the primitive local process "STOP" is used to terminate the execution of the program.

5   Security Threats/Vulnerabilities and their Management Control

When dealing with the security threats and vulnerabilities in a system like Key2phone, which controls the entrance of various premises, people's physical safety occupies a top priority. By physical safety, we mean protecting against the occurrence of any fatalities. Similarly, security also encompasses protection against any misuse by the authorised users.

For the elicitation of safety and security requirements, firstly we identified different actors, preconditions, and assumptions in each case of the scenario. This is followed by expert group opinions. In the first phase of expert opinions, our team (comprising six security and usability researchers) listed out the safety and security requirements for each case. In the second phase two external field experts participated to identify if there are any missing or unnecessary requirements. Last it was decided that a verifiable and verified design should be among our target.

The final list of threats and vulnerabilities against which the Key2phone system has to act, along with their management control, are presented in Table 1.

Table 1. Security threats and vulnerabilities and their management control

Security Threats/Vulnerabilities	Management Control
Human physical safety	*Implement safety measures*
1.1. It will be inconvenient for a user to dial the door number to open it during emergency situations, e.g., a fire breaks into the building and people are in panic.	Use different sensors; however, which sensor(s) will be considered will depend on the necessity of the user. When a sensor is triggered, the door opens automatically to facilitate the escape of people inside the premises. However, it is necessary to avoid nuisance or false alarms and handle no-alarm situations (i.e., sensors fail to act due to worn out batteries or faulty loose connections)
1.2. People can be trapped in-between or under the doors while closing them.	Include door entrapment protection mechanisms, such as motion or proximity detectors, to determine (and inform) when it is safe to close the door.
Follow on attack or tailgating	*Use automatic locking system*
1.3. People may enter the premises immediately behind an authorised user when it takes time to close the door.	Use automatic locking system to lock the door automatically, soon after it closes.
Lost , theft, misplace of mobile phone	*Use mechanism to authenticate user*
1.4. The mobility nature of mobile phone makes it vulnerable to loss or theft. Misplacing it, even temporarily, due to the owner's carelessness, it can be exposed to unauthorised access.	Use PIN and password to authenticate the system' users. There is a possibility that authorised users may forget their PIN and password. Hence, PIN or password reset mechanism can be implemented. Some alternatives can be graphical password, e-tokens, and biometrics but they come with inherent limitations, extra cost and several of the mobile phones will not support them.

Table 1. (*Continued*)

Password cracking	Strengthen the authentication mechanism
1.5. Even when the device is properly secured by PIN or password, it is possible for a determined attacker to intercept it when the user enters it [10]. Attackers can employ techniques, such as brute force attacks, password guess, and dictionary attacks in order to crack the password (paraphrase) or PIN used for authentication.	Users must select *high entropy* password. Entropy of a password can be increased by using an uncommon and lengthy composition of characters (both uppercase and lowercase), integers, and special characters. However, such password will decrease its usability. Besides, users can be blocked after three consequent attempts of incorrect PIN or password. A danger is that anyone can abuse it, when adopting account lockout to lock a legitimate user's account. An alternative can be introducing a delay of 5 sec for the first wrong entry and after every wrong entry the delay is increased by 5 sec [11].
Bluetooth hacked	Improve Bluetooth pairing protocol
1.6. Hackers can intercept the Bluetooth signal to hack into mobile phone and gain full control of it. They can employ different types of attack, such as BlueBug, HeloMoto, Bluesnarf, Bluesnarf++, and Bluebugging to take control of victim's phone. These attacks are possible when Bluetooth is left exposed and under full connection facility. Further, many times mobile phone users do not change their Bluetooth passkey and leave the default one provided by the company. Such users are easy prey to hackers.	Use the latest version of Bluetooth and always turn off its discovery and connect modes when they are not needed [12, 13, 14]. Also use strong passkey (length and randomness) used for Bluetooth pairing [12, 13, 14]. More importantly, verifier should not accept unknown claimant [14]. Furthermore, Bluetooth specification time-out period between repeated attempts can be set that will increase exponentially [12] to protect from Bluesnarf attack by guessing the device's Media Access Control (MAC) address via a vicious and enforced attack.
Caller ID spoofing	Implement caller ID verification mechanisms
1.7. Attackers can employ 'caller ID spoofing' to fake the authorised mobile number to open the door.	A solution can be 'CallerDec' that builds a trusted covert channel between the person called (callee) and the claimed caller, and uses timing estimation together with the call status to verify indeed the claimed caller is calling [15]. In the case of Key2phone, simply authenticating the caller as mentioned in 1.4 before opening the door can protect against 'caller ID spoofing'.
Attacks during data transmission	Use of crypto graphical measures
1.8. User's phone identification is based on phone number or phone's Bluetooth address. Attackers can use man-in-the-middle attacks, or packet sniffing, or eavesdropping to intercept data packets travelling over network.	IPSec, e.g., TSL/SSL can be used for web-based configuration. Similarly, an upgraded version of Cellular Message Encryption Algorithm (CMEA), such as ECMEA and SCMEA [16] can be used in mobile data transmission. Further, mobile end-to-end protection can be used. In case of Bluetooth, it offers built-in security measures at the link level; for example, in the Security Mode 3 of Bluetooth, the link-level authentication and encryption methods are used for all connections to and from the device.

Table 1. (*Continued*)

Disruption of service to authorized users	*Implement network protection*
1.9. Attackers can employ Denial-of-Service (DoS), Distributed Denial of Service (DDoS), network congestion, server crashing, signal jamming, false information passed to the piconet members, etc. to prevent legitimate users from accessing the service.	Mechanisms for integrity management, intrusion or anomaly detection systems, *timeliness detection* of data, and originality of data [17] can be implemented. Further, security defense techniques (e.g., Firewall, Intrusion Detection System, and other) can be applied at multi-level and at each level they should be dissimilar to each other. Blacklisting the connection request in a suspicious manner can help to prevent from such attacks to an extent.
Intentional/accidental attacks by authorised users	*Design suitable policies and ensure that user adheres to them; implement authorisation and ensure accountability*
1.10. An authorised user can deliberately misuse and conceal any service or device. Moreover, there is an equal chance that s/he accidentally misuses it and does not realise it.	Apply the *least privilege principle* for authorisation. Maintaining logs or audit trails can help to record each activity of an authorised user and improve accountability. Moreover, users who are allowed access for a limited time should be immediately removed as soon as the permitted time completes. Finally, designing suitable policies for the authorised user and ensuring that they all understand and adhere to the policies can help to prevent from accidental misuse.
Attacks using phishing to hack Bluetooth or obtain PIN and password	*Employ security software; design suitable policies and ensure that users adhere to them; educate and bring awareness in users; implement authorization; and use simple design for security related operations*
1.11. Attackers can use technical subterfuge like keylogger and malware to steal password. Furthermore, they can employ social skills to lure potential victims and hack their Bluetooth. Similar acts can be deployed even to know the password or PIN from the users. In fact, social engineering is a key threat in information security. Humans can be the weakest link in information security [18, 19, 20, 21]. They can easily be manipulated and are prone to errors.	It is advisable to use security software like firewall, anti-virus, and anti-phishing software and keep them up-to-date. Further, human can become the strongest link [20]. Design suitable policies and ensure that users understood and practiced them. Educating and bringing awareness in users about the risks can help in preventing them from falling for social engineering tricks. Further, equipping users with simple and intuitive design and usability in security related tasks [21, 22] can also help in social engineering cases. In case anyone becomes a victim of social engineering, implementing the least privilege principle will limit the compromise.

Table 1. (*Continued*)

Vulnerabilities in software and hardware	Use high quality hardware and software
1.12. Attackers exploit vulnerabilities in the software. Likewise, quality of the hardware against below freezing temperature as well as above temperature, high humidity, power loss problems, and many other situations are vital from security perspective.	Integrate safety and security requirements with the system requirements and design process for validation and verification from the early stage of the system development [23, 24, 25] and obey secure coding principles and practices to write software code [26]. In case of hardware, design verification and hardware testing before purchasing can help to improve the hardware quality [27]. Performing regular tests using diversified real time scenarios can help to recognise the bugs and limitations and fix them on time that is before the product reaches the users.

6   Formal Specification of the Key2phone System

The main idea behind formalising these specifications using FSP and LTSA is to increase their computationality/formality and understanding and describe the evolutionary nature of the requirements under analysis. Running the FSP notation in LTSA utilising its animation and FSM draw features can help the user to get clearer picture of the specifications and the ways they interact when implemented in the system.

We start the formalisation of specification with *authorisation* function, which can be a possible mitigation for 1.10 (Table 1). Along with that, the activities of user are also registered in a log-file in order to guarantee *accountability*.

Regarding authorisation, there are *primary key bearer* and *non-primary key bearer*. The primary key bearer is the administrative rights holder whilst the non-primary key bearer is a general user.

```
/*Declarations of constant, range, and Boolean.*/
const MAXATTEMPT=3
range ATTEMPTRANGE=1..MAXATTEMPT
const MAXHOUR=8
range HOURRANGE=1..MAXHOUR
range BOOL=0..1


/* When an authorised user sends requests for open-
close door operation or mode change, the door control
module processes the requests. */
DOOR_OPERATION= (process->KEY),

/*Users can be a primary key bearer (administrator) or
a non primary key bearer (general user). */
KEY= ( primaryKey->ADMINISTRATOR
```

```
|nonPrimaryKey->GENERAL_USER),
```

The primary key bearer is authorised to the following operations: *manage mode, move mode, remote mode, sleep mode, normal mode,* and *emergency mode.* In contrast, the non-primary key bearer is authorised to only *normal mode, move mode* and *emergency mode.*

```
/*The administrator is authorised to: configure
settings (manage mode); enable and disable modes like
move mode, sleep mode, and remote mode; open and close
door (normal mode), and receive alerts during emergency
situations (emergency mode)*/
ADMINISTRATOR= ( managementOperation->MANAGE_MODE
               |moveOperation->MOVE_MODE
               |sleepOperation->SLEEP_MODE
               |remoteOperation->REMOTE_MODE
               |defaultOperation->NORMAL_MODE
               |emergencyOperation->EMERGENCY_MODE),
```

```
/* A general user is authorised to: open and close door
(normal mode); enable and disable move mode; and
receive alerts during emergency situations (emergency
mode).*/
GENERAL_USER= ( defaultOperation->NORMAL_MODE
              |moveOperation->MOVE_MODE
              |emergencyOperation->EMERGENCY_MODE),
```

In *manage mode,* the primary key bearer can add any new non-primary users, update or delete the existing non-primary users, download report, and configure security management rules through *configuration management system.* Security management rules can be related to *sleep mode, remote mode,* and other, for example, at what time the *sleep mode* should be enabled or disabled. The primary key bearer must be authenticated to perform these administrative activities.

But to identify different user types and to prevent misuse from 1.4 (Table 1), it necessitates authenticating users. For an authentication purpose, username-password pair can be used, since it is simple to implement and does not add extra costs [28, 29]. However, a delay of a few seconds can be introduced when an incorrect entry is made, which again exponentially increases after every incorrect attempt to countermeasure 1.5 (Table 1). The idea is that if somebody employs techniques like *dictionary attack* or *brute-force attack* or *password-guess* for password cracking, the attacker will have to wait for the failed delay, thus, forcing them to spend more time for the task. The National Institute of Standards and Technology [11] recommends a delay of 5 sec for the first wrong entry and after every next wrong entry the delay is increased by 5 sec.

```
/*To perform the management, the administrator has to
be logged-in using username-password pair. */
MANAGE_MODE=(authenticateAdmin-> ADMIN_AUTHENTICATION),
```

```
/*A delay of a few seconds, which will increase
exponentially is introduced for every incorrect login
attempt.*/
ADMIN_AUTHENTICATION= (
     correctCredentials->performManagement->
     MANAGEMENT_ACTIVITY
    |incorrectCredentials->introduceExponentialDelay->
     allowRetry-> ADMIN_AUTHENTICATION),
/*During manage mode, the administrator can add new
users; delete or edit the existing users; download
reports; and configure security rules for remote mode
and sleep mode. */
MANAGEMENT_ACTIVITY= ({addUser,removeUser,updateUser,
downloadReport, configureSecurityRules}->
maintainLogEntry->(loginStatus[l:BOOL]->
   if l==1 then
      (continue->MANAGEMENT_ACTIVITY)
   else
      (logOut->DOOR_OPERATION))),
```

A user can enable or disable *move mode* only after entering the correct PIN code (again PIN code is simple to implement and does not add extra costs) through the *Key2phone Bluetooth application*. In order to improve the security and protect from attacks like *brute force attack*, *password guess*, and *dictionary attack*, we have limited the interaction to only three consecutive attempts of incorrect PIN code before the number is blocked from opening the door as well as changing the mode. The number can be unblocked via the *web-based configuration management system*. A danger when adopting account lockout could be that anyone can easily abuse it to lock an authorised user's account. However, in this case it is difficult, since, the attacker will first need access to the mobile phone of an authorised user to abuse it.

When enabling the *move mode*, the mobile-phone's Bluetooth is also set discoverable and connectable after the correct PIN code is entered.   A time has to be set for which the *move mode* has to remain in enabled state. On the one hand it will relieve the user from separately pressing a button to enable Bluetooth while on the other hand it will help in protecting against Bluetooth hacking, since the rest of the time when Bluetooth is not required (i.e., *move mode* is disabled) it will remain undiscovered and thus not connectable to counteract 1.6 (Table 1).

The *move mode* is activated when a user requires frequent door opening. In this mode, a user is able to open the door just by pressing a button. The door opens when a valid Bluetooth comes into the door proximity and open-button in the *Key2phone Bluetooth application* is pressed. Thus, it will prevent users from a tiresome task of entering the PIN code each time they open the door.

```
/*Move mode is used for the occasions when frequent
opening of the door is required. During move mode, a
user can simply dial the door number or reach the door
proximity, select the door he wants to open and press
open-door button in the Key2phone Bluetooth application
to open the door*/
```

```
MOVE_MODE= (moveModeStatus [m: BOOL] ->
  if m==1 then
      (dialDoorNumber->openDoor->maintainLogEntry->
      protectDoorEntrapment->DOOR_CLOSE
      |bluetoothInRange->selectDoor->pressButton->
      openDoor->maintainLogEntry->
      protectDoorEntrapment-> DOOR_CLOSE)
  else
      (authenticateUser-> MODE_AUTHENTICATION)),
/*To set move mode, the user has to first authenticate
by entering correct PIN code, and provide the time for
which move mode will remain enabled. Moreover, after
the correct PIN code, the user's mobile phone Bluetooth
will set to discoverable and connectable. */
MODE_AUTHENTICATION= (
  correctPIN->setOnShowBluettooth->setTime->moveMode->
  maintainLogEntry ->DOOR_OPERATION
  |incorrectPIN [k: ATTEMPTRANGE]->ATTEMPT_CHECK [k]),

/*When authenticating with PIN code, only three
incorrect attempts are allowed after that the number is
blocked. The number can be unblocked via configuration
management system*/                      ATTEMPT_CHECK
[1: ATTEMPTRANGE] = (
  when (1 <MAXATTEMPT)
      allowRetry-> MODE_AUTHENTICATION
  |when (1 >= MAXATTEMPT)
      blockNumber->STOP),
```

The *sleep mode* defines the operational behaviour of the door-lock system during the night time. The security management rules set by the primary key bearer for this mode get activated. For example, the primary key bearer can define the time after which the door has to be locked with no more operation.

```
/*Sleep mode for the night time, i.e., how the door
operation should behave during the night time. The
primary key bearer can set security rules via the
configuration management system, which will be
activated during sleep mode*/
SLEEP_MODE= (sleepModeStatus[s: BOOL] ->
  if s==1 then
      (applySleepModePolicy->protectDoorEntrapment->
      DOOR_CLOSE)
  else
      (checkWithinSleepTime[c:BOOL]->
        if c==1 then
          (applySleepModePolicy->
          protectDoorEntrapment-> DOOR_CLOSE)
        else
          (default->DOOR_OPERATION))),
```

The *remote mode* allows an ability to control the door from remote locations. For example, when the *remote mode* is activated, the pre-defined security rules are automatically loaded and taken into use in order to keep doors locked until the primary key bearer is approaching. Further, for the functioning of the *remote mode*, it is necessary to detect the administrator's location. Thus, the administrator has to either manually enable the remote mode when s/he wants or implement geo-location service, which in turn will continuously record his or her current location and will enable remote mode when s/he is outside of the city.

```
/*Remote mode is for the time when the administrator is
out of the town. The primary key bearer can set
security rules via the configuration management system,
which will be activated during remote mode. In order to
know the location of the administrator, his location at
a respective time is recorded.*/
REMOTE_MODE=(adminLocation->respectivTime-> leaveHome
[l:BOOL]->
  if l==1 then
    (activateRemoteModeSecurity->
    protectDoorEntrapment-> DOOR_CLOSE)
  else
    (default-> DOOR_OPERATION)),
```

Normal mode allows users to open the door after entering the correct PIN code. For example, during the day time an authorised user can dial the door number or reach the door proximity with Bluetooth enabled and can enter the correct PIN code to open the door.

```
/*During normal mode, users can open the door by
dialing the door number or reach the door proximity
with Bluetooth enabled; but in this case the users will
also need to authenticate by entering the PIN code.*/
NORMAL_MODE= (normalModeStatus [n: BOOL] ->
  if n==1 then
    (correctPIN->openDoor->maintainLogEntry->
    protectDoorEntrapment->DOOR_CLOSE
    |inCorrectPIN[i:ATTEMPTRANGE]->
    AUTHENTICATE_USER[i])
  else
    (protectDoorEntrapment->DOOR_CLOSE)),
/*When authenticating with PIN code, only three
incorrect attempts are allowed after that the number is
blocked. The number can be unblocked via configuration
management system*/
AUTHENTICATE_USER [a: ATTEMPTRANGE] = (
  when ( a <MAXATTEMPT)
    allowRetry-> NORMAL_MODE
```

```
|when (a >= MAXATTEMPT)
    blockNumber->STOP),
```

During the *emergency mode* the system notifies the people inside the premise and opens the door automatically to facilitate them in escaping the premise in a short time, which is a solution for 1.1 (Table 1). This mode is enabled when there are serious situations, for instances when the building is on fire or there is an earthquake. To correctly operate the *emergency mode*, it requires additional sensors, e.g. smoke sensors, to be deployed and connected with the Key2phone system. But the sensor-system has to protect from nuisance or false alarms and at the same time it must trigger when there is any true cause. A sensor which automatically adjusts the sensitivity without affecting its performance during no-alarm situations can prove to be extremely helpful.

```
/*Emergency mode is activated during any serious
situation, like, building on fire or there is an
earthquake. During this mode, all the users are alerted
and the door opens automatically.*/
EMERGENCY_MODE= (notifyEmergency->openDoor->STOP),
```

When closing the door, it is necessary to protect any entrapment in between the door, i.e. a solution for 1.2 (Table 1).

```
/*When closing the door, it first checks for any object
in-between the door to prevent entrapment.*/
DOOR_CLOSE=(objectInBetweenDoorStatus [o:BOOL]->
  if o==1 then
    (openDoor->DOOR_CLOSE)
  else
    (closeDoor->DOOR_OPERATION)).
```

The authentication mechanism will also prevent *caller ID spoofing,* i.e., 1.7 (Table 1), since fake caller will fail to open the door without a valid PIN code. Moreover, blocking the mobile number dialing the door in suspicious ways can help in protecting from DoS and DDoS attacks, a mitigation for 1.9 (Table 1). Likewise, open-door operation has always been immediately followed by close-door operation, which can be helpful to prevent tailgating, a solution for 1.3 (Table 1).

The remaining vulnerabilities 1.8, 1.11, and 1.12 (Table 1) are not included in the FSP notations since they deal with data transmission, people, and employed hardware/software. In practice, service from third party SSL/TLS provider is used to encrypt transmitted data to maintain their confidentiality and integrity and, therefore 1.8 (Table 1) is out of our scope. Similarly, identifying vulnerabilities in people, i.e., 1.11 (Table 1) to suggest suitable mitigations for them is a wide domain and will need a separate future study, so even in the Table 1 we suggested general but generic mitigations. Last, vulnerabilities due to the quality of hardware and software are again a domain which will need a separate study to suggest appropriate mitigations. Thus, only formal abstraction suggestions are included in the table.

Fig 1 is the FSM model of door operation. State '0' is the initial state and state '2' is the final state of the non-primary key bearer whereas state'3' is the final state of the primary key bearer. State '-1' is the unreachable state which occurred in the figure because it is a result of executing only a part of the FSP notation encoded of the Key2phone system. The complete FSM model resulted by executing the complete FSP notation encoded of the Key2phone system (where state '-1' does not occur) cannot be fitted in this paper in a readable clear form because the graphical model is too large and abstract with complex graphical detail. For example, in Fig 3 which presents the FSM model of the *emergency mode* the resulted graph was obtained by executing its complete code and, thus, does not have '-1' state. In order to obtain the complete FSM, it simply requires copying all the aforementioned code snippets (of the current section) sequentially and executing it using LTSA.

The FSM in the Fig 1 conveys that when the door operation is processed, if it is the primary key bearer it moves to state '3' otherwise state'2'. From state '3' administrative activities can be performed whereas from state '2' only activities authorised to a general user can be performed.

Likewise, Fig 2 is the respective animation of the FSM in Fig 1. Clicking the checkbox with a checkmark, which also means selecting an activity, will lead to the activity which has to be performed next. For example, in the beginning the checkmark was in 'process' through which, when clicked checkmark moves to 'primarykey' and 'nonprimarykey' conveying the same information as the FSM. This increases the understandability and simplicity of the formal FSM-based specifications, since a user does not have to understand each code, but can instead just watch the animation of the specification.

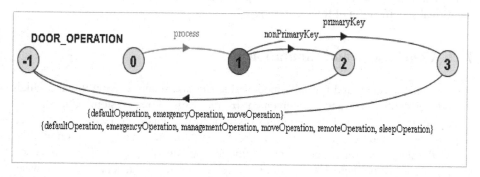

Fig. 1. FSM of Door Operation showing the authorisation provided to the primary key and non-primary key bearers. State '0' is the initial state and states '2' and '3' are the final state of the non-primary key and primary key bearers respectively. State '-1' is *unreachable* state.

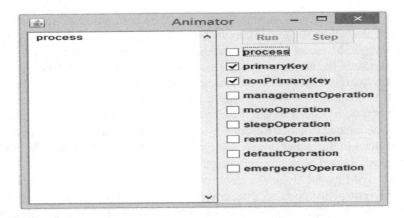

Fig. 2. Animation of Door Operation in which clicking the checkbox with check mark (i.e., selecting activity) will proceed to the activity which has to be performed next

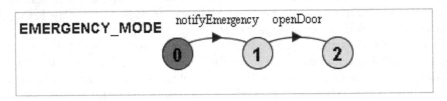

Fig. 3. FSM of Emergency Mode in which state '0' is the initial state and state '2' is the final state

Figures 1-3 above are just a small sample of the graphs generated while executing the formal specification of this case study.

7   Conclusions and Limitations

We elicited, analysed, and formally modelled safety and security requirements, which should be deliberated and implemented in the Key2phone system. Further, we described and represented the requirements in a formal language [see e.g. reference 30] and automated tool that cater for formal system specification. In relation to personal safety, we suggested i) an automatic opening of door during emergency situations and ii) the inclusion of a door entrapment protection mechanism. Likewise, we expressed and analysed security concerns for the protection against physical, syntactic, and semantic attacks. In physical attacks we consider, for instance, theft or misplace of mobile phone. Similarly, in syntactic attacks we raised the issues primarily associated with integrated technologies, such as Bluetooth and mobile technology data transmission. Regarding semantic attacks, we support that measures merely focused on system's design are not adequate because they cannot eliminate all the possible risks and vulnerabilities. Therefore, the respective organizations should have suitable policies and ways to ensure that those policies are adhered by the users.

Moreover, to facilitate users in implementing safety and security measures consistently and correctly, the usability of the interaction interface has to be such that it will i) lessen the users' burden and ii) protect the system from users' (conscious or unconscious) aggressive behaviour [31].

An important fact to remember while applying safety and security design principles is that they are contextual. So the respective persons/organisations have to determine which level of safety and security is appropriate for them. Furthermore, different countries have their own recommended standard(s) for door functioning, so it is necessary to follow them. Meanwhile, an implementation of safety and security requirements, counter actions and counter measures comes with cost. In general, safety and security features are not cost-effective. Therefore, selecting the degree of safety and security depending on the sensitivity and contextual background of user scenarios can result in reduced (unnecessary) expenses.

An equally important reality is that a mobile phone device is battery powered. Any unnecessary activities (e.g., enabling Bluetooth all the time or running the application even when it is not needed ...) will also strain the battery. Further, any intensive computing tasks related to security checks (e.g., use of biometrics for authentication, unnecessary code execution ...) can result in an accelerated battery drain.

Our work does not discuss in detail the severity of the mentioned safety and security issues; the main aim has so far been to provide design solution based on formal specification, which would naturally lead to system automation. Our design solution also does not cover risks from Subscriber Identity Module (SIM) cloning, and limitations in mobile phone technology such as threats from malicious software. A feature called 'remote mode' learns the location and the respective time of the primary user. This can raise complications for users who consider it a privacy breach. Last but not least, our work does not consider the impact in people with hearing or vision disability who also need to open doors in their daily life. Ongoing and future R&D work will deal with the above and also concentrate on the proposed algorithm's computational complexity, delay measurements, and energy spending.

Acknowledgments. This work has financially been supported by TEKES (The National Research Agency of Finland) and is of the DIGILE Internet-of-Things (IoT) research programme. The content is a deliverable of the WP4: Human Interaction. We sincerely thank Professor Maria Papadopouli from The University of Crete and Ms Yan Zhao as Nokia corporation's ex-employee for their useful insights and very constructive feedback.

References

1. Finwe Ltd.: Key2phone Mobile Access Solution, http://key2phone.com/english_index.html (cited February 23, 2014)
2. Magee, J., Kramer, J.: Concurrency: State Models & Java Programs, 2nd edn. John Wiley & Sons (2006) ISBN: 0470093552
3. Imperial College, London: FSP Notation, http://www.doc.ic.ac.uk/~jnm/LTSdocumention/FSP-notation.html (cited February 23, 2014)

4. Labelled Transition System Analyser V3.0, `http://www.doc.ic.ac.uk/~jnm/book/ltsa/LTSA_applet.html` (cited February 23, 2014)
5. Sommerville, I.: Software Engineering: Dependability and Security Specification, 9th edn., pp. 309–340. Pearson Education Inc. (2011) ISBN-13: 978-0-13-703515-1
6. Magee, J., Maibaum, T.: Towards Specification, Modelling and Analysis of Fault Tolerance in Self Managed Systems. In: Proceedings of the International Workshop on Self-Adaptation and Self-Managing Systems, Shanghai, China, May 21-22, pp. 30–36 (2006), doi:10.1145/1137677.1137684
7. Kaisar, E., Austin, M., Papadimitriou, S.: Formal Development and Evaluation of Narrow Passageway System Operations. European Transport Trasporti Europei 34, 88–104 (2006)
8. Orgi, U.J., Okwong, D.E.B., Etim, A.: Designing and Construction of Door Locking Security System Using GSM. IJECS 2(7), 2235–2257 (2013) ISSN: 2319-7242
9. Bauer, L., Cranor, L.F., Reiter, M.K., Vaniea, K.: Lessons Learned from the Deployment of a Smartphone-Based Access-Control System. In: Proceedings of Symposium on Usable Privacy and Security (SOUPS), Pittsburgh, PA, USA, July 18-20, pp. 64–75 (2007), doi:10.1145/1280680.1280689
10. Symantec Inc.: Bluetooth Security Review, `http://www.symantec.com/connect/articles/bluetooth-security-review-part-1` (cited February 23, 2014)
11. Scarfone, K., Souppaya, M.: Guide to Enterprise Password Management: Recommendations of the National Institute of Standards and Technology. National Institute of Standard and Technology (NIST) Special Publication 800-118 (2009) `http://csrc.nist.gov/publications/drafts/800-118/draft-sp800-118.pdf` (cited February 3, 2014)
12. Scarfone, K., Padgette, J.: Guide to Bluetooth Security: Recommendations of the National Institute of Standards and Technology. NIST Special Publication 800-121 (2008), `http://csrc.nist.gov/publications/drafts/800-121r1/Draft-SP800-121_Rev1.pdf` (cited February 3, 2014)
13. National Security Agency (NSA): Bluetooth Security, `http://www.nsa.gov/ia/_files/factsheets/i732-016r-07.pdf` (cited February 2, 2014)
14. Singelée, D., Preneel, B.: Improved pairing protocol for bluetooth. In: Kunz, T., Ravi, S.S. (eds.) ADHOC-NOW 2006. LNCS, vol. 4104, pp. 252–265. Springer, Heidelberg (2006)
15. Mustafa, H., Sadeghi, A.R., Schulz, S., Xu, W.: You Can Call But Can't Hide: Detecting Called ID Spoofing Attacks. In: The Proceedings of 44th Annual IEEE/IFIP International Conference on Dependable Systems and Networks (DSN), Atlanta Georgia USA, June 23-26 (2014)
16. Cryptome: Common Cryptographic Algorithms. Revision D.1 publication version. Report no. TR45.AHAG (2000), `http://cryptome.org/espy/TR45-ccad1.pdf` (cited January 4 2014)
17. Frantti, T., Savola, R., Hietalahti, H.: A Risk-Driven Security Analysis and Metrics Development for WSN-MCN Router. In: Proceedings of ICTC 2013, pp. 342–347 (2013), doi:10.1109/ICTC.2013.6675370
18. Bagnall, P.: Improving Visibility. ITNOW 54(3), 30–32 (2012), doi:10.1093/itnow/bws063
19. Sasse, M.A., Brostoff, S., Weirich, D.: Transforming the 'Weakest Link'- A Human/Computer Interaction Approach to Usable and Effective Security. BT Technology Journal 19(3), 122–131 (2001), doi:10.1023/A:1011902718709
20. Niblett, G.: Securing the Human. ITNOW 54(3), 25 (2012), doi: 10.1093/itnow/bws063

21. Whitten, A., Tygar, J.D.: Usability of Security: A Case Study. Carnegie Mellon University, CMU-CS-98-155 (1998), http://reports-archive.adm.cs.cmu.edu/anon/1998/abstracts/98-155.html (cited February 2, 2014)
22. Schultz, E.E., Proctor, R.W., Lien, M.C., Salvendy, G.: Usability and Security an Appraisal of Usability Issues in Information Security. Computer & Security 20(7), 620–634 (2001) ISSN: 0167-4048/01
23. Leveson, N.G.: Intent Specifications: An Approach to Building Human-Centered Specifications. IEEE Transactions on Software Engineering SE-26 (2000)
24. Zafar, S., Dormey, R.G.: Integrating Safety and Security Requirements into Design of an Embedded System. In: The Proceedings of 12th Asia Pacific Software Engineering Conference, Taipei, Taiwan, December 15-17 (2005)
25. Flechais, I.: Integrating security and usability into the requirements and design process. Int. J. Electronic Security and Digital Forensics 1(1) (2007)
26. Graff, M.G., van Wyk, K.R.: Secure Coding Principles and Practices. O'Reilly (June 2003) ISBN: 978-0-596-55601-3
27. Martin, R.J., Mathur, A.P.: Software and Hardware Quality Assurance: Towards a Common Platform for High Reliability. In: Proceedings of IEEE International Conference on Communications 1990, Atlanta Georgia, USA, April 16-19, vol. 4, pp. 1324–1328 (1990), doi:10.1109/ICC.1990.117284
28. Li, L., Berki, E., Helenius, M., Savola, R.: New Usability Metrices for Authentication Mechanisms. In: Proceedings of SQM 2012, Tampere, Finland, August 20-23, pp. 239–250 (2012)
29. Bonneau, J., Herley, C., Oorschot, P.C., Stanjano, F.: A Quest to Replace Passwords: A Framework for Comparative Evaluation of Web Authentication Schemes. In: Proceedings of IEEE Symposium on Security and Privacy, pp. 553–567 (2012), doi:10.1109/SP.2012.44(2012)
30. Diller, A.: Z: An Introduction to Formal Methods, 2nd edn. John Wiley & Sons Ltd., Chichester (1994) ISBN: 978-0-471-93973-3
31. Kainda, R., Flechais, I., Roscoe, A.W.: Security and Usability. In: Proceedings of ARES 2010, pp. 275–282 (2010), doi:10.1109/ARES.2010.77

Timed Mobility and Timed Communication for Critical Systems

Bogdan Aman$^{(\boxtimes)}$ and Gabriel Ciobanu

Romanian Academy, Institute of Computer Science,
Blvd. Carol I no.11, 700506, Iaşi, Romania
baman@iit.tuiasi.ro, gabriel@info.uaic.ro

Abstract. We present a simple but elegant prototyping language for describing real-time systems including specific features as timeouts, explicit locations, timed migration and timed communication. The parallel execution of a step is provided by multiset labelled transitions. In order to illustrate its features, we describe a railway control system. Moreover, we define some behavioural equivalences matching multisets of actions that could happen in a given range of time (up to a timeout). We define the strong time-bounded bisimulation and the strong open time-bounded bisimulation, and prove that the latter one is a congruence. By using various bisimulations over the behaviours of real-time systems, we can check which behaviours are closer to an optimal and safe behaviour.

1 Introduction

To emphasize real-time aspects in critical systems, we use our prototyping language called rTiMo (real Timed Mobility) having specific features as timeouts, explicit locations, timed migration and timed communication. The timed constraints on migration and communication are used to coordinate interactions among various processes in time-aware systems. A notable advantage of using rTiMo to describe real-time critical systems is the possibility to express natural compositionality, explicit mobility, parallel execution of actions, scalable specification of complex systems in a modular fashion, and behavioural equivalences between matching multisets of actions that could happen in a given range of time (up to a timeout). Moreover, describing processes in rTiMo allows an automatic verification by using the model checking capabilities of UPPAAL [1]. Here we emphasize on the behaviours of the critical systems depending not only on the order of actions, but also on the time at which the actions are performed. Thus, correctness and performances issues are closely related. When choosing which behavioural equivalence relation to adopt for a certain time-aware system, we should decide what properties should be preserved by the equivalence relation and how behaves the reliable system taken as reference. On the other hand, all the equivalence relations should be compositional with respect to the main constructs of the language: for example, if two systems are equivalent, then they remain equivalent when composed in parallel with the same third system. This allows compositional reasoning, and so each parallel component can be substituted by equivalent ones.

M. Núñez and M. Güdemann (Eds.): FMICS 2015, LNCS 9128, pp. 146–161, 2015.
DOI: 10.1007/978-3-319-19458-5_10

In critical systems the time issues are essential. A correct evolution depends not only on the actions taken, but also when the actions happen. A system may crash if an action is taken too early or too late. We illustrate how rTiMo works by describing a railway control system, a well-known example of a real-time system [11]. The system used in this paper is composed of two railways that intersect on a mobile bridge, together with several trains that want to cross the bridge. The mobile bridge is used to allow ships sail on the river below. The most important security rule is to avoid collision by prohibiting more than one train to cross the bridge at any given moment. The railway crossing is equipped with a controller that either allows or stops trains from crossing, depending on the state of the bridge (up or down). We use new temporal bisimilarities to define equivalence classes of trains offering similar services with respect to the waiting time (possibly up to an acceptable time difference). By using various bisimulations over the behaviours of real-time critical systems, we can identify which behaviours are closer to an optimal and safe behaviour (i.e., reductions work as expected) and compare it with sub-optimal ones containing faults (unacceptable reductions). The bisimulations can return some useful information about the compared processes: a qualitative indication that a sub-optimal behaviour might be present, and also quantitative information about the possible location or moment of a fault.

2   rTiMo : Syntax and Semantics

In rTiMo the processes can migrate between different locations of a distributed environment consisting of a number of explicit distinct locations. Timing constraints over migration and communication actions are used to coordinate processes in time and space. The passage of time in rTiMo is described with respect to a real-time global clock, while migration and communication actions are performed in a maximal parallel manner. Timing constraints for migration allow one to specify a temporal timeout after which a mobile process must move to another location. Two processes may communicate only if they are present at the same location. In rTiMo, the transitions caused by performing actions with timeouts are alternated with continuous transitions. The semantics of rTiMo is provided by multiset labelled transitions in which multisets of actions are executed in parallel (in one step).

Timing constraints applied to mobile processes allow us to specify how many time units are required by a process to move from one location to another. A timer in rTiMo is denoted by $^{\Delta t}$, where $t \in \mathbb{R}_+$. Such a timer is associated with a migration action such as $go^{\Delta t}bridge$ then P indicating that process P moves to location $bridge$ after t time units. A timer $^{\Delta 5}$ associated with an output communication process $a^{\Delta 5}!\langle z \rangle$ then P else Q makes the channel a available for communication (namely it can send z) for a period of 5 time units. It is also possible to restrict the waiting time for an input communication process $a^{\Delta 4}?(x)$ then P else Q along a channel a; if the interaction does not happen before the timeout 4, the process gives up and continues as the alternative process Q.

The syntax of rTiMo is given in Table 1, where the following are assumed:

- a set *Loc* of locations, a set *Chan* of communication channels, and a set *Id* of process identifiers (each $id \in Id$ has its arity m_{id});
- for each $id \in Id$ there is a unique process definition $id(u_1, \dots, u_{m_{id}}) \stackrel{def}{=} P_{id}$, where the distinct variables u_i are parameters;
- $a \in Chan$ is a communication channel; l is a location or a location variable;
- $t \in \mathbb{R}_+$ is a *timeout* of an action; u is a tuple of variables;
- v is a tuple of expressions built from values, variables and allowed operations.

Table 1. rTiMo Syntax

Processes	P, Q	$::=$	$a^{\Delta t}!\langle v \rangle$ then P else Q		(output)
			$a^{\Delta t}?(u)$ then P else Q		(input)
			$go^{\Delta t}l$ then P		(move)
			0		(termination)
			$id(v)$		(recursion)
			$P \mid Q$		(parallel)
Located Processes	L	$::=$	$l[[P]]$		
Systems	N	$::=$	$L \mid L \mid N$		

The only variable binding constructor is $a^{\Delta t}?(u)$ then P else Q that binds the variable u within P (but *not* within Q). $fv(P)$ is used to denote the free variables of a process P (and similarly for systems); for a process definition, is assumed that $fv(P_{id}) \subseteq \{u_1, \dots, u_{m_{id}}\}$, where u_i are the process parameters. Processes are defined up-to an alpha-conversion, and $\{v/u, \dots\}P$ denotes P in which all free occurrences of the variable u are replaced by v, eventually after alpha-converting P in order to avoid clashes.

Mobility is provided by a process $go^{\Delta t}l$ then P that describes the migration from the current location to the location indicated by l after t time units. Since l can be a variable, and so its value is assigned dynamically through communication with other processes, this form of migration supports a flexible scheme for the movement of processes from one location to another. Thus, the behaviour can adapt to various changes of the distributed environment. Processes are further constructed from the (terminated) process 0, and parallel composition $P \mid Q$. A located process $l[[P]]$ specifies a process P running at location l, and a system is built from its components $L \mid N$. A system N is well-formed if there are no free variables in N.

Operational Semantics. The first component of the operational semantics of rTiMo is the structural equivalence $\equiv$ over systems. The structural equivalence is the smallest congruence such that the equalities in Table 2 hold. Essentially, the role of $\equiv$ is to rearrange a system in order to apply the rules of the operational semantics given in Table 3. Using the equalities of Table 2, a given system N can always be transformed into a finite parallel composition of located processes of the form $l_1[[P_1]] \mid \dots \mid l_n[[P_n]]$ such that no process P_i has the parallel composition operator at its topmost level. Each located process $l_i[[P_i]]$ is called a component of N, and the whole expression $l_1[[P_1]] \mid \dots \mid l_n[[P_n]]$ is called a *component decomposition* of the system N.

Table 2. rTiMo Structural Congruence

(NNULL)	$N \mid l[[0]] \equiv N$
(NCOMM)	$N \mid N' \equiv N' \mid N$
(NASSOC)	$(N \mid N') \mid N'' \equiv N \mid (N' \mid N'')$
(NSPLIT)	$l[[P \mid Q]] \equiv l[[P]] \mid l[[Q]]$

The operational semantics rules of rTiMo are presented in Table 3. The multiset labelled transitions of form $N \xrightarrow{\Lambda} N'$ use a multiset Λ to indicate the actions executed in parallel in one step. When the multiset Λ contains only one action λ, in order to simplify the notation, $N \xrightarrow{\{\lambda\}} N'$ is simply written as $N \xrightarrow{\lambda} N'$. The transitions of form $N \xrightarrow{t} N'$ represent a time step of length t.

Table 3. rTiMo Operational Semantics

(STOP)	$l[[0]] \not\rightarrow$ (DSTOP) $l[[0]] \xrightarrow{t} l[[0]]$
(DMOVE)	if $t \geq t'$ then $l[[go^{\Delta t}l'$ then $P]] \xrightarrow{t'} l[[go^{\Delta t - t'}l'$ then $P]]$
(MOVE0)	$l[[go^{\Delta 0}l'$ then $P]] \xrightarrow{l \triangleright l'} l'[[P]]$
(COM)	$l[[a^{\Delta t}!\langle v \rangle$ then P else $Q \mid a^{\Delta t'}?(u)$ then P' else $Q']] \xrightarrow{\{v/u\}@l} l[[P \mid \{v/u\}P']]$
(DPUT)	if $t \geq t' > 0$ then $l[[a^{\Delta t}!\langle v \rangle$ then P else $Q]] \xrightarrow{t'} l[[a^{\Delta t - t'}!\langle v \rangle$ then P else $Q]]$
(PUT0)	$l[[a^{\Delta 0}!\langle v \rangle$ then P else $Q]] \xrightarrow{a!^{\Delta 0}@l} l[[Q]]$
(DGET)	if $t \geq t' > 0$ then $l[[a^{\Delta t}?(u)$ then P else $Q]] \xrightarrow{t'} l[[a^{\Delta t - t'}?(u)$ then P else $Q]]$
(GET0)	$l[[a^{\Delta 0}?(u)$ then P else $Q]] \xrightarrow{a?^{\Delta 0}@l} l[[Q]]$
(DCALL)	if $l[[\{v/x\}P_{id}]] \xrightarrow{t} l[[P'_{id}]]$ and $id(v) \overset{def}{=} P_{id}$ then $l[[id(v)]] \xrightarrow{t} l[[P'_{id}]]$
(CALL)	if $l[[\{v/x\}P_{id}]] \xrightarrow{id@l} l[[P'_{id}]]$ and $id(v) \overset{def}{=} P_{id}$ then $l[[id(v)]] \xrightarrow{id@l} l[[P'_{id}]]$
(DPAR)	if $N_1 \xrightarrow{t} N'_1$, $N_2 \xrightarrow{t} N'_2$ and $N_1 \mid N_2 \not\rightarrow$ then $N_1 \mid N_2 \xrightarrow{t} N'_1 \mid N'_2$
(PAR)	if $N_1 \xrightarrow{\Lambda_1} N'_1$ and $N_2 \xrightarrow{\Lambda_2} N'_2$ then $N_1 \mid N_2 \xrightarrow{\Lambda_1 \cup \Lambda_2} N'_1 \mid N'_2$
(DEQUIV)	if $N \equiv N'$, $N' \xrightarrow{t} N''$ and $N'' \equiv N'''$ then $N \xrightarrow{t} N'''$
(EQUIV)	if $N \equiv N'$, $N' \xrightarrow{\Lambda} N''$ and $N'' \equiv N'''$ then $N \xrightarrow{\Lambda} N'''$

In rule (MOVE0), the process $go^{\Delta 0}l'$ then P migrates from location l to location l' and evolves as process P. In rule (COM), a process $a^{\Delta t}!\langle v \rangle$ then P else Q located at location l, succeeds in sending a tuple of values v over channel a to process $a^{\Delta t}?(u)$ then P' else Q' also located at l. Both processes continue to execute at location l, the first one as P and the second one as $\{v/u\}P'$. If a communication action has a timer equal to 0, then by using the rule (PUT0) for output action or the rule (GET0) for input action, the generic process $a^{\Delta 0} *$ then P else Q where $* \in \{!\langle v \rangle, ?(x)\}$ continues as the process Q. Rule (CALL) describes the evolution of a recursion process. The rules (EQUIV) and (DEQUIV) are used to rearrange a system in order to apply a rule. Rule (PAR) is used to compose larger systems from smaller ones by putting them in parallel, and considering the union of multisets of actions.

The rules devoted to the passing of time are starting with D. For instance, in rule (DPAR), $N_1 \mid N_2 \not\xrightarrow{\lambda}$ means that no action λ (i.e, an action labelled by $l' \triangleright l$, $\{v/u\}@l$, $id@l$, $go^{\Delta 0}@l$, $a?^{\Delta 0}@l$ or $a!^{\Delta 0}@l$) can be applied in the system $N_1 \mid N_2$. Negative premises are used to denote the fact that the passing to a new step is performed based on the absence of actions; the use of negative premises does not lead to an inconsistent set of rules.

A complete computational step is captured by a derivation of the form:

$$N \xrightarrow{\Lambda} N_1 \xrightarrow{t} N'.$$

This means that a complete step is a parallel execution of individual actions of Λ followed by a time step. Performing a complete step $N \xrightarrow{\Lambda} N_1 \xrightarrow{t} N'$ means that N' is directly reachable from N. If there is no applicable action ($\Lambda = \emptyset$), $N \xrightarrow{\Lambda} N_1 \xrightarrow{t} N'$ is written $N \xrightarrow{t} N'$ to indicate (only) the time progress.

Proposition 1. *For all systems N, N' and N'', the following statements hold:*

1. *If $N \xrightarrow{t} N'$ and $N \xrightarrow{t} N''$, then $N' \equiv N''$;*
2. *$N \xrightarrow{(t+t')} N'$ if and only if there is a N'' such that $N \xrightarrow{t} N''$ and $N'' \xrightarrow{t'} N'$.*

The first item of Proposition 1 states that the passage of time does not introduce any nondeterminism into the execution of a process. Moreover, if a process is able to evolve to a certain time t, then it must evolve through every time moment before t; this ensures that the process evolves continuously.

3 Modelling Critical Systems by Using rTIMO

The use of rTIMO for specifying critical systems is illustrated by considering a railway bridge controller, a real-time problem concerned with the control of accessing a mobile bridge by several trains according to the rule that the bridge can be accessed only by one train at a time. The system is defined as a number of trains (we use three trains), two railways (each divided into two sections on each side of the bridge), and a mobile bridge that can allow ships to sail on the river below (the bridge is up) or not (the bridge is down). This is a simplified version of the system described in [11]. Since not all the actions can take place simultaneously, their delays are modelled by timers.

The initial system is described in rTIMO by:

$$railway1a[[train1 \mid train3]] \mid railway1b[[0]] \mid railway2a[[train2]] \mid railway2b[[0]]$$
$$\mid bridge[[operate \mid control_1]],$$

where the processes placed inside locations are as defined below.

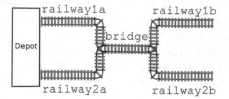

Fig. 1. A railway crossing

In what follows branches that continue with a 0 process are omitted. Waiting indefinitely on a channel a is abstracted by using the timer $\Delta\infty$.

$train1 = go^{\Delta 15}bridge\ then\ appr^{\Delta 20}!\langle train1, railway1a, railway1b\rangle$
$\quad\ |\ stop^{\Delta 25}?(x)\ then\ move^{\Delta\infty}?(y)$
$\qquad\qquad\qquad\quad then\ (go^{\Delta 3}bridge\ then\ go^{\Delta 7}railway1b\ then\ train1'$
$\qquad\qquad\qquad\qquad\quad |\ go^{\Delta 10}bridge\ then\ leave^{\Delta 1}!\langle train1\rangle)$
$\qquad\qquad\qquad\quad else\ (go^{\Delta 2}bridge\ then\ go^{\Delta 7}railway1b\ then\ train1'$
$\qquad\qquad\qquad\qquad\quad |\ go^{\Delta 9}bridge\ then\ leave^{\Delta 1}!\langle train1\rangle)$

$train2 = go^{\Delta 11}bridge\ then\ appr^{\Delta 20}!\langle train2, railway2a, railway2b\rangle$
$\quad\ |\ stop^{\Delta 21}?(x)\ then\ move^{\Delta\infty}?(y)\ then\ (go^{\Delta 2}bridge$
$\qquad\qquad\qquad\quad then\ go^{\Delta 6}railway2b\ then\ train2'$
$\qquad\qquad\qquad\qquad\quad |\ go^{\Delta 8}bridge\ then\ leave^{\Delta 1}!\langle train2\rangle)$
$\qquad\qquad\qquad\quad else\ (go^{\Delta 1}bridge\ then\ go^{\Delta 6}railway1b\ then\ train2'$
$\qquad\qquad\qquad\qquad\quad |\ go^{\Delta 7}bridge\ then\ leave^{\Delta 1}!\langle train2\rangle)$

$train3 = go^{\Delta 1}bridge\ then\ appr^{\Delta 20}!\langle train3, railway1a, railway2b\rangle$
$\quad\ |\ stop^{\Delta 11}?(x)then\ move^{\Delta\infty}?(y)$
$\qquad\qquad\qquad\quad then\ (go^{\Delta 1}bridge\ then\ go^{\Delta 5}railway2b\ then\ train3'$
$\qquad\qquad\qquad\qquad\quad |\ go^{\Delta 6}bridge\ then\ leave^{\Delta 1}!\langle train3\rangle)$
$\qquad\qquad\qquad\quad else\ (go^{\Delta 0.5}bridge\ then\ go^{\Delta 5}railway1b\ then\ train3'$
$\qquad\qquad\qquad\qquad\quad |\ go^{\Delta 5.5}bridge\ then\ leave^{\Delta 1}!\langle train3\rangle)$

$operate = down^{\Delta\infty}?(v)\ then\ up^{\Delta\infty}?(w)\ then\ operate$
$control_1 = appr^{\Delta\infty}?(x_1, y_1, z_1)\ then\ (down^{\Delta 1}!\langle x_1\rangle\ |\ control_0\ |\ control_2)$
$control_0 = leave^{\Delta\infty}?(x)\ then\ (up^{\Delta 1}!\langle x_1\rangle\ |\ unblock^{\Delta\infty}!\langle x_1\rangle)$
$control_i = appr^{\Delta\infty}?(x_i, y_i, z_i)$
$\qquad\qquad then\ [go^{\Delta 0}y_i\ then\ stop^{\Delta 1}!\langle x_i\rangle\ |\ go^{\Delta 10i}y_i\ then\ move^{\Delta 1}!\langle x_i\rangle$
$\qquad\qquad\quad |\ wait^{\Delta 10i}?(x)\ then\ 0\ else\ (down^{\Delta 10}!\langle x_1\rangle\ |\ control_0)$
$\qquad\qquad\qquad |\ unblock^{\Delta 1}?(z)\ then\ control_{i-1}\ else\ control_{i+1}]$

A train movement is abstractly modelled using go actions to describe the migrations between the locations of the system (the parts of the railways and the bridge). The synchronization between the controllers operating the bridge and the trains is modelled by communication actions. When a train is approaching, it communicates with the $control_i$ on channel $appr$, announcing the name of the train, the current location and the destination. The timer $\Delta 20$ means that the $control_i$ has to acknowledge in at most 20 units of time that the train is approaching. If the bridge is occupied, the train has to be stopped in 10 units of time from the receiving of the approach message; otherwise the train goes to location $bridge$. When the $control_i$ decides to stop a train, it does it by synchronizing on channel *stop* at the train location. After a train was stopped, it waits for the synchronization on the channel *move* allowing it to cross the bridge. It can be noticed that if a train is stopped, then it takes a longer period of time to cross the *bridge*.

The *bridge* has to ensure the following safety properties: the *bridge* is down whenever a train is at the crossing, and it prevents trains crossing when another train is engaged in crossing. The controller $control_i$ interacts with the incoming trains, instruct them what to do (e.g., *stop* or *move*) and sends messages to control the operation of the bridge (either *up* or *down*).

In what follows are written some evolution steps for the system described above. For each process are written only the actions to be applied next (e.g., the *train1* process is represented as $train1 = go^{\Delta 15}bridge\ldots \mid stop^{\Delta 25}?(x)\ldots)$. In order to follow easily the evolution, the reductions are performed one after another instead of an entire multiset of reductions; the whole parallel step is delimited by the time steps $\overset{t}{\leadsto}$. To ease the reading, we bold the actions or the processes that are executed in the next step. We illustrate only a few reductions just to give an idea how the system evolves.

$railway1a[[train1 \mid train3]] \mid railway2a[[train2]] \mid railway1b[[0]] \mid railway2b[[0]]$
$\quad \mid bridge[[operate \mid control_1]]$
$\overset{1}{\leadsto} railway1a[[go^{\Delta 14}bridge\ldots \mid stop^{\Delta 24}?(x)\ldots$
$\qquad\qquad \mid \mathbf{go^{\Delta 0}bridge}\ldots \mid stop^{\Delta 10}?(x)\ldots]]$
$\quad \mid railway2a[[go^{\Delta 10}bridge\ldots \mid stop^{\Delta 20}?(x)\ldots]]$
$\quad \mid railway1b[[0]] \mid railway2b[[0]] \mid bridge[[operate \mid control_1]]$
$\xrightarrow{railway1a\triangleright bridge} railway1a[[go^{\Delta 14}bridge\ldots \mid stop^{\Delta 24}?(x)\ldots \mid stop^{\Delta 10}?(x)\ldots]]$
$\quad \mid railway2a[[go^{\Delta 10}bridge\ldots \mid stop^{\Delta 20}?(x)\ldots]] \mid railway1b[[0]] \mid railway2b[[0]]$
$\quad \mid bridge[[operate \mid \mathbf{control_1} \mid \mathbf{appr^{\Delta 20}!\langle train3, railway1a, railway2b\rangle}]]$
$\xrightarrow{\{(train3,railway1a,railway2b)/(x_1,y_1,z_1)\}@bridge}$
$\quad railway1a[[go^{\Delta 14}bridge\ldots \mid stop^{\Delta 24}?(x)\ldots \mid stop^{\Delta 10}?(x)\ldots]]$
$\quad \mid railway2a[[go^{\Delta 10}bridge\ldots \mid stop^{\Delta 20}?(x)\ldots]] \mid railway1b[[0]] \mid railway2b[[0]]$
$\quad \mid bridge[[\mathbf{operate} \mid \mathbf{down^{\Delta 1}!\langle train3\rangle}$
$\quad \mid \{(train3, railway1a, railway2b)/(x_1, y_1, z_1)\}control_0$
$\quad \mid \{(train3, railway1a, railway2b)/(x_1, y_1, z_1)\}control_2]]$
$\xrightarrow{\{train3/v\}@bridge} railway1a[[go^{\Delta 14}bridge\ldots \mid stop^{\Delta 24}?(x)\ldots \mid stop^{\Delta 10}?(x)\ldots]]$
$\quad \mid railway2a[[go^{\Delta 10}bridge\ldots \mid stop^{\Delta 20}?(x)\ldots]] \mid railway1b[[0]] \mid railway2b[[0]]$
$\quad \mid bridge[[up^{\Delta \infty}?(w)\ldots \mid \{(train3, railway1a, railway2b)/(x_1, y_1, z_1)\}control_0$
$\qquad\qquad \mid \{(train3, railway1a, railway2b)/(x_1, y_1, z_1)\}control_2]]$
$\overset{10}{\leadsto}\ldots$

An important advantage of using rTiMo to describe time-aware systems is the possibility to verify certain interesting real-time properties such as safety properties (a specified error cannot occur) and bounded liveness properties (configuration reachability within a certain amount of time) by using the model checking capabilities of the software tool Uppaal. This is possible due to the relationship between rTiMo and timed safety automata presented in [1], allowing a natural use of the software tool Uppaal for verification of critical systems described in rTiMo.

4   Real-Time Behavioral Equivalences in rTiMo

Bisimulation is one of the important notion related to concurrent complex systems [15]. We focus here on behavioural equivalences over multiset labelled transition systems; unlike the classical definition in which two systems are equivalent if they match each other's actions, in this paper we consider that two systems are equivalent if they match each other's multiset of actions. Moreover, this could happen in a certain range of time (up to a timeout). An advantage of equivalences defined in this way is that one could aim at obtaining a correspondence between processes that otherwise would not be equivalent (by using already existing equivalences where the order of compared actions has to be the same, at the same moment of time). The multisets of actions could be considered as timely equivalent if they are in a similar interval of time, without imposing a strict moment for each action. Bisimilarity could be also useful when reasoning about behavioural equivalences of processes: given a process, one can check if it is behaving as intended (optimal behaviour) or not (sub-optimal behaviour). Two processes are said to be equivalent if they are able to "simulate" each others' actions, step by step, and continue to be equivalent after each such step [14].

When choosing which equivalence relation to adopt for a given system, one needs to decide what properties should be preserved by the equivalence relation. It is an advantage if the equivalence relations are compositional with respect to the main constructs of the formalism, and so allowing the components to be substituted by equivalent ones without any side-effect.

Definition 1. *A* **timed bisimulation** $\mathcal{R}$ *over* rTiMo *systems using a set Act of actions is a symmetrical binary relation satisfying the conditions:*

- *for all* $(N_1, N_2) \in \mathcal{R}$, *if* $N_1 \xrightarrow{\lambda} N_1'$ *for* $\lambda \in Act$ *and* N_1', *then* $N_2 \xrightarrow{\lambda} N_2'$ *and* $(N_1', N_2') \in \mathcal{R}$ *for some* N_2'.
- *for all* $(N_1, N_2) \in \mathcal{R}$, *if* $N_1 \xrightarrow{t} N_1'$ *for* $t \in \mathbb{R}_+$ *and* N_1', *then* $N_2 \xrightarrow{t} N_2'$ *and* $(N_1', N_2') \in \mathcal{R}$ *for some* N_2'.

Two rTiMo *systems are* **timed bisimilar** *iff there is a timed bisimulation relation containing them.*

In a similar way as in timed distributed π-calculus [4], the standard notion of bisimilarity is extended to take into account timed transitions and multisets of actions. For a set A, A^* denotes the set of all multisets over A. For a multiset of actions $\Lambda = \{\lambda_1, \ldots, \lambda_n\} \in A^*$, the sequence $\xrightarrow{\lambda_1} \ldots \xrightarrow{\lambda_n}$ is denoted by $\xrightarrow{\Lambda}$.

The **identity relation** over the set $\mathcal{L}$ of located processes is id $\overset{def}{=} \{(L, L) \mid L \in \mathcal{L}\}$. The **inverse of a relation** $\mathcal{R}$ is $\mathcal{R}^{-1} \overset{def}{=} \{(L_2, L_1) \mid (L_1, L_2) \in \mathcal{R}\}$. The **composition of relations** $\mathcal{R}_1$ and $\mathcal{R}_2$ is $\mathcal{R}_1\mathcal{R}_2 \overset{def}{=} \{(L, L'') \mid \exists L' \in \mathcal{L} \text{ such that} (L, L') \in \mathcal{R}_1 \text{ and } (L', L'') \in \mathcal{R}_2\}$.

Definition 2. *A binary relation* $\mathcal{R} \subseteq \mathcal{L} \times \mathcal{L}$ *is called a* **timed simulation** *(T simulation) if when* $(l[[P]], l[[Q]]) \in \mathcal{R}$ *and* $\Lambda \in \{id@l, \{v/u\}@l, go^{\Delta 0}@l, a?^{\Delta 0}@l, a!^{\Delta 0}@l\}^*$:

- if $l[[P]] \xrightarrow{\Lambda} \xrightarrow{l \triangleright l'} l'[[P']] \mid l[[P'']]$ then $\exists Q', Q''$ s.t. $l[[Q]] \xrightarrow{\Lambda} \xrightarrow{l \triangleright l'} l'[[Q']] \mid l[[Q'']]$, $(l'[[P']], l'[[Q']]) \in \mathcal{R}$ and $(l[[P'']], l[[Q'']]) \in \mathcal{R}$;
- if $l[[P]] \xrightarrow{\Lambda} \xrightarrow{t} l[[P']]$ then $\exists Q'$ s.t. $l[[Q]] \xrightarrow{\Lambda} \xrightarrow{t} l[[Q']]$ and $(l[[P']], l[[Q']]) \in \mathcal{R}$.

If $\mathcal{R}$ and $\mathcal{R}^{-1}$ are timed simulations, then $\mathcal{R}$ is called a **timed bisimulation** (T bisimulation). **Strong timed bisimilarity** (ST bisimulation) $\sim$ is defined by

$$\sim \stackrel{def}{=} \{(l[[P]], l[[Q]]) \in \mathcal{L} \times \mathcal{L} \mid \exists T \text{ bisimulation } \mathcal{R} \text{ and } (l[[P]], l[[Q]]) \in \mathcal{R}\}.$$

This definition treats timed transitions as normal transitions, and so it coincides with the original notion of bisimulation over a labelled transition system.

Remark 1. $\sim$ is an equivalence relation, and also the largest ST bisimulation.

Example 1. Inspired by the railway system of Subsection 3, consider the following simplified two located processes:

$L_1 = railway1a[[stop^{\Delta 5}?(x)$ then $(go^{\Delta 3}bridge$ then $go^{\Delta 7}railway1b)$
$\quad\quad\quad\quad\quad\quad\quad\quad else$ $(go^{\Delta 2}bridge$ then $go^{\Delta 7}railway1b)]]$

$L_2 = railway1a[[stop^{\Delta 5}?(x)$ then $(go^{\Delta 2}bridge$ then $go^{\Delta 6}railway1b)$
$\quad\quad\quad\quad\quad\quad\quad\quad else$ $(go^{\Delta 1}bridge$ then $go^{\Delta 6}railway1b)]]$

If the trains reach *bridge* after different numbers of time units, the two located processes are not strong timed bisimilar, i.e., $(L_1 \not\sim L_2)$, because they have different evolutions in time (after 7 units of time).

$L_1 \xrightarrow{5} railway1a[[stop^{\Delta 0}?(x)$ then $(go^{\Delta 3}bridge$ then $go^{\Delta 7}railway1b)$ $\quad$ (DPAR)
$\quad\quad\quad\quad\quad\quad\quad\quad else$ $(go^{\Delta 2}bridge$ then $go^{\Delta 7}railway1b)]]$

$\xrightarrow{stop?^{\Delta 0}@railway1a} railway1a[[go^{\Delta 3}bridge$ then $go^{\Delta 7}railway1b]]$ $\quad$ (GET0)

$\xrightarrow{2} railway1a[[go^{\Delta 1}bridge$ then $go^{\Delta 7}railway1b]]$ $\quad$ (DPAR)

$\xrightarrow{1} railway1a[[go^{\Delta 0}bridge$ then $go^{\Delta 7}railway1b]]$ $\quad$ (DPAR)

$L_2 \xrightarrow{5} railway1a[[stop^{\Delta 0}?(x)$ then $(go^{\Delta 2}bridge$ then $go^{\Delta 6}railway1b)$ $\quad$ (DPAR)
$\quad\quad\quad\quad\quad\quad\quad\quad else$ $(go^{\Delta 1}bridge$ then $go^{\Delta 6}railway1b)]]$

$\xrightarrow{stop?^{\Delta 0}@railway1a} railway1a[[go^{\Delta 2}bridge$ then $go^{\Delta 6}railway1b]]$ $\quad$ (GET0)

$\xrightarrow{2} railway1a[[go^{\Delta 0}bridge$ then $go^{\Delta 6}railway1b]]$ $\quad$ (DPAR)

$\xrightarrow{railway1a \triangleright bridge} bridge[[go^{\Delta 7}railway1b]]$ $\quad$ (MOVE0)

Strong timed equivalences require an exact matching between the multisets of transitions of two located processes, for the entire evolution. Sometimes these requirements are too strong. According to [12], there are problems in computer science and artificial intelligence where only the timed behaviour within a given amount of time t is of interest. Sometimes one needs to see if two critical systems have the same behaviour for a predefined period of time and not for their entire evolution (e.g., trains that behave equivalently only between two locations, regardless of what happens for the rest of their evolutions). That is why in what follows the equivalences are restricted to a given time range $[0, t]$, thus defining **time-bounded** equivalences.

Definition 3. *The binary relations $\mathcal{R}_t \subseteq \mathcal{L} \times \mathcal{L}$, $t \in \mathbb{R}_+$ over located processes are called **time-bounded simulations** (TB simulations) if for $t \in \mathbb{R}_+$, whenever $(l[[P]], l[[Q]]) \in \mathcal{R}_t$ and $\Lambda \in \{id@l, \{v/u\}@l, go^{\Delta 0}@l, a?^{\Delta 0}@l, a!^{\Delta 0}@l\}^*$:*

- if $l[[P]] \xrightarrow{A} \xrightarrow{l \triangleright l'} l'[[P']] \mid l[[P'']]$ then $\exists Q', Q''$ such that $l[[Q]] \xrightarrow{A} \xrightarrow{l \triangleright l'} l'[[Q']] \mid$
  $l[[Q'']]$, $(l'[[P']], l'[[Q']]) \in \mathcal{R}_t$ and $(l[[P'']], l[[Q'']]) \in \mathcal{R}_t$;
- $\forall t' \leq t, t' \in \mathbb{R}_+$ if $l[[P]] \xrightarrow{A} \overset{t'}{\rightsquigarrow} l[[P']]$ then $\exists Q'$ such that $l[[Q]] \xrightarrow{A} \overset{t'}{\rightsquigarrow} l[[Q']]$
  and $(l[[P']], l[[Q']]) \in \mathcal{R}_{t-t'}$.

If $\mathcal{R}_t$ and $\mathcal{R}_t^{-1}$, with $t \in \mathbb{R}_+$, are time-bounded simulations, then $\mathcal{R}_t$ is a **time-bounded bisimulation** *(TB bisimulation)*. **Time-bounded bisimilarities** $\simeq_t$ are defined by

$$\simeq_t \overset{def}{=} \{(l[[P]], l[[Q]]) \in \mathcal{L} \times \mathcal{L} \mid \exists \ TB \ bisimulation \ \mathcal{R}_t \ and \ (l[[P]], l[[Q]]) \in \mathcal{R}_t\}.$$
$(l[[P]], l[[Q]]) \in \simeq_t$ can be written also as $l[[P]] \simeq_t l[[Q]]$.

Example 2. Consider the two located processes of Example 1. Even if those systems have different definitions, they are time-bounded bisimilar before time unit 7 ($L_1 \simeq_7 L_2$) since they have the same evolutions during this period at location $railway1a$. Hence L_1 and L_2 cannot be identified by timed bisimulation, but this is possible by using time-bounded bisimulation for the time range $[0, 7]$. However, if $t > 7$, then $L_1 \not\simeq_t L_2$.

Time-bounded bisimulation satisfies the following properties showing that an equivalence $\simeq_t$ includes the equivalence $\simeq_u$ for any $u \leq t$. This result is consistent with the continuity of time. This means that if two processes are time-bounded equivalent in a finite time range $[0, t]$, then they are time-bounded equivalent in any finite time range $[0, u]$, $u \leq t$.

Lemma 1. *For any processes P and Q, location l, and any $u, t \in \mathbb{R}_+$:*
  If $l[[P]] \simeq_t l[[Q]]$, then for any $u \leq t$ it holds that $l[[P]] \simeq_u l[[Q]]$.

A useful question to ask about an rTiMo located process is the reachability of a given process within a given amount of time. In what follows l and l' denote the same or different locations:

Definition 4. *Given $t \in \mathbb{R}_+$ and $l[[P]], l'[[Q]] \in \mathcal{L}$, the t-bounded reachability problem asks if there exists a computation leading from $l[[P]]$ to $l'[[Q]]$ in at most t units of time.*

The next lemma states that time-bounded bisimulation is adequate to check t-bounded reachability on arbitrary located processes.

Lemma 2. *If $l[[P]] \simeq_t l[[Q]]$, then $l'[[R]]$ is reachable from $l[[P]]$ in at most t units of time iff $l'[[R]]$ is reachable from $l[[Q]]$ in at most t units of time.*

Using the TB bisimulations $\simeq_t$, a specific relation of bisimilarity is defined, called strong time-bounded bisimilarity, satisfying Proposition 2.

Definition 5. Strong time-bounded bisimilarity *(STB bisimulation), denoted $\simeq$, is defined by:*
  $\simeq = \{(l[[P]], l[[Q]]) \in \mathcal{L} \times \mathcal{L} \mid \exists t \in \mathbb{R}_+ \ and \ a \ TB \ bisim. \ \simeq_t \ s.t. \ (l[[P]], l[[Q]]) \in \simeq_t\}.$

Proposition 2. *The following statements hold:*

1. $\simeq$ *is a TB bisimulation;*
2. $\simeq$ *is closed to identity, inverse, composition and union;*
3. $\simeq$ *is the largest TB bisimulation;*
4. $\simeq$ *is an equivalence.*

Using the fact that $\simeq$ is an equivalence can be used to partition a state space into equivalence classes such that states in the same class are observationally equivalent with respect to the system's behaviour. This leads to a reduction of the state space prior to model checking.

4.1   Strong Open Time-Bounded Equivalences

Bisimulation as a congruence is a desirable feature for any (real-time) language for critical systems because it can be used in checking compositionally whether two critical systems are behaving similarly. This means that the specifications related by a bisimulation relation $\mathcal{R}$ can be used interchangeably as parts of a larger process without affecting the overall behaviour of the latter (as depicted in Figure 2). In this paper behavioural equivalences are based on the observable transitions of processes, rather than on their states (as done in timed automata and time/timed Petri nets).

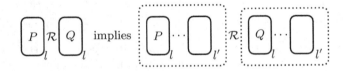

Fig. 2. Interchangeably equivalent parts of a larger system

In this section we define such a relation for rTiMo, a relation inspired by the *open bisimilarity* [14]. In this kind of bisimilarity, all names that occur in a system are potentially replaceable (all free names are treated as variables). The newly defined open bisimilarity is necessary since, according to the following example, the TB equivalence is not closed under arbitrary substitutions.

Example 3. Consider that *train1* from Subsection 3 is located in the depot (has not entered yet either *railway1a* or *railway2a* of the two railways to which the depot is connected) and wants to reach *railway2b*. In order to reach the destination it is necessary to use either *railway1a* or *railway2a*. It has to take a decision on which of the these two railways its journey starts. In order to decide on this aspect it sends a *query* to the depot in order to receive an answer that can help it in making this decision. There are two situations: the *train1* decides either to use the received information (process P_1) or not (process P_2).

$P_1 = newrail^{\Delta 0}?(railway1a)$ then $query^{\Delta 2}!\langle railway1a\rangle$
    $|\ query^{\Delta 5}?(u)$ then $(go^{\Delta 3}u$ then $train1).$
$P_2 = newrail^{\Delta 0}?(railway1a)$ then $query^{\Delta 2}!\langle railway1a\rangle$
    $|\ query^{\Delta 5}?(u)$ then $(go^{\Delta 3}railway1a$ then $train1).$
For any $t \in \mathbb{R}_+$, it holds that $station[[P_1]] \simeq_t station[[P_2]]$ because

$station[[P_1]] \xrightarrow{newrail?^{\Delta 0}@station} \xrightarrow{\{railway1a/u\}@station}$
        $station[[go^{\Delta 3}railway1a$ then $train1]],$ and
$station[[P_2]] \xrightarrow{newrail?^{\Delta 0}@station} \xrightarrow{\{railway1a/u\}@station}$
        $station[[go^{\Delta 3}railway1a$ then $train1]].$

After communicating on channel $query$, results the same process and thus $station[[P_1]] \simeq_t station[[P_2]]$. However, if in these two processes, P_1 and P_2, the free names are rewritten by the substitution $\sigma = \{railway2a/railway1a\}$ (meaning that name $railway2a$ is communicated instead of $railway1a$), then

$station[[P_1\sigma]] \xrightarrow{newrail?^{\Delta 0}@station} \xrightarrow{\{railway1a/u\}@station}$
        $station[[go^{\Delta 3}railway1a$ then $train1]],$ and
$station[[P_2\sigma]] \xrightarrow{newrail?^{\Delta 0}@station} \xrightarrow{\{railway1a/u\}@station}$
        $station[[go^{\Delta 3}railway2a$ then $train1]].$

These processes have different behaviours, and so
$$station[[P_1]] \not\simeq_t station[[P_2]].$$

Following the style presented in [15], we define the following bisimilarity that becomes a congruence by closing the bisimilarity under arbitrary substitutions.

Definition 6. *The binary relations* $\mathcal{R}_t^o \subseteq \mathcal{L} \times \mathcal{L}$, $t \in \mathbb{R}_+$ *over located processes are called* **open time-bounded simulations** *(OTB simulations) if for* $t \in \mathbb{R}_+$, *whenever* $(l[[P]], l[[Q]]) \in \mathcal{R}_t^o$, *then for any substitution* σ *and* $\Lambda \in \{id@l, \{v/u\}@l, go^{\Delta 0}@l, a?^{\Delta 0}@l, a!^{\Delta 0}@l\}^*$ *it holds:*

- *if* $l[[P\sigma]] \xrightarrow{\Lambda} \xrightarrow{l\triangleright l'} l'[[P']] \mid l[[P'']]$ *then* $\exists Q', Q''$ *such that* $l[[Q\sigma]] \xrightarrow{\Lambda} \xrightarrow{l\triangleright l'} l'[[Q']] \mid l[[Q'']]$, $(l'[[P']], l'[[Q']]) \in \mathcal{R}_t^o$ *and* $(l[[P'']], l[[Q'']]) \in \mathcal{R}_t^o$;
- $\forall t' \leq t$, $t' \in \mathbb{R}_+$ *if* $l[[P\sigma]] \xrightarrow{\Lambda} \overset{t'}{\rightsquigarrow} l[[P']]$ *then* $\exists Q'$ *such that* $l[[Q\sigma]] \xrightarrow{\Lambda} \overset{t'}{\rightsquigarrow} l[[Q']]$ *and* $(l[[P']], l[[Q']]) \in \mathcal{R}_{t-t'}^o$.

If $\mathcal{R}_t^o$ *and* $(\mathcal{R}_t^o)^{-1}$ *are open time-bounded simulations for* $t \in \mathbb{R}_+$, *then* $\mathcal{R}_t^o$ *are called* **open time-bounded bisimulations** *(OTB bisimulations).* **Open time-bounded bisimilarities** $\simeq_t^o$ *are defined by*

$$\simeq_t^o \overset{def}{=} \{(l[[P]], l[[Q]]) \in \mathcal{L} \times \mathcal{L} \mid \exists\ OTB\ bisimulation\ \mathcal{R}_t^o\ and\ (l[[P]], l[[Q]]) \in \mathcal{R}_t^o\}.$$
$(l[[P]], l[[Q]]) \in \simeq_t^o$ *can be written as* $l[[P]] \simeq_t^o l[[Q]]$.

The intuition is that two located processes are equivalent whenever all possible instantiations (substitutions of their free names) have matching transitions.

The next result is consistent with the continuity of time: an open time-bounded equivalence $\simeq_0^t$ includes the open time-bounded equivalence $\simeq_0^u$, for any $u \leq t$. This means that if two processes are open time-bounded equivalent in a finite time range $[0, t]$, then they are open time-bounded equivalent in any finite time range $[0, u]$, $u \leq t$.

Lemma 3. *For any processes P and Q, location l, and any $u, t \in \mathbb{R}_+$: if $l[[P]] \simeq_t^o$ $l[[Q]]$, then for any $u \leq t$ it holds that $l[[P]] \simeq_u^o l[[Q]]$.*

Using the OTB bisimulations $\simeq_t^o$, a specific relation of bisimilarity is defined, called strong open time-bounded bisimilarity; this relation satisfies the statements of Proposition 3.

Definition 7. Strong open time-bounded bisimilarity *(SOTB bisimulation), denoted $\simeq^o$, is defined by:*

$$\simeq^o = \{(l[[P]], l[[Q]]) \in \mathcal{L} \times \mathcal{L} \mid \exists t \in \mathbb{R}_+ \text{ and a OTB bisim. } \simeq_t^o \text{ s.t. } (l[[P]], l[[Q]]) \in \simeq_t^o\}.$$

The following results present some properties of the SOTB equivalences.

Proposition 3.   *The following statements hold:*

1. *$\simeq^o$ is a OTB bisimulation;*
2. *$\simeq^o$ is closed to identity, inverse, composition and union;*
3. *$\simeq^o$ is the largest OTB bisimulation;*
4. *$\simeq^o$ is an equivalence.*

Definition 8. *A binary relation $\mathcal{R}$ is said to be **closed under substitutions** if whenever $(l[[P]], l[[Q]]) \in \mathcal{R}$, then $(l[[P\sigma]], l[[Q\sigma]]) \in \mathcal{R}$ for any substitution σ. Formally,*

$$\text{clos}(\mathcal{R}) \stackrel{def}{=} \{(l[[P\sigma]], l[[Q\sigma]]) \mid (l[[P]], l[[Q]]) \in \mathcal{R}$$
$$\text{and } \sigma \text{ is an arbitrary substitution}\}.$$

The connections between $\simeq$ and $\simeq^o$ are illustrated in the next result. The second item states that $\simeq^o$ is included in $\simeq$, namely if $l[[P]] \simeq^o l[[Q]]$ implies that $l[[P]] \simeq l[[Q]]$.

Lemma 4.   *1. If $\simeq$ is closed under substitution, then $\simeq = \simeq^o$.*
 2. $\simeq^o \subseteq \simeq$.

The following result states that the SOTB equivalence $\simeq^o$ is preserved by migration, communication and parallel composition.

Lemma 5. *For $P, P', Q, Q' \in \mathcal{P}$ and $l, l' \in Loc$, if $l[[P]] \simeq^o l[[P']]$ then*

1. *$l[[P \mid Q]] \simeq^o l[[P' \mid Q]]$;*
2. *$l[[a^{\Delta t'}?(u) \text{ then } P \text{ else } Q]] \simeq^o$*
   $l[[a^{\Delta t'}?(u) \text{ then } P' \text{ else } Q]]$;
3. *$l[[go^{\Delta t'} l' \text{ then } P]] \simeq^o l[[go^{\Delta t'} l' \text{ then } P']]$.*

As a consequence of Lemmas 3 and 5, the main result of the paper is obtained.

Theorem 1. *$\simeq^o$ is a congruence.*

When choosing which bisimulation to adopt in certain situation one needs to decide what kind of properties should be preserved by the equivalence relation. If the bisimulation is not a congruence then the bisimilar systems can still be distinguished by putting them in appropriate contexts. On the other hand, if the bisimulation is a congruence, this means that the systems that are related by a congruence relation, e.g., $\simeq^o$ in our case, can be used interchangeably as parts of a larger system without affecting the overall behaviour of the latter (as depicted in Figure 2). For this reason, usually one needs to ensure that he defines equivalences that are in fact congruences. In this way theories can be constructed that support modular description and verification of critical systems. Thus, it should be possible to use the congruence relation $\simeq^o$ in computer simulations and model checkers for real-time systems with timed migration and communication.

5   Conclusion and Related Work

Several proposals for real-time modelling and verification have been presented in the literature (e.g., [16]). A comprehensive overview of the development of an algebraic theory of processes with time is given in [3]. In this paper we used a prototyping language rTiMo for describing real-time critical systems. It emphasizes the essential aspects, and is different from all these previous approaches since it encompasses specific features as timeouts, explicit locations, timed migration and communication. Starting from a first version of TiMo proposed in [6], several variants were developed during the last years in order to model various complex systems; we mention the access permissions given by a type system in perTiMo [7]. TiMo is a simpler version of timed distributed π-calculus [8]. Inspired by TiMo, a flexible software platform was introduced in [5] to support the specification of agents allowing timed migration in a distributed environment. Interesting properties as bounded liveness and optimal reachability are presented in [2]. A verification tool called TiMo@PAT is presented in [9]; it was developed by using an extensible platform for model checkers called PAT.

In this paper rTiMo is used for comparing in a formal way the behaviours of critical systems. In particular, we have presented an example of applying rTiMo to the distributed railway bridge system, illustrating that rTiMo provides a natural framework for modelling and reasoning about critical systems with timed migration and concurrency given by interaction/communication. This leads to a compositional approach of verifying concurrent critical systems, in opposition to the noncompositional approach provided by inductive assertion method and Hoare logic.

Behavioural equivalences are useful to define some observational criteria that processes should fulfil. Several behavioural equivalences over $tD\pi$ and TiMo are studied in [4]. In practice, even though several processes can be valid solutions to a given problem, some processes may be preferable to others. For example, a faster or less resource consuming process is often preferred to one that is slower or demanding more resources, respectively. In fact, there are many ways to evaluate processes. An important goal of defining bisimulations is to obtain refinements and equivalence relations that can reduce state space to their equivalence classes, in order to facilitate a more efficient (automated) verification.

We defined two bisimulations ($\simeq$ and $\simeq^o$) over real-time distributed processes, and illustrated them by using a distributed railway control system involving a mobile bridge and several trains. The behavioural equivalences are established in terms of relative time (timeouts) and locations, and are also used to distinguish between optimal and sub-optimal behaviours. We prove that $\simeq^o$ is a congruence, allowing a compositional reasoning of complex real-time systems in terms of their observable parallel behaviours. The first equivalence ($\simeq$) resembles the finite-horizon bisimulation defined over time-inhomogeneous Markov chains [10], in the sense that they also consider a threshold in time when comparing two systems.

The strong bisimulations studied in the paper are useful but their usage is somehow limited in the sense that at each moment either the time elapse or the multiset of actions should coincide. A weaker version of these bisimulations could be defined, having a more practical use in real problems: e.g., to distinguish between trains having the same route, but different moving time depending on the type of the train (e.g., InterRegio or InterCity). Such weak bisimulations in rTiMo and verification of realistic scenarios with a powerful model-checker like UPPAAL [13] represent a future work. The capabilities of UPPAAL allow verification of various properties: reachability of desired configurations (e.g., several mobile elements being close to each other at some time instance), the fact that the system does not block, and whether an error occurs (e.g., two trains collide).

Acknowledgements. The work was supported by a grant of the Romanian National Authority for Scientific Research, CNCS-UEFISCDI, project number PN-II-ID-PCE-2011-3-0919.

References

1. Aman, B., Ciobanu, G.: Real-Time Migration Properties of rTiMo Verified in UPPAAL. In: Hierons, R.M., Merayo, M.G., Bravetti, M. (eds.) SEFM 2013. LNCS, vol. 8137, pp. 31–45. Springer, Heidelberg (2013)
2. Aman, B., Ciobanu, G., Koutny, M.: Behavioural Equivalences over Migrating Processes with Timers. In: Giese, H., Rosu, G. (eds.) FORTE 2012 and FMOODS 2012. LNCS, vol. 7273, pp. 52–66. Springer, Heidelberg (2012)
3. Baeten, J.C.M., Middelburg, C.A.: Process Algebra with Timing. In: Monographs in Theoretical Computer Science, An EATCS Series. Springer, Berlin (2002)
4. Ciobanu, G.: Behaviour Equivalences in Timed Distributed π-Calculus. In: Wirsing, M., Banâtre, J.-P., Hölzl, M., Rauschmayer, A. (eds.) Software Intensive Systems. LNCS, vol. 5380, pp. 190–208. Springer, Heidelberg (2008)
5. Ciobanu, G., Juravle, C.: Flexible Software Architecture and Language for Mobile Agents. Concurrency and Computation: Practice and Experience 24, 559–571 (2012)
6. Ciobanu, G., Koutny, M.: Modelling and Verification of Timed Interaction and Migration. In: Fiadeiro, J.L., Inverardi, P. (eds.) FASE 2008. LNCS, vol. 4961, pp. 215–229. Springer, Heidelberg (2008)

7. Ciobanu, G., Koutny, M.: Timed Migration and Interaction With Access Permissions. In: Butler, M., Schulte, W. (eds.) FM 2011. LNCS, vol. 6664, pp. 293–307. Springer, Heidelberg (2011)
8. Ciobanu, G., Prisacariu, C.: Timers for Distributed Systems. Electronic Notes in Theoretic Computer Science 164(3), 81–99 (2006)
9. Ciobanu, G., Zheng, M.: Automatic Analysis of TiMo Systems in PAT. In: Proc. 18th International Conference on Engineering of Complex Computer Systems, pp. 121–124. IEEE Computer Society (2013)
10. Han, T., Katoen, J.-P., Mereacre, A.: Compositional Modeling and Minimization of Time-Inhomogeneous Markov Chains. In: Egerstedt, M., Mishra, B. (eds.) HSCC 2008. LNCS, vol. 4981, pp. 244–258. Springer, Heidelberg (2008)
11. Heitmeyer, C., Lynch, N.: The Generalized Railroad Crossing: A Case Study in Formal Verification of Real-Time Systems. In: Proc. of IEEE Real-Time Systems Symposium, pp. 120–131 (1994)
12. Kamide, N.: Bounded Linear-Time Temporal Logic: A Proof-Theoretic Investigation. Annals of Pure and Applied Logic 163, 439–466 (2012)
13. Larsen, K.G., Petterson, P., Yi, W.: UPPAAL in a Nutshell. International Journal on Software Tools for Technology Transfer 1(2), 134–152 (1997)
14. Milner, R.: Communicating and Mobile Systems: the π-calculus. Cambridge University Press (1999)
15. Sangiorgi, D.: Introduction to Bisimulation and Coinduction. Cambridge University Press, New York (2011)
16. Yi, W., Pettersson, P., Daniels, M.: Automatic Verification of Real-time Communicating Systems by Constraint-Solving. In: International Conference on Formal Description Techniques, pp. 223–238 (1994)

On the Formal Analysis of Photonic Signal Processing Systems

Umair Siddique[✉], Sidi Mohamed Beillahi, and Sofiène Tahar

Department of Electrical and Computer Engineering,
Concordia University, Montreal, Canada
{muh_sidd,beillahi,tahar}@ece.concordia.ca

Abstract. Photonic signal processing is an emerging area of research, which provides unique prospects to build high-speed communication systems. Recent advancements in fabrication technology allow on-chip manufacturing of signal processing devices. This fact has lead to the widespread use of photonics in industrial critical applications such as telecommunication, biophotonics and aerospace. One the most challenging aspects in the photonics industry is the accurate modeling and analysis of photonic devices due to the complex nature of light and optical components. In this paper, we propose to use higher-order-logic theorem proving to improve the analysis accuracy by overcoming the known limitations of incompleteness and soundness of existing approaches (e.g., paper-and-pencil based proofs and simulation). In particular, we formalize the notion of transfer function using the signal-flow-graph theory which is the most fundamental step to model photonic circuits. Consequently, we formalize and verify the important properties of the stability and the resonance of photonic systems. In order to demonstrate the effectiveness of the proposed infrastructure, we present the formal analysis of a widely used double-coupler double-ring (DCDR) photonic processor.

Keywords: Photonic signal processing · Signal-flow-graph · Theorem proving · HOL light

1   Introduction

Recent advances in communication technology resulted in the development of sophisticated devices such as multifunction routers and personal digital assistants (PDAs); which brought additional challenges of high-speed, low power and huge bandwidth requirements. However, traditional electronic communication has already reached a point where such issues cannot be addressed. On the other hand, photonics technology offers promising solution to resolve these bottlenecks and provides the better convergence of computation and communication, which is a key to cope with future communication challenges. Although, the complete replacement of existing communication systems is not possible at this point, future communication systems will be based on electronic-photonic convergence as mentioned in the MIT's first Communications Technology Roadmap (CTR)

© Springer International Publishing Switzerland 2015
M. Núñez and M. Güdemann (Eds.): FMICS 2015, LNCS 9128, pp. 162–177, 2015.
DOI: 10.1007/978-3-319-19458-5_11

[7]. Moreover, some feasibility studies have been conducted to demonstrate the realization of large scale (100,000-node) photonic networks which indicate that photonics has the capabilities to interconnect thousands of computing nodes with an ultimate goal of building Exaflops/second links [19]. The main requirement of designing such systems is to process light waves (counterpart of electronic signals) to achieve the desired functionality such as light amplification, filtering and ultrashort pulse generation. Photonic signal processing (PSP) [5] is an active area of research which offers an efficient framework to process high bandwidth signals with low power consumption. The demand of miniaturized communication devices and recent advances in fabrication technology resulted in the development of very large scale integrated (VLSI) photonic circuits [10]. One of the core steps in photonic systems development life cycle is the physical modeling of fundamental building-blocks such as photonic filters and amplifiers [5]. A significant portion of time is spent finding bugs through the validation of such models in order to minimize the failure risks and monetary loss. In particular, this step is more important in industrial applications, where failures directly lead to safety issues such as in aerospace and biomedical devices. For example, the mission management system of Boeing F/A-18E is linked using a photonic network [25]. In general, there are several aspects of light-wave systems which need to be analyzed; however, the focus of this paper is photonic signal processing which forms the core of modern communication devices.

The first step to analyze the behavior of PSP systems is to obtain the transfer function which relates the input and output signals (light-waves). Consequently, the test for the stability (which ensures that the system output is always finite) and resonance (which ensures the oscillation of light waves at certain frequencies) conditions of the photonic circuit can be identified which are the foremost design criterion. One primary analytical approach is to compute the transfer function by explicitly writing node and loop equations which can further be utilized to analyze some physical aspects (e.g., transfer intensity and dispersion [9]) of photonic systems. Recently, however, the signal-flow graph (SFG) theory (originally proposed by Mason [17]) has been extensively used to compute the transfer function of PSP systems. The main motivation of this choice was inspired by its successful applications in electrical and control systems. Indeed, the problem of finding the transfer function reduces to the computation of the forward paths and loops which further can be plugged into the Mason's gain formula (MSG) [17] (which provides an easy way to find the transfer function). The analysis of complex photonic systems using paper-and-pencil based proofs [5] and computer algorithms [11] is not rigorous and sound and thus cannot be recommended for safety critical applications. We believe that there is a dire need of an accurate framework to build high assurance photonic systems.

The main focus of this paper is to formalize the signal-flow-graph theory along with the Mason's gain formula and strengthen the formal reasoning support in the area of photonic signal processing. Indeed, our current work is at the intersection of two ongoing projects[1][2], i.e., the formalization of different theories of optics and the formal analysis of signal processing systems. As a first step towards our ultimate goal, we present in this paper the higher-order logic formalization of signal-flow-graph theory and Mason's gain formula for the computation of transfer functions in HOL Light theorem prover [12]. Next, we formalize the notion of stability and resonance along with the formal verification of some important properties such as the finiteness and the cardinality of the set of poles (complex-valued parameters at which the system becomes unstable) and zeros (parameters which determine the resonance condition in the system). In order to show the practical utilization of our work, we formally verify the transfer function of a double-coupler double-ring (DCDR) circuit [5], which is a widely used photonic signal processor. Consequently, we derive the general stability and resonance conditions (for both coherent and incoherent operation [5]), which greatly simplifies the verification for any given DCDR configuration. The rigor of higher-order-logic theorem proving allows us to unveil all the hidden assumptions in the paper-and-pencil based approach reported in [5]. Moreover, we also found some incorrect stability conditions and we formally prove that these conditions lead to an unstable operation of the DCDR circuit. The source code of our formalization is available for download [3] and can be utilized by other researchers and engineers for further developments and the analysis of more practical systems.

The rest of the paper is organized as follows: we highlight the most relevant work about the formal analysis of optical and photonic systems in Section 2. Some fundamentals of signal-flow-graph theory and the Mason's gain formula are reviewed in Section 3. We present the formal analysis framework for the photonic signal processing systems along with highlights of our higher-order logic formalization in Section 4. We describe the analysis of the DCDR photonic processor as an illustrative practical application in Section 5. Finally, Section 6 concludes the paper and provides hints for some future directions.

2   Related Work

In the last decade, formal methods based techniques have been proven to be an effective approach to analyze physical, hybrid and digital engineering systems. Here, we describe the most relevant works for analyzing optical systems using theorem proving. The pioneering work about the formal analysis of optical waveguides has been reported in [13]. However, this work is primarily based on real analysis in HOL4 which is insufficient to capture the dynamics of the real photonic systems which involve complex-valued electric and magnetic fields. In [20], a preliminary infrastructure has been developed in HOL Light to verify some fundamental properties (e.g., ray confinement or stability) of optical systems based on ray optics which can only be used when the size of involved optical components is much larger than the wavelength of light. However, the

---

[1] http://hvg.ece.concordia.ca/projects/optics/

[2] http://hvg.ece.concordia.ca/projects/signal-processing/

physical meaning of stability considered in [20] and in the current paper are totally different, as the first is related to the ray confinement conditions inside a cavity and later deals with the finite output response. In [22], a preliminary formalization of photonic microresonators has been reported which is only focused towards the transmission and reflection properties of light-waves. This work cannot be used to analyze many signal processing properties of optical systems particularly stability and resonance. A more recent work about quantum formalization of coherent light has been reported in [15], with potential applications in the development of future quantum computers. Other interesting works are the formalization of Laplace transform [23] and Z-transform [21] in the HOL Light. Both of these transformations are less popular in the photonic community due to the additional overhead of transforming back-and-forth from time to frequency domain. On the other hand, most PSP systems can directly be described using the SFG theory where properties of interest (such as stability and resonance) can be analyzed [5]. This is the main motivation of choosing the signal-flow-graph approach to model photonic processing systems in our work.

3   Signal-Flow-Graph Theory and Mason's Gain Formula

A signal-flow graph (SFG) [17] is a special kind of directed graph which is widely used to model engineering systems. Mathematically, it represents a set of linear algebraic equations of the corresponding system. An SFG is a network in which nodes are connected by directed branches. Every node in the network represents a system variable and each branch represents the signal transmission from one node to the other under the assumption that signals flow only in one direction. An example of an SFG is shown in Figure 1 consisting of six nodes. An input (*source node*) and an output (*sink node*) are those which only have outgoing branches and incoming branches, respectively (e.g., node 1 and node 6 in Figure 1). A branch is a directed line from node i to j and the gain of each branch is called the *transmittance* which is represented by t_{ij} as shown in Figure 1. A *path* is a traversal of connected branches from one node to the other and if no node is crossed more than once and it connects the input to the output then the path is called *forward path* otherwise if it leads back to itself without touching any node more than once it is considered as a *feedback path* or a *loop*. The loop containing only one node is called *self loop* and any two loops in the SFG are said to be *touching loops* if they have any common node. The total gain of forward path and a loop can be computed by multiplying the transmittances of each traversed branch.

In the analysis of practical engineering systems, the main task is to characterize the relation among system input and output which is called transfer function. The total transmittance or gain between two given nodes (usually input and output) describes the transfer function of the corresponding system. Mason [17] proposed a computational procedure (also called Mason's gain formula) to obtain the total gain of any arbitrary signal-flow-graph. The formula

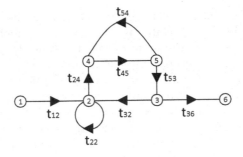

Fig. 1. Signal-Flow-Graph

is described as follows [16]:

$$G = \sum_k \frac{G_k \Delta_k}{\Delta} \tag{1}$$

$$\Delta = 1 - \sum_m P_{m1} + \sum_m P_{m2} - \sum_m P_{m3} + \ldots + (-1)^n \sum \ldots \tag{2}$$

where Δ represents the determinant of the graph, Δ_k represents the value of Δ for the part of graph that is not touching the kth forward path and it is called the cofactor of forward path k, P_{mr} is the gain product of mth possible combination of r non-touching loops. The gain of each forward path is represented by G_k.

4   Proposed Formal Analysis Framework

The proposed framework for the analysis of photonic signal processing systems, given in Figure 2, outlines the necessary steps to encode theoretical fundamentals in higher-order logic. In order to represent a given system in HOL, the first step is the formalization of the signal-flow-graph theory which consists of some new type definitions and the implementation of an algorithm which computes all the elementary circuits (i.e., forward paths and loops). Consequently, this can be used to formalize the Mason's gain formula. The next step is the formalization of the transfer function and its corresponding properties describing different situations such as systems with no forward paths or no touching loops, etc. In order to facilitate the formal modelling of the system properties and reasoning about their satisfaction in the given system model, the last step is to provide the necessary support to express system properties in HOL, i.e., their formal definitions and most frequently used theorems. These system properties are *stability*, which ensures the finite behavior of the system, *resonance*, which provides the basis to derive the suitable parameters at which the photonic circuit can resonate, and *frequency response*, which is necessary to evaluate the frequency dependent system response such as group delay. Finally, we apply the above mentioned steps to develop a library of frequently used photonic signal processing components, such as the double-coupler double-ring [5] or the add-drop filter [26].

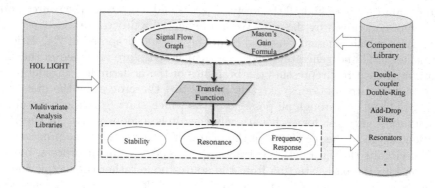

Fig. 2. Proposed Analysis Framework for Photonic Signal Processing Systems

4.1   Formalization of Signal-Flow-Graphs and Mason's Gain

In this section, we only present a brief overview of the formalization developed in our framework (Figure 2). A more detailed description can be found in [4].

We model a single branch as a triplet (a, t_{ab}, b), where a, t_{ab} and b represent the start node, the transmittance and the end node, respectively. Consequently, a path can be modeled as a list of branches and furthermore an SFG can be defined as a composition of a path along with the information about the total number of nodes in the circuit, sink and source nodes at which we want to compute light amplitudes. As mentioned in Section 3, nodes and transmittance represent the system variable and gain, respectively. These parameters are indeed complex valued, i.e., $a, t_{ab}, b \in \mathbb{C}$ in the context of photonic systems. However, the information about the nodes is just used to find properties of signals (light-waves) transmission and they do not appear in the gain and transfer function computation using Mason's gain formula. So, we adopted the same approach as proposed by Mason [17], where nodes of an SFG are represented by natural numbers ($\mathbb{N}$). In order to simplify the reasoning process, we encode the above information by defining three type abbreviations in HOL Light[3], i.e., branch, path and signal-flow-graph as follows:

Definition 1 (Branch, Path and SFG).
```
new_type_abbrev ("branch", ':N × C × N')
new_type_abbrev ("path", ':(branch)list')
new_type_abbrev ("sfg", ':path × N × N × N')
```

where **branch** represents a triplet (a, t_{ab}, b). The second element of **sfg** represents the total number of nodes whereas the third and fourth elements represent the input and output nodes of a signal-flow-graph, respectively.

---

[3] Note that throughout this paper, we used minimal HOL Light syntax in the presentation of definitions and theorems to improve the readability and for a better understanding without prior experience of HOL Light notations.

Our main task is to find all the forward paths and loops from the source node to the sink node given by the user. We implemented a procedure to extract this information which is mainly inspired from the method proposed in [24]. Briefly, we take an SFG and generate a matrix in which nodes are arranged in the first column and each row represents the branches of the node under consideration. In elementary circuits (loops) extraction, we start the process by the first node of the SFG and go through all possible paths which start from the node under consideration and test for each path whether it is a loop or not. In the next iteration, we go to the next node of the graph and repeat the same process. For forward circuits (forward paths) extraction, we repeat a similar process, but we only consider the paths starting from the source node rather than exploring all the nodes. For the sake of conciseness, we give the following two main definitions of our formalization where more details can be found in [3].

Definition 2 (Elementary Circuits).
⊢ ∀(system : sfg). EC system = if (fst_of_four system = [ ]) then [ ]
    else all_loops (EC_MAIN system) system

Here, the function EC_MAIN accepts an SFG, (system : path × $\mathbb{N}$ × $\mathbb{N}$ × $\mathbb{N}$) and returns the list of loops in which each loop is represented as a list of nodes only, and all_loops takes the result of EC_MAIN and an SFG (system) and returns the list of loops in the standard format where each branch represents a triplet. Finally, the main function EC returns an empty list if the system has no branches otherwise it gives the list of all loops in the system.

Definition 3 (Forward Circuits).
⊢ ∀(system : sfg). FC system = if (fst_of_four system = [ ]) then [ ]
    else forward_paths (FC_MAIN system) system

where the function FC_MAIN accepts an SFG (system) and returns the list of forward paths in which each forward path is considered as a list of nodes. Then the function forward_paths takes the result of FC_MAIN and system and returns the list of forward paths, such that each forward path is a list of branches.

Finally, we utilize above described definitions to formalize the Mason's gain formula given in Equation 1, as follows:

Definition 4 (Mason's gain formula).
⊢ ∀(system : sfg). Mason_Gain system =

$$\frac{\text{product\_gain\_det (EC system) (FC system)}}{\text{determinant (EC system)}}$$

where the function Mason_Gain accepts an SFG (system, which is a model of the given system in our case) and computes the Mason's gain as given in Equation 1. Note that the function product_gain_det accepts the list of loops (Definition 2) and forward paths (Definition 3) in the system and computes $\sum_{k \in system} G_k \Delta_k$, where G_k and Δ_k represent, respectively, the product of all forward path gains and the determinant of the kth forward path considering the elimination of all loops touching the kth forward path as described in Section 3. The function determinant takes the list of loops and gives the determinant of the system as given in Equation (2).

We developed some simplification tactics for the loops and forward paths extraction and Mason's gain computations. For example, MASON_SIMP_TAC accepts a list of theorems (or definitions) and automatically proves or simplify the goal (more details can be found in the source code [3,4]). Next, we present the formalization of the transfer functions which is the second part of the proposed framework (Figure 2).

4.2 Formalization of the Transfer Function

In practice, the physical behavior of any photonic signal processing system is described by the transmittance of each path (or a single branch) involved in the signal-flow-graph. We can consider each path as a system component which processes the input light signal to achieve the desired functionality such as amplification, attenuation or delay [5]. The general expression for the photonic transmittance is given as follows:

$$T_i = t_{a_i} G_i z^{m_i} \tag{3}$$

where i corresponds to the ith path, ta_i is the transmission coefficient for each path expressed as the same path t_a, the parameter G_i is the optical intensity gain factor and m_i is the delay factor of the ith path described as the power of complex-valued parameter z. Note that the parameters t_{a_i} and G_i are constants whereas z is a variable quantity in the system. Indeed, the signal-flow-graph of the given photonic system is expressed as function of z and we need to consider this physical aspect in the formalization of the transfer function which describes the overall behavior of the system. It is mentioned in Section 3 that the Mason's gain formula describes the total gain between the input and the output of the system and hence it can be used to describe the transfer function of the photonic system provided the given signal flow graph can be described as a function of a complex parameter (z). We use the Mason's gain formalization and the above description to formalize the transfer function of a photonic system as follows:

Definition 5 (Photonic System Transfer Function).

⊢ ∀system. transfer_function system = Mason_Gain (λz. system z)

where the function transfer_function accepts a system which has type $\mathbb{C} \to$ sfg and returns a complex ($\mathbb{C}$) quantity which represents the transfer function of the photonic system (system). Next, we define the following two helper functions which simplify the formalization of the stability and resonance.

⊢ ∀sys. numerator sys = product_gain_det (EC sys) (FC sys)
⊢ ∀sys. denominator sys = determinant EC sys

Finally, we verify that any photonic transfer function can be described in terms of the `numerator` and `denominator` as follows:

Theorem 1 (Transfer Function).

$\vdash \forall$`system z`. `transfer_function (system z)` $= \dfrac{\texttt{numerator (system z)}}{\texttt{denominator (system z)}}$

4.3   Formalization of System Properties

To this point, we covered the two components of the proposed framework (Figure 2) which concern the process of formal modeling of the photonic system description provided by the physicists or optical system designers. In order to verify that the given model meets its specification, we need to build the foundations based on which we can formally describe the main system properties (i.e., stability, resonance and frequency response) in HOL. Physically, the stability and resonance are concerned with the identification of all values of z for which the system transfer function becomes infinite and zero, respectively. In the signal processing literature, these values are called *system poles* and *system zeros* which can be computed by the denominator and numerator of the transfer function, respectively. Furthermore, all poles and zeros need to be inside the unit circle which means that their magnitude should be less than 1. The frequency response of the system can be computed by considering the parameter z as a complex exponential $exp(jw)$, where exp, j and w represent the base of logarithm, the imaginary unit $\sqrt{-1}$ and the angular frequency, respectively. We formalize the above mentioned informal description of the system properties in HOL as follows:

Definition 6 (System Poles).

$\vdash \forall$`system`. `poles system` $=$ `{z | z`$\neq 0 \wedge$`denominator (system z)`$= 0$`}`

$\vdash \forall$`system`. `zeros system` $=$ `{z | z`$\neq 0 \wedge$`numerator (system z)`$= 0$`}`

where the functions `poles` and `zeros` take the `system` as a parameter and return the set of poles and zeros, respectively. Note that we do not consider the case `z` $= 0$ because it leads to unconditional stable or resonant system (i.e., 0 is always inside the unit circle). Next, we formalize the notion of stability and resonance as follows:

Definition 7 (System Stability and Resonance).

$\vdash \forall$`system`. `is_stable_psp system` $\Leftrightarrow$

$\qquad \forall$`p. p` $\in$ `(poles system)` $\Longrightarrow \| \texttt{p} \| < 1$

$\vdash \forall$`system`. `is_resonant_psp system` $\Leftrightarrow$

$\qquad \forall$`z. z` $\in$ `(zeros system)` $\Longrightarrow \| \texttt{z} \| < 1$

where the predicate `is_stable_psp` accepts the photonic system (`system`) and verifies that the magnitude (norm of a complex number, $\| \texttt{p}_i \|$) of each element

p_i of the set of poles $\{p_0, ..., p_n\}$ is smaller than 1. The function is_resonant_psp is defined in a similar way by considering the zeros of the system.

Next, we verify two important theorems which describe that if the denominator or the numerator of the transfer function is a polynomial of order n, it will always have a finite number of poles or zeros and the cardinality of the set of poles and zeros can only be equal or less than n.

Theorem 2 (Finiteness and Cardinality of Poles).

$\vdash \forall n$ c system. $\neg(\forall i.\ i\ \in \{0, 1, ..., n\}\ \Rightarrow c\ i = 0)\land$

$(\forall z.$ denominator (system z) $= \sum_{i\in\{0,1,...,n\}}(\lambda i.\ c\ i * z^i)) \implies$

FINITE (poles (system z)) $\land$ CARD (poles (system z)) $\leq n$

where n represents the order of the complex polynomial function c. The function $\sum_s$ takes two parameters, i.e., s which specifies the set over which the summation occurs and an arbitrary function $f : (A \to \mathbb{R}^N)$. The functions FINITE and CARD, represent the finiteness and cardinality of a set, respectively. We also prove the same theorem for the set of zeros of a system, where more details can be found in [3]. We formalize the frequency response of a photonic system, group delay and dispersion [8] in terms of the transfer function where more details can be found in [3].

5 Application: Analysis of Photonic Signal Processors

Photonic signal processors process light-waves to achieve different functionalities such as switching, filtering and amplification. In practice, photonic signal processors are of two types (coherent and incoherent) depending upon the nature of light source used in the system. In incoherent photonic processors, the coherence time (i.e., the interval within which the phase of light signal can be predictable) [5] of the light source is much shorter than the unit time delay (or sampling period). On the other hand, coherent processors require the coherence time of the light source to be much longer than the basic time delay to achieve coherent interference of the delayed signals. Both types of photonic processors have wide application domains, e.g., incoherent systems are more stable and mostly used as light amplifiers, whereas coherent integrated optical processors are used in microwave communication systems [5]. The design and analysis of photonic processors mainly involves three steps, i.e., specification of the desired properties of the system, modeling using transfer function and the realization of overall structure (parallel, cascaded, etc.). Given the processor specifications in terms of nature of light sources, transmission powers and optical intensity, the first step is to represent the system as an SFG, the identification of all forward paths and feedback loops and then to compute the system transfer function. Consequently, stability, resonance and frequency response analysis and architectural optimization (possibility of reducing the total number of involved system components) can be performed based on the given specifications. Our proposed framework (Figure 2) allows us to perform these steps (for both coherent and incoherent signal processing) within HOL Light.

The double-coupler double-ring (DCDR) [5] is a widely used processor in the domain of photonics due to its unique features such as compact size, low cost and better compatibility with fiber communication devices. It also has many important physical characteristics due to which it has been used as a photonic filter [5], interferometer [6] and photonic switch [5]. Generally, a DCDR is composed of two main components: (1) Optical directional coupler which are optical devices that transfer the maximum possible optical power from one or more optical devices to another one in a selected direction; and (2) Microring (or cavity) which consists of a fiber ring and confine the light in a very small volume to perform different operations such as light amplification and wavelength filtering.

Using the proposed framework, we formally analyze the DCDR circuit as both coherent and incoherent signal processor. However, we present the analysis of incoherent case while more details about the coherent case can be found in [3]. The schematic diagram of the DCDR circuit is shown in Figure 3 which consists of two directional couplers interconnected with three optical fiber forward and feedback paths. The fiber paths ③-⑥ and ④-⑤ are the forward paths of the circuit while the path ⑦-② is the feedback path of the circuit. The parameters (k_1, k_2), and (T_1, T_2, T_3) represent the power coupling coefficients of the two couplers and the transmission functions of the forward paths, respectively. The photonic transmittance can be expressed as $T_i = t_{a_i} G_i z^{m_i}$ for the ith forward path as described in Section 4.2. The parameters (k_1, k_2) are the deciding factor whether the processor is coherent or incoherent. Typically, for incoherent systems, $k_1 = 1 - k_2$ and for coherent systems $k_1 = \sqrt{1-k}$ and $k_2 = -j\sqrt{k}$, where k is the intensity coupling coefficient [5].

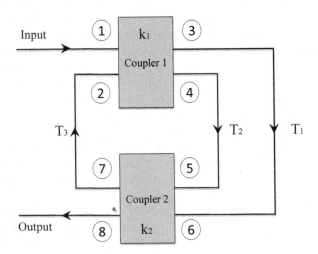

Fig. 3. Double-Coupler Double-Ring Schematic Architecture

The SFG representation of the DCDR circuit is shown in Figure 4 which consists of the same number of nodes as in the block diagram representation in Figure 3. Our main interest is to evaluate the circuit behavior at the output node which is represented by node ⑧, when the signal is applied at the input, i.e., node ①. We keep all above mentioned parameters in general form which further can be used to model different DCDR configurations. We formally define the SFG of the DCDR as follows:

Definition 8 (DCDR Model).

⊢ $\forall T_1\ T_2\ T_3\ k_1\ k_2\ \in \mathbb{C}$.

DCDR_model $T_1\ T_2\ T_3\ k_1\ k_2 = [(1, 1 - k_1, 3); (3, T_1, 6); (6, 1 - k_2, 8); (1, k_1, 4);$

$(4, T_2, 5); (5, k_2, 8); (6, k_2, 7); (7, T_3, 2); (2, k_1, 3); (2, 1 - k_1, 4); (5, 1 - k_2, 7)], 8, 1, 8$

where DCDR_model accepts complex-valued transmittances and coupling coefficients, and returns the signal-flow-graph which has a total number of 8 nodes, where 1 and 8 represent the input and output nodes as shown in Figure 3.

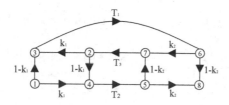

Fig. 4. Signal-Flow-Graph Model of the DCDR

Next, we verify the transfer function of the DCDR circuit as follows:

Theorem 3 (Transfer Function of DCDR).

⊢ $\forall T_1\ T_2\ T_3\ k_1\ k_2\ \in \mathbb{C}$.

transfer_function (DCDR_model $T_1\ T_2\ T_3\ k_1\ k_2$) =

$$\frac{(1 - k_1) * (1 - k_2) * T_1 + k_1 * k_2 * T_2 - (1 - 2 * k_1) * (1 - 2 * k_2) * T_1 * T_2 * T_3}{1 - k_1 * k_2 * T_1 * T_3 - (1 - k_1) * (1 - k_2) * T_2 * T_3}$$

The proof of this theorem is mainly based on the extraction of forward paths and loops in the circuit and then using Mason's gain formula. In fact, we developed some simplification tactics [4] which can find elementary and forward circuits to automate the parts of the proof in HOL Light. The transfer function verified in Theorem 3 can be used to analyze four different configurations of DCDR as given in Table 1. One of the most widely used case is when every path has unity delay. Such DCDR circuits are usually used as data processing elements in the photonic communication. The second case of Table 1 describes the conditions when one of the paths in the circuit (Figure 3) amplifies the light signals.

The DCDR circuit operates in passive mode when there is no light amplification in the circuit. Finally, the last case describes the circuit operation when each path can have different delays.

Table 1. DCDR Configurations (parameters G_i and m_i correspond to Eq. 3)

DCDR Configuration	Parameters
Active DCDR Circuit with Unit Delay	$m1 = m_2 = m_3 = 1$
Optical Amplifier in the Fiber Path	$(m1 = m_2 = m_3 = 1) \wedge (G_i > 1)$
Passive DCDR Circuit	$G1 = G_2 = G_3 = 1$
DCDR with Multiple Delay	m_i can have different combinations

In the case of unit delay, the denominator of transfer function of the DCDR can be represented as a second order polynomial which leads to the useful information that the DCDR can have 2 poles at maximum according to Theorem 2. Next, we present the verification of the stability conditions of the DCDR circuit under unit delay conditions as follows:

Theorem 4 (Stability Conditions for Incoherent DCDR).

$\vdash \forall G_1\ G_2\ G_3\ k_1\ k_2\ \in \mathbb{C}.$
$\| \sqrt{k_1 * k_2 * G_1 * G_2 + (1 - k_1) * (1 - k_2) * G_2 * G_3} \| \le 1\ \wedge$
$(k_1 * k_2 * G_1 * G_2 + (1 - k_1) * (1 - k_2) * G_2 * G_3) \ne 0$
$\implies \text{is\_stable\_psp}\quad (\lambda z.\ \text{DCDR}\ (G_1 * \frac{1}{z})\ (G_2 * \frac{1}{z})\ (G_3 * \frac{1}{z})\ k_1\ k_2)$

where $\| \cdot \|$ and $\sqrt{\cdot}$ represent the complex norm and complex square root, respectively. The first assumption ensures that both poles are inside the unit circle, whereas the second assumption is required to prove that the poles are indeed valid. Similarly, we verify the second important result, i.e., the resonance condition for the DCDR circuit as follows:

Theorem 5 (Resonance Conditions for Incoherent DCDR).

$\vdash \forall G_1\ G_2\ G_3\ k_1\ k_2 \in \mathbb{C}.\ \| \sqrt{\frac{((1 - 2*k_1) * (1 - 2*k_2) * G_1 * G_2 * G_3)}{((1 - k_1) * (1 - k_2) * G_1 + k_1 * k_2 * G_2)}} \| \le 1\ \wedge$
$((1 - 2 * k_1) * (1 - 2 * k_2) * G_1 * G_2 * G_3) \ne 0\ \wedge$
$(1 - k_1) * (1 - k_2) * G_1 + k_1 * k_2 * G_2) \ne 0$
$\implies \text{is\_resonant\_psp}\quad (\lambda z.\ \text{DCDR}\ (G_1 * \frac{1}{z})\ (G_2 * \frac{1}{z})\ (G_3 * \frac{1}{z})\ k_1\ k_2)$

where all assumptions in this theorem are required to ensure that zeros of the DCDR are valid and inside the unit circle.

Similarly, we verify the stability and the resonance conditions of the other DCDR configurations as described in Table 1. One of the main strengths of theorem proving based approach is to unveil all the assumptions under which a theorem can be verified. For example, the second assumption of Theorem 4, and the last two of Theorem 5 are not mentioned in the paper-and-pencil based approach reported in [5]. However, without these assumptions Theorems 4 and 5 cannot be verified. Moreover, our results are verified for universally quantified parameters and the problem of finding the stability and resonance conditions reduces to just ensuring that the values of the system parameters satisfy both assumptions. In an effort to validate the stability results provided in [5], we discovered that both given values of poles cannot satisfy the stability conditions. We formally proved the instability of the DCDR in case of passive operation (i.e., $G1 = G_2 = G_3 = 1$) with $k1 = k2 = 0.9$ as follows:

$\vdash$ unstable_psp (λz. DCDR $\frac{1}{z}$ $\frac{1}{z}$ $\frac{1}{z}$ 0.9 0.9 [0.905539; −0.905539])

where unstable_psp sys = $\neg$(is_stable_psp sys) as described in Definition 7. This demonstrates the importance of using higher-order-logic theorem proving to unveil such discrepancies. In fact, incorrect stability conditions can lead to the instability of the photonic processor which is hazardous in industrial critical systems which are related to both cost and human safety.

This completes our formal analysis of the DCDR which is a practical photonic processor with vast industrial applications in photonic and microwave communication systems. The stability and resonance conditions have been verified under the general parameters of the DCDR circuit (e.g., k_1, k_2) which is not possible in the case of simulation [5], where these properties are verified for the particular values of k_1 and k_2. Note that the signal-flow-graph model of the DCDR processor involves 8 nodes, however, our formalization is general and can be applied for an arbitrary number of nodes. For example, we formally verified the transfer function of a quadruple optical ring resonator based filter which consists of 20 nodes and 14 complex-valued parameters [8]. We also formalized and verified another important photonic processor namely the add-drop filter [26] which is widely used as a filtering element in biosensors and wavelength division multiplexing (WDM). Some remarkable features of our formalized libraries of SFG and corresponding properties are the generic nature and reusability as the formal specification and verification of above mentioned case studies require minimal efforts. Moreover, we have also made efforts to provide effective automation using derived rules and tactics, so that the application to a particular system does not involve the painful manual proofs often required with interactive (higher-order logic) theorem proving. The source code of the add-drop filter and the quadruple optical ring resonator specification along with their analyses in HOL Light is available at [3]. A brief summary of developed tactics can be found in the Appendix I of [4].

We believe that the formal analysis of above mentioned real-world photonic processors provides two main insights: theorem proving systems have reached to the maturity, where complex physical models can be expressed with less efforts than ever before; and formal methods can assist in the verification of futuristic photonic processors in particular and quantum computers in general. However, the utilization of higher-order-logic theorem proving in industrial settings (particularly, physical systems) is always questionable due to the huge amount of time required to formalize the underlying theories. Another, important factor is the gap between the theorem proving and engineering communities which limits its usage in industry. For example, it is hard to find engineers (or physicists) with theorem proving background and vice-versa. On the other hand, the use of formal methods for safety-critical systems is recommended by different industrial standards like IEC 61508 [14] for electrical and electronics systems, or DO178-B [18] for aviation. In the last decade, some major iconic companies (e.g., Intel [2] and IBM [1]) have established research centers to build revolutionary future computing and communication systems based on the recent advancements in silicon photonics. We believe that applying formal methods to certify photonic designs will be an interesting and challenging future research direction for the formal methods community. Our reported work can be considered as a one step towards an ultimate goal of using theorem provers as a complementary tool in the field of photonics which is one of the rapidly growing high-tech industries in the world today.

6   Conclusion

In this paper, we reported a new application of formal methods in the domain of photonic signal processing. We presented a formal analysis framework based on higher-order logic which provides the required expressiveness and soundness to formally model and verify physical aspects of photonics. In particular, we formalized the signal-flow-graph theory along with Mason's gain formula and transfer functions. Consequently, we presented the formalization of the properties of photonic signal processing systems (such as stability, resonance and frequency response). Finally, we described the formal analysis of the stability and resonance conditions of the double-coupler double-ring photonic processor.

Our immediate future work is to explore the formal relation among the signal-flow-graph representation and the Z-transform [21]. A potential utilization of our formalization and developed automation tactics is to build a framework to certify the results produced by informal tools such as MATLAB based SFG analysis program (available at [11]). Other interesting directions are the application of the current work to formally verify control and digital signal processing systems which are usually modeled as signal-flow-graphs.

References

1. IBM: Silicon photonics (2015),
   http://www.zurich.ibm.com/st/photonics/silicon.html
2. Intel-based Optical PCI Express (2015), http://www.intel.com/content/www/us/en/research/intel-labs-silicon-photonics-optical-pci-express-server.html
3. Beillahi, S.M., Siddique, U.: Formal Analysis of Photonic Signal Processing Systems (2015), http://hvg.ece.concordia.ca/projects/optics/psp.html
4. Beillahi, S.M., Siddique, U., Tahar, S.: On the Formalization of Signal-Flow-Graphs in HOL. Technical report, Department of Electrical and Computer Engineering, Concordia University, Montreal, QC, Canada (November 2014)
5. Binh, L.N.: Photonic Signal Processing: Techniques and Applications. Optical Science and Engineering. Taylor & Francis (2010)

6. Harvey, D., Millar, C.A., Urquhart, P.: Fibre Reflection Mach-Zehnder Interferometer. Optics Communcation 70, 304–308 (1989)
7. MIT's CTR (2015), https://mphotonics.mit.edu/ctr-documents
8. Dey, S.B., Mandal, S., Jana, N.N.: Quadruple Optical Ring Resonator based Filter on Silicon-on-insulator. Optik - International Journal for Light and Electron Optics 124(17), 2920–2927 (2013)
9. Emelett, S., Soref, R.: Synthesis of Dual-Microring-Resonator Cross-Connect Filters. Optics Express 13(12), 4439–4456 (2005)
10. Driessen, A., et al.: Microresonators as Building Blocks for VLSI Photonics. AIP Conference Proceedings 709(1), 1–18 (2004)
11. Signal Flow Graph Simplification Program for MATLAB (2015), http://www.mathworks.com/matlabcentral/fileexchange/22-mason-m
12. Harrison, J.: HOL Light: A Tutorial Introduction. In: Srivas, M., Camilleri, A. (eds.) FMCAD 1996. LNCS, vol. 1166, pp. 265–269. Springer, Heidelberg (1996)
13. Hasan, O., Khan Afshar, S., Tahar, S.: Formal Analysis of Optical Waveguides in HOL. In: Berghofer, S., Nipkow, T., Urban, C., Wenzel, M. (eds.) TPHOLs 2009. LNCS, vol. 5674, pp. 228–243. Springer, Heidelberg (2009)
14. Ladkin, P.B.: An Overview of IEC 61508 on EEPE Functional Safety (2008)
15. Yousri Mahmoud, M., Tahar, S.: On the Quantum Formalization of Coherent Light in HOL. In: Badger, J.M., Rozier, K.Y. (eds.) NFM 2014. LNCS, vol. 8430, pp. 128–142. Springer, Heidelberg (2014)
16. Mason, S.J.: Feedback Theory, Further Properties of Signal Flow Graphs. In: Proceeding of IRE, vol. 44, pp. 920–926 (July 1956)
17. Mason, S.J.: Feedback Theory, Some Properties of Signal Flow Graphs. In: Proceeding of IRE, vol. 41, pp. 1144–1156 (September 1953)
18. RTCA/DO-178B: Software Considerations in Airborne Systems and Equipment Certification (1992)
19. Rumley, S., Glick, M., Dutt, R., Bergman, K.: Impact of Photonic Switch Radix on Realizing Optical Interconnection Networks for Exascale Systems. In: IEEE Optical Interconnects Conference, pp. 98–99 (2014)
20. Siddique, U., Aravantinos, V., Tahar, S.: Formal Stability Analysis of Optical Resonators. In: Brat, G., Rungta, N., Venet, A. (eds.) NFM 2013. LNCS, vol. 7871, pp. 368–382. Springer, Heidelberg (2013)
21. Siddique, U., Mahmoud, M.Y., Tahar, S.: On the Formalization of Z-Transform in HOL. In: Klein, G., Gamboa, R. (eds.) ITP 2014. LNCS, vol. 8558, pp. 483–498. Springer, Heidelberg (2014)
22. Siddique, U., Tahar, S.: Towards the Formal Analysis of Microresonators Based Photonic Systems. In: IEEE/ACM Design Automation and Test in Europe, pp. 1–6 (2014)
23. Taqdees, S.H., Hasan, O.: Formalization of Laplace Transform Using the Multivariable Calculus Theory of HOL-Light. In: McMillan, K., Middeldorp, A., Voronkov, A. (eds.) LPAR-19 2013. LNCS, vol. 8312, pp. 744–758. Springer, Heidelberg (2013)
24. Tiernan, J.C.: An Efficient Search Algorithm to Find the Elementary Circuits of a Graph. Communnications of the ACM 13(12), 722–726 (1970)
25. Weaver, T.: High-Flying Photonics. SPIE OE Magazine (2004), http://spie.org/x17123.xml
26. Yupapin, P.P., Li, C., Saeung, P.: Characteristics of Complementary Ring-Resonator Add/Drop Filters Modeling by Using Graphical Approach. Optics Communications 272(1), 81–86 (2007)

Verification

Automated Verification of Nested DFS

Jaco C. van de Pol[✉]

Formal Methods and Tools, Department of Computer Science,
CTIT, University of Twente, Enschede, The Netherlands
j.c.vandepol@utwente.nl

Abstract. In this paper we demonstrate the automated verification of
the Nested Depth-First Search (NDFS) algorithm for detecting accepting
cycles. The starting point is a recursive formulation of the NDFS algorithm. We use Dafny to annotate the algorithm with invariants and a
global specification. The global specification requires that NDFS indeed
solves the accepting cycle problem. The invariants are proved automatically by the SMT solver Z3 underlying Dafny. The global specifications,
however, need some inductive reasoning on paths in a graph. To prove
these properties, some auxiliary lemmas had to be provided. The full
specification is contained in this paper. It fits on 4 pages, is verified by
Dafny in about 2 minutes, and was developed in a couple of weeks.

1 Introduction

Model checking is an attractive verification technique because it is fully automatic. Since model checking is memory and time intensive, scalability of model
checking to industrial systems requires sophisticated algorithms and high-perfor-
mance implementations. This makes the construction of model checkers intricate
and error prone. When model checkers are used for the verification of industrial
critical systems, they themselves become part of the critical engineering infrastructure. This motivated several efforts to verify the verification algorithms and
tools themselves.

Recently, model checkers have been verified using *interactive theorem provers*.
Here users are responsible for creating a proof, which is then checked by the
machine. Examples include the verification of a μ-calculus model checker in
Coq [14], compositional model checkers in ACL2 [12], and a depth-first search
algorithm for strongly connected components in Coq [11]. Probably the largest
piece of work in this direction is the development of a reasonably efficient, certified automata-based LTL model checker in Isabelle/HOL [4]. This includes the
translation of LTL properties to Büchi automata, and an algorithm to detect
accepting cycles in the result graph.

The purpose of the current paper is to raise the level of automation. We investigated whether full functional correctness of graph-based verification algorithms
can be established by *automatic program verifiers*. These tools depend on user
added annotations to a program, like pre- and postconditions and loop invariants. The program verifier then generates proof obligations, which are discharged
automatically by an SMT solver.

© Springer International Publishing Switzerland 2015
M. Núñez and M. Güdemann (Eds.): FMICS 2015, LNCS 9128, pp. 181–197, 2015.
DOI: 10.1007/978-3-319-19458-5_12

Concretely, this paper demonstrates how the Nested Depth-First Search algorithm (NDFS) can be expressed in DAFNY, and how it can be verified in an incremental manner. The complete specification (Section A) demonstrates that NDFS correctly decides if the input graph contains an accepting cycle. DAFNY is an automatic program verifier created by Rustan Leino and relies on the workhorse Z3 as the underlying SMT solver. We took inspiration from the verification of the Schorr-Waite graph algorithm, also by Leino [10]. However, we insist on the natural recursive formulation of NDFS.

As far as we know, we provide the first verification of *full correctness* of a model checking algorithm by an *automatic program verifier*. A related approach [6] applied automatic program verifiers to distributed state space generators (but not on the model checking algorithm). Another approach based on annotations is the PAT model checker, model checking its own annotations [15] (but not full functional correctness).

2   Nested Depth-First Search and Dafny

2.1   Dafny

DAFNY [10] provides a straightforward imperative programming language. It supports sequential programs, with classes and dynamic allocation. The program can be mixed freely with specification annotations, like preconditions (requires), postconditions (ensures) and invariants. Loops and recursion require termination metrics (decreases) to ensure termination. In order to support modularity, framing conditions restrict read and write permissions on objects.

The specification language is quite liberal: specifications can introduce ghost variables in program text, mathematical functions, and built-in value types like sets and sequences. We heavily depend on these features.

DAFNY parses and type-checks the program, and generates proof obligations to guarantee absence of runtime errors, termination, and the validity of all specification annotations. DAFNY works in a modular fashion, method by method. It relies on the SMT solver Z3 [3] to discharge the proof obligations, and reconstructs sensible error messages at the program level when verification fails.

2.2   Nested Depth-First Search

The automata based approach [16] reduces the LTL model checking problem to the detection of *accepting cycles*. Given a graph $G = (V, E, s_0, A)$, with nodes V, edges E, root $s_0 \in V$ and accepting states $A \subseteq V$, the question is whether there exists a reachable accepting cycle, i.e. a state $t \in A$ with $s_0 E^* t$ and $t E^+ t$. The famous linear-time algorithm to detect accepting cycles on-the-fly is called Nested Depth-First Search [2]. NDFS performs a first (blue) DFS to detect accepting states, and a second (red) search to identify cycles on those states. Both searches visit nodes at most once, by colouring them cyan/blue and pink/red.

NDFS is heavily used as the core algorithm of LTL model checkers, starting with SPIN model checker [7], and also forms the basis of parallel LTL model checking in LTSmin [8]. Its memory overhead is negligible: only two bits per state [13]. The version verified in this paper is the new NDFS [13] without early cycle detection, and with a distinction in pink and red nodes. It corresponds to the sequential version of the parallel algorithm in [8]. We claim that the pink colour not only helped in parallelizing NDFS, but is also instrumental in the formal verification proof.

2.3   Formulation of the NDFS Algorithm in Dafny

```
1   datatype Color = white | cyan | blue | pink | red;
2
3   class Node {
4     var next: seq<Node>;
5     var accepting: bool;
6     var color1: Color;
7     var color2: Color;
8   }
9
10  method ndfs(root:Node) returns (found:bool)
11  { found := dfsblue(root); }
12
13  method dfsblue(s:Node) returns (found:bool)
14  { s.color1 := cyan;
15    var i := 0;
16    while (i < |s.next|)
17    { var t := s.next[i];
18      i := i+1;
19      if (t.color1 = white)
20      { found := dfsblue(t);
21        if (found) { return; }
22      }
23    }
24    if (s.accepting)
25    { found := dfsred(s);
26      if (found) { return; }
27    }
28    s.color1 := blue;
29    return false;
30  }
31
32  method dfsred(s:Node) returns (found:bool)
33  { s.color2 := pink;
34    var i := 0;
35    while (i < |s.next|)
36    { var t := s.next[i];
37      i := i+1;
38      if (t.color1 = cyan) { return true; }
39      if (t.color2 = white)
40      { found := dfsred(t);
41        if (found) { return; }
42      }
43    }
44    s.color2 := red;
45    return false;
46  }
```

Fig. 1. Expressing the plain NDFS algorithm in DAFNY syntax

Figure 1 introduces the recursive formulation of the NDFS algorithm in DAFNY syntax. After introducing the enumerated datatype Color (ℓ. 1), the class Node of nodes in the underlying graph is defined (ℓ. 3-8). Each node is equipped with a sequence next of successors in the graph and a Boolean accepting. These attributes will never be changed. Two colours are introduced as well, which will be manipulated by the algorithm. Alternatively, one could introduce distinct types for bluish and reddish colours.

The main algorithm is method ndfs (ℓ. 10,11). Its single argument is the root:Node where the algorithm starts, and its return value found:Bool indicates whether an accepting cycle was found. Return values are named in DAFNY, so they can be referred to in the postcondition of the specification. They can be used as normal local variables in the method body. The main method just calls method dfsblue. The reason to have ndfs as a separate method is to be able to attach the top-level specification to it later.

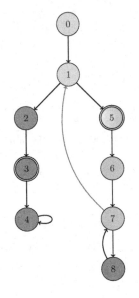

The recursive formulation of method dfsblue (s:Node) (ℓ. 13-30) closely follows the textbook description, see for instance [13, Fig 3.]. After marking s cyan (ℓ. 14), all successor nodes t of s are iterated over (ℓ. 15-18). If t is seen for the first time (ℓ. 19), it is processed recursively (ℓ. 20) and the result is stored in found. As soon as an accepting cycle has been found, the search can be terminated (ℓ. 21); note that return is an abbreviation for return found in Dafny, since we named the return value found.

After processing all successors of s, the red search is started with dfsred(s) (ℓ. 25), provided that s is accepting (ℓ. 24). Again, if an accepting cycle is found we return immediately. When no cycle is found, node s is coloured blue and the procedure returns (ℓ. 28-29).

The method dfsred(s:Node) (ℓ. 32-46) performs the red search in a similar fashion. Initially, nodes are coloured pink (ℓ. 33). All successors t are processed sequentially (ℓ. 34-37). If t is cyan, a cycle has been found and is reported (ℓ. 38). Otherwise, the procedure continues recursively and the results are propagated (ℓ. 39-41). Finally, when no cycle has

Fig. 2. Illustrating NDFS

been found at all, node s is coloured red and the procedure returns (ℓ. 44-45).

Figure 2 illustrates the colours. Cyan and pink nodes are still in progress. After backtracking from the search, nodes are coloured blue or red. So for these colours we can establish strong invariants.

3   Developing the Correctness Proof

The verification was carried out incrementally. First, runtime errors are eliminated by appropriate preconditions, then termination is addressed. To verify the algorithm, the key approach was to identify invariants on the *local* properties of the colours in the graph. These invariants can be checked easily. Similar invariants played a crucial role in the manual proof of parallel NDFS [8]. Finally, completeness and soundness of NDFS are proved using auxiliary lemmas, which reason on global properties of paths and cycles in the graph.

3.1   Absence of Runtime Errors

Even though we did not specify any requirements on NDFS, the code in Figure 1 is not regarded correct by DAFNY. It does not report syntax or type check errors, but the verifier complains (ℓ. 14, 33):

```
Error: assignment may update an object not in ... modifies clause
Error: target object may be null
```

First, in order to allow for modular verification, DAFNY uses dynamic frames, insisting on explicit permissions to modify objects. In Figure 3, we added the permissions to modify the color-fields only (ℓ. 10, 16, 22). Note that dfsred only modifies color2.

In order to guarantee absence of runtime errors, DAFNY has generated some implicit proof obligations. In our case, runtime errors could occur due to *null dereferences* (e.g. in s.color1) and *out-of-bound indexing* (e.g. in next[i]). The latter is excluded, since DAFNY easily deduces $0 \le i < |$s.next$|$ from the loop bounds. However, if initially s:Node = null, indeed s.next would lead to a run-time error.

In order to solve both problems, we use the technique explained in [10] in the verification of the Schorr-Waite graph algorithm. We extend the specification as indicated in Figure 3. We define a ghost variable G:set<Node> (ℓ. 1), indicating the universe of all (reachable) nodes in the graph. As a ghost variable, G can only be used in specification annotations; it cannot modify the program execution. Next, the predicate graph(G) is defined (ℓ. 3-5). G is a valid graph if its nodes are non-null records and their successors are in G again. We equip all methods with a precondition that requires that the start node is contained in the valid graph G (e.g., ℓ. 14-15). Since graph(G) is closed, there is no risk to run into null nodes anymore.

3.2   Termination

Still, DAFNY is not satisfied. In order to guarantee total correctness, it insists on termination. Termination of the while loops in our case (cf. Figure 1, ℓ. 16, 35) is easily discharged automatically. However, the recursive calls (ℓ. 20, 40) lead to the following complaint:

```
Error: cannot prove termination; try supplying a decreases clause
```

```
1   ghost var  G: set<Node>;
2
3   predicate  graph(G: set<Node>)
4      reads G;
5   { ∀ m • m ∈ G ⟹ (m ≠ null ∧ ∀ n • n ∈ m.next ⟹ n ∈ G) }
6
7   method ndfs(root:Node) returns (found:bool)
8      requires  graph(G);
9      requires  root ∈ G;
10     modifies  G'color1 , G'color2 ;
11  { ... }
12
13  method dfsblue(s:Node) returns (found:bool)
14     requires  s ∈ G;
15     requires  graph(G);
16     modifies  G'color1 , G'color2 ;
17  { ... }
18
19  method dfsred(s:Node) returns (found:bool)
20     requires  s ∈ G;
21     requires  graph(G);
22     modifies  G'color2 ;
23  { ... }
```

Fig. 3. Specifying a well-defined and closed graph

So why does NDFS terminate at all? Basically, because every node is visited at most twice: once during `dfsblue` and once during `dfsred`. This is realized by the colours: we only recurse on `white` nodes, and immediately colour them `cyan`. We specify this insight by declaring that the function G-Cyan(G) decreases for each call to `dfsblue` (ℓ. 11 in Figure 4), where the set Cyan(G) is defined as those nodes $n \in G$ with n.color1=cyan (ℓ. 1-3)[1]. We add similar definitions and annotations for pink nodes in `dfsred`.

DAFNY is not yet convinced: We clearly need to require that initially all nodes are `white` (ℓ. 6) and we only meet `white` nodes along the way (ℓ. 10), otherwise the termination function wouldn't decrease. Moreover, recursive calls to `dfsblue` could manipulate the Cyan set arbitrarily in principle, leading to non-termination for calls to subsequent successors. To exclude this, `dfsblue` must ensure that it will leave the Cyan set unchanged (ℓ. 12). Note that this is realized in (ℓ. 23), but only in case no accepting cycle is found. An invariant (ℓ. 15) is required to reason about the value of Cyan during and after the loop.

We are nearly there, but not quite! The preconditions lead to new proof obligations. Obviously, the recursive call to `dfsblue(t)` (ℓ. 18) satisfies the precondition that t.color1=white. However, DAFNY points out that at (Figure 4, ℓ. 21) there is a call to `dfsred`, but the precondition t.color2=white at (Figure 4, ℓ. 28) is not guaranteed:

```
Error: A precondition for this call might not hold.
Related location: This is the precondition that might not hold.
```

---

[1] An alternative is to introduce and manipulate a ghost variable Cyan in the method body, but we prefer our more declarative approach, since it does not clutter the code.

```
1    function Cyan(G: set ⟨Node⟩): set ⟨Node⟩
2       reads G; requires graph(G);
3    { set n | n ∈ G ∧ n.color1 = cyan • n }
4
5    method ndfs(root:Node) returns (found:bool)
6       requires ∀ s • s ∈ G ⟹ s.color1 = s.color2 = white;
7    { ... }
8
9    method dfsblue(s:Node) returns (found:bool)
10      requires s.color1 = white;
11      decreases G − Cyan(G);
12      ensures ¬found ⟹ old(Cyan(G)) = Cyan(G);
13   { ...
14      while (i < |s.next|)
15      invariant Cyan(G) = old(Cyan(G)) ∪ {s};
16      { ...
17         if (t.color1 = white)
18         { found := dfsblue(t);
19         ...
20      if (s.accepting)
21         { found := dfsred(s); // still to prove: why is s.color2 white?
22         ...
23      s.color1 := blue;
24      return false;
25   }
26
27   method dfsred(s:Node) returns (found:bool)
28      requires s.color2 = white;
29      decreases G − Pink(G);
30      ensures ¬found ⟹ old(Pink(G)) = Pink(G);
31   { ... }
```

Fig. 4. Specifying decreasing termination functions

Indeed, the insight that the red search does not escape the blue territory is subtle. It depends on the very depth-first nature of NDFS! Proving the main invariants on the NDFS colours will also complete the termination proof.

3.3 Main Local Invariants on NDFS Colours

In order to prove the main invariant Red ⊆ Blue we have to provide several additional invariants. These invariants are needed in the termination proof, but they will be reused in the completeness proof of NDFS. All invariants in this section can be proved locally, without reasoning about the whole graph.

We now come to the formulation of the main invariants. They capture the very basic idea of Depth-First Search: A node is only coloured blue if its successors are processed, i.e. they are coloured blue or cyan. Similarly, all successors of red nodes are red or pink. We express these invariants concisely with a special predicate Next, where Next (G, X, Y) indicates that all successors in G of nodes X are in Y. See Figure 5 for the statement of the main invariants.

Another important local property is that there will never be an edge from a red node to a cyan node, Next(G, Red(G), G-Cyan(G)). This is guaranteed by the cycle detection in dfsred at (Section A.5, ℓ. 38).

For the complete proof we refer to Section A. One of the subtleties is that in dfsred (Section A.5, ℓ. 50) we colour the start node red, just before it

```
1   predicate Next(G:set⟨Node⟩,X:set⟨Node⟩,Y:set⟨Node⟩)
2      reads G; requires graph(G);
3   { ∀ n,i • n ∈ G ∧ 0 ≤ i < |n.next| ⟹ ( n ∈ X ⟹ n.next[i] ∈ Y ) }
4   ...
5   invariant Red(G) ⊆ Blue(G);
6   invariant Next(G, Blue(G), Blue(G) ∪ Cyan(G));
7   invariant Next(G, Red(G) , Red(G) ∪ Pink(G));
8   invariant Next(G, Red(G) , G − Cyan(G));
```

Fig. 5. Stating the main local invariants on the colours in NDFS

becomes blue, temporarily violating the main invariant. This is solved by re-membering the starting point of dfsred in a ghost variable ghost root:Node (Section A.5, ℓ. 1). The invariants on Blue in dfsred are modified to Blue ∪ {root} (Section A.5, ℓ. 8, 10, 19, 32). Also, we must explicitly state that all successors of s up to i are in Blue ∪ Cyan (Section A.4, ℓ. 33), or Red ∪ Pink (Section A.5, ℓ. 29), respectively. In order to prove this under the given condi-tions, we introduce an invariant on the exact types that the two colour variables may assume (Section A.1, ℓ. 16-20).

Adding the invariants expands the DAFNY code considerably, since most in-variants must be repeated six times: before and after each recursive call, and in the while loops. See for instance the six occurrences of invariant types(G) in Section A.4, A.5.

At this point, DAFNY is happy, since the code is guaranteed to terminate with-out run time errors. This run takes about 10 seconds (on a 2.7GHz Macbook).

Dafny program verifier finished with 13 verified, 0 errors

3.4   Completeness

We can now proceed to specify and prove that NDFS accomplishes a useful task. The correctness criterion is that the result found indicates correctly whether the graph G has an accepting cycle. In order to specify this, we first define the notions of paths and cycles, in terms of sequences of nodes, Figure 6.

A sequence of nodes p is a path from x to y in graph G if it starts with x, ends with y, and successive members are linked by an edge in G. A reachable accepting cycle is defined as a lasso: a path p from root x to accepting state y, and the cycle is a non-empty path q from y to itself.

Next, correctness of ndfs is ensured, distinguishing soundness and complete-ness. In the rest of this section, we prove completeness, i.e. the algorithm does not miss an accepting cycle. To this end we state the key invariant (Figure 6, ℓ. 13-15). The completeness proof consists of two parts: proving the key invari-ant, that no blue nodes can have an accepting cycle, and proving that all nodes will be blue if ndfs terminates with found=false.

Let us see what we know after dfsblue(root) terminates with found=false; we refer to the line numbers in Section A.4. We have already proved the invariant Next(G,Blue(G),Blue(G) ∪ Cyan(G)) (ℓ. 16). Since Old(Cyan)=Cyan (ℓ. 19) and Cyan={} initially (nodes start white), we obtain

```
1   function  Path (G: set ⟨Node⟩ ,x : Node, y : Node, p : seq ⟨Node⟩ ) : bool
2      reads G;  requires  graph(G);
3   {  |p| > 0 ∧ p[0] = x ∧ p[|p|−1] = y
4      ∧ ∀ i • 0 ≤ i < |p|−1 ⟹ p[i] ∈ G ∧ p[i+1] ∈ p[i].next }
5
6   function  Cycle (G: set ⟨Node⟩ ,x : Node, y : Node, p : seq ⟨Node⟩ ,q : seq ⟨Node⟩ ) : bool
7      reads G;  requires  graph(G);
8   {  Path (G,x,y,p) ∧ Path (G,y,y,q) ∧ |q| > 1 ∧ y. accepting }
9
10  ensures  found  ⟹ (∃ a,p,q • Cycle (G, root ,a,p,q));   // soundness
11  ensures  (∃ s,p,q • Cycle (G, root ,s,p,q)) ⟹ found;    // completeness
12
13  function  KeyInvariant (G: set ⟨Node⟩ ) : bool
14     reads G;  requires  graph(G);
15  {  ∀ s • s ∈ Blue(G) ∧ s. accepting ⟹ ¬ ∃ p • |p| > 1 ∧ Path (G,s,s,p) }
```

Fig. 6. Specification of the full functional correctness and key invariant of NDFS

Next (G, Blue (G) , Blue (G)). Since root . color1=blue (ℓ. 18), we can now prove inductively that all reachable nodes are indeed in Blue (G). So if the Key Invariant holds, there cannot be an accepting cycle.

Since finding inductive proofs is beyond the capabilities of DAFNY, we must prove this with a separate lemma. In DAFNY, an inductive proof corresponds to a recursive function that establishes the correct post condition. Function NoCycle (Section A.2, ℓ. 15-21) represents a proof by induction over the reachable nodes that the key invariant indeed implies that there is no accepting cycle. Note that we have to explicitly apply this lemma in ndfs (Section A.3, ℓ. 9).

Next we must still prove the Key Invariant (ℓ. 10, 23, 38). The crucial step is just before we assign s.color1 = blue for an accepting state s (ℓ. 58). At this point we apply a new lemma, NoPath, which basically reasons about the result of dfsred, with another inductive argument.

So what do we know after calling dfsred when found=false? We now refer to line numbers in Section A.5. We already proved Next (G, Red (G) , Red (G) ∪ Pink (G)) (ℓ. 18). Since Old (Pink) =Pink (ℓ. 16) and Pink={} before the call (Section A.4, ℓ. 31) we obtain Next (G, Red (G) , Red (G)). Since s. color2=red (ℓ. 15), we can now prove inductively that all reachable nodes are in Red (G). One of our main invariants on colours is that there is no edge between red nodes and cyan nodes (ℓ. 11). So indeed, the root node, which is still cyan, is not reachable.

Again, this requires an inductive argument, which is provided by the recursive function NoPath (Section A.2, ℓ. 5-13) that establishes the correct postcondition.

3.5   Soundness

The final task is to prove soundness, i.e., if ndfs reports found=true, then there exists an accepting cycle. This is intuitively an easy task, since the stack of the program execution corresponds to the accepting cycle (cf. the cyan and pink nodes in Figure 2). However, we have no access to the stack. Actually, the soundness proof posed some verification challenges to the underlying Z3 SMT solver, since it introduces quantifications over sequences. To limit the search

```
1   method ndfs(root:Node)
2   { try
3     { dfsblue(root);
4       assert ¬CycleExists;
5     }
6     catch CycleFound ⇒ { assert CycleExists; }
7   }
8
9   method dfsblue(s:Node) raises CycleFound
10  { s.color1 := cyan;
11    var i := 0;
12    while (i < |s.next|)
13    { var t := s.next[i];
14      i := i+1;
15      if (t.color1 = white) { dfsblue(t); }
16    }
17    if (s.accepting) { dfsred(s); }
18    s.color1 := blue;
19  }
20
21  method dfsred(s:Node) raises CycleFound
22  { s.color2 := pink;
23    var i := 0;
24    while (i < |s.next|)
25    { var t := s.next[i];
26      i := i+1;
27      if (t.color1 = cyan) { raise CycleFound; }
28      if (t.color2 = white) { dfsred(t); }
29    }
30    s.color2 := red;
31  }
```

Fig. 7. Specification in DAFNY language extended with exceptions

space, DAFNY does not try extensively to find a witness to an obligation of the form `exists p:seq<<Node>>`. So at certain places in the program we must add assertions, to suggest the correct witnesses. Alternatively, one could add ghost variables to manipulate paths explicitly, as done in [10].

The blue search ensures that when `found=true`, there is indeed an accepting cycle (Section A.4, ℓ. 22). The assertion at (ℓ. 46) shows how this cycle is constructed from the path obtained from the recursive call. In the other case, at (ℓ. 55), the situation is less trivial. Here we apply `lemma CycleFoundHere` to reconstruct the cycle.

Let us first consider this situation. Assume that the blue search started in node s, calls the red search from an accepting node t, which hits a cyan state r. Note that r is not necessarily accepting. In this case, the accepting cycle consists of the prefix s to t, followed by the loop t to r back to t ($s = 0$, $t = 5$, $r = 1$ in Figure 2).

The fact that there is a path from r to t is not obvious. We added a new precondition (Section A.4, ℓ. 11) that from any cyan state c (in particular r) there is a path to the current state s. When we color s cyan, the path is trivial, but still we must assert it (ℓ. 26). Before the recursive call (ℓ. 43) we use `lemma NextCyan` (Section A.2, ℓ. 23-29) to tell DAFNY how the path to the next cyan node is constructed by concatenation.

To reconstruct the path from t to some r, the red search ensures that if `found=true`, there is a path from the current state to some cyan state

(Section A.5, ℓ. 21). The assertion at (ℓ. 39) indicates how this path is constructed in case the cyan state is found, and (ℓ. 45) indicates how the path is created from the path obtained in the recursive call.

Lemma CycleFoundHere (Section A.2, ℓ. 31-41) checks the reasoning that we sketched above. It was fairly non-trivial to convince DAFNY that this construction is correct, even though it is basic first-order reasoning without induction. Actually, the interaction with DAFNY at this point was quite inconvenient: DAFNY just tells that the proof does not go through, and the user has to find out, via numerous assertions, which facts DAFNY does or does not see. This small part of the proof would have been easier with an interactive theorem prover. But then it is extra rewarding to see (in 2 minutes):

```
Dafny program verifier finished with 22 verified, 0 errors
```

4 Conclusion

The main conclusion is that verification of recursive graph algorithms with automatic program verifiers is feasible. In particular, the functional correctness proof of NDFS with DAFNY was successful.

Success Factors. One of the success factors is the rich specification language of DAFNY. We heavily depended on set values (for sets of nodes with a particular colour) and sequence values (representing paths and cycles in the graph). We also made extensive use of quantifiers. We feel that every line of the specification is straightforward and understandable. Also, the recursive nature of the algorithm did not pose any problem.

Another success factor is the power of the SMT solver Z3, and the error reporting by DAFNY. In nearly all cases of a failed verification DAFNY came back with a line number and a diagnosis of the cause, on which the user could take action.

This was the first experience with DAFNY by the author, or with any automatic program verifier at all. Still it took only a couple of weeks to finish the complete proof. Here it should be noted that the author was already familiar with the details of the NDFS algorithm, and also with interactive theorem provers.

Finally, the proof strategy to split local invariants on colours from inductive arguments on paths helped to structure the proof. These invariants contribute to the global understanding of the NDFS algorithm. Also, the modular approach was essential to build up the specification incrementally, even though DAFNY does not provide extra support for specification refinement. But also it was necessary to keep the verification task manageable.

Useful Extensions to DAFNY. There are still a few issues where DAFNY could be improved to be even more useful. The complete verification takes about 2 minutes, which is fine. However, when the user checks intermediate attempts frequently, 2 minutes imply a considerable slowdown. But even worse, DAFNY (or rather Z3) chokes on failed proof attempts: DAFNY simply does not come back at all within a reasonable amount of time. This was the main reason to follow an incremental approach. Maybe the IDE interface to DAFNY would have better supported an incremental approach.

There are also two reasons why the specification has increased more than necessary. First, many invariants are repeated six times: in both while-loops, and before and after each recursive procedure. This could be mitigated by allowing an invariant keyword for recursive functions. A more drastic solution would be to generate invariants, possibly guided by some hints. For example, specify once hint types(G); instead of six times as in Section A.4, A.5.

The other extension on the wish list is exceptions. Several lines in the plain code (Figure 1) just handle return values. A more natural coding would use exceptions, as illustrated in (Figure 7). This is probably a non-trivial extension to the verification condition generator in DAFNY.

Finally, SMT solving for full first-order logic is necessarily incomplete. So, when DAFNY reports that an assertion at some line number fails, that assertion may hold or not. No further diagnostic information is given. At one place we struggled hard to come up with the three intermediate assertions to convince DAFNY, cf. CycleFoundHere in (Section A.2, ℓ. 38-40). It would be nice if the user had the possibility to fall back on an interactive proof session to deal with such cases, in order to avoid blind guessing.

Perspectives for Future Work. It is now possible to easily play with variants of NDFS, for instance those introduced by [5]. After submission of the paper, the author modified the code and proof in a couple of hours to the 2-bit version of [13], basically by replacing the pink colour by a ghost variable OnStack. The basic setup might also be reused to automate the verification of other DFS algorithms, e.g. SCC-based algorithms [9]. A more challenging assignment would be to include partial-order reduction, the LTL-to-Büchi translation, or the operational semantics of a modeling language. It is not clear that these tasks are in the scope of an automatic program verifier right now.

The most useful extension would be the application to parallel graph algorithms, like the parallel NDFS in [8]. This would require a program verifier for multi-threaded programs that synchronize by reading and writing colours on a shared graph. Such a tool would help researchers in developing parallel graph algorithms, especially when small input graphs could be generated as counter examples for faulty programs.

Acknowledgement. The author is grateful to the organisers and participants of Dagstuhl Seminar 14171 [1] in April 2014 on Software Verification System benchmarks, which initiated this research. In particular, the author is thankful to Rustan Leino for creating DAFNY, and supporting the author during and after the workshop. The reviewers of this paper provided several useful suggestions to improve the presentation.

References

1. Beyer, D., Huisman, M., Klebanov, V., Monahan, R.: Evaluating Software Verification Systems: Benchmarks and Competitions (Dagstuhl Reports 14171). Dagstuhl Reports 4(4), 1–19 (2014)
2. Courcoubetis, C., Vardi, M.Y., Wolper, P., Yannakakis, M.: Memory-Efficient Algorithms for the Verification of Temporal Properties. Formal Methods in System Design 1(2/3), 275–288 (1992)
3. de Moura, L.M., Bjørner, N.: Z3: an efficient SMT solver. In: Ramakrishnan, C.R., Rehof, J. (eds.) TACAS 2008. LNCS, vol. 4963, pp. 337–340. Springer, Heidelberg (2008)
4. Esparza, J., Lammich, P., Neumann, R., Nipkow, T., Schimpf, A., Smaus, J.-G.: A fully verified executable LTL model checker. In: Sharygina, N., Veith, H. (eds.) CAV 2013. LNCS, vol. 8044, pp. 463–478. Springer, Heidelberg (2013)
5. Gaiser, A., Schwoon, S.: Comparison of Algorithms for Checking Emptiness on Büchi Automata. CoRR, abs/0910.3766 (2009)
6. Gava, F., Fortin, J., Guedj, M.: Deductive verification of state-space algorithms. In: Johnsen, E.B., Petre, L. (eds.) IFM 2013. LNCS, vol. 7940, pp. 124–138. Springer, Heidelberg (2013)
7. Holzmann, G.J., Peled, D., Yannakakis, M.: On Nested Depth First Search. In: The Spin Verification System, pp. 23–32. American Mathematical Society (1996)
8. Laarman, A.W., Langerak, R., van de Pol, J.C., Weber, M., Wijs, A.: Multi-Core Nested Depth-First Search. In: Bultan, T., Hsiung, P.-A. (eds.) ATVA 2011. LNCS, vol. 6996, pp. 321–335. Springer, Heidelberg (2011)
9. Lammich, P.: Verified efficient implementation of Gabow's strongly connected component algorithm. In: Klein, G., Gamboa, R. (eds.) ITP 2014. LNCS, vol. 8558, pp. 325–340. Springer, Heidelberg (2014)
10. Leino, K.R.M.: Dafny: An automatic program verifier for functional correctness. In: Clarke, E.M., Voronkov, A. (eds.) LPAR-16 2010. LNCS, vol. 6355, pp. 348–370. Springer, Heidelberg (2010)
11. Pottier, F.: Depth-first search and strong connectivity in Coq. Journées Francophones des Langages Applicatifs (JFLA 2015) (January 2015)
12. Ray, S., Matthews, J., Tuttle, M.: Certifying compositional model checking algorithms in ACL2. In: IW on ACL2 Theorem Prover and its Applications (2003)
13. Schwoon, S., Esparza, J.: A note on on-the-fly verification algorithms. In: Halbwachs, N., Zuck, L.D. (eds.) TACAS 2005. LNCS, vol. 3440, pp. 174–190. Springer, Heidelberg (2005)
14. Sprenger, C.: A verified model checker for the modal μ-calculus in Coq. In: Steffen, B. (ed.) TACAS 1998. LNCS, vol. 1384, pp. 167–183. Springer, Heidelberg (1998)
15. Sun, J., Liu, Y., Cheng, B.: Model checking a model checker: A code contract combined approach. In: Dong, J.S., Zhu, H. (eds.) ICFEM 2010. LNCS, vol. 6447, pp. 518–533. Springer, Heidelberg (2010)
16. Vardi, M.Y., Wolper, P.: An automata-theoretic approach to automatic program verification. In: LICS, pp. 332–344. Cambridge (1986)

A   Full NDFS Proof in Dafny

This section contains the full specification of the NDFS algorithm and is completely verified with DAFNY. The verification was run with DAFNY version 1.8.2.10419 on a Macbook 2.7 GHz Intel Core i7 processor with 8GB RAM under MacOS 10.10.1 and Mono version 3.2.5. The verification time varies around 2 minutes. The code in this section has been typeset with dafny.sty by Rustan Leino, obtained from https://searchcode.com/codesearch/view/28108731/.

A.1   Basic Definitions

```
1   datatype Color = white | cyan | blue | pink | red;
2
3   class Node {
4     var next: seq⟨Node⟩;
5     var accepting: bool;
6     var color1: Color;
7     var color2: Color;
8   }
9
10  ghost var G: set⟨Node⟩;
11
12  predicate graph(G: set⟨Node⟩)
13    reads G;
14  { ∀ m • m ∈ G ⟹ (m ≠ null ∧ ∀ n • n ∈ m.next ⟹ n ∈ G) }
15
16  predicate types(G: set⟨Node⟩)
17    reads G; requires graph(G);
18  { ∀ m • m ∈ G ⟹
19      m.color1 ∈ {white, cyan, blue}
20      ∧ m.color2 ∈ {white, pink, red}}
21
22  function Cyan(G: set⟨Node⟩): set⟨Node⟩
23    reads G; requires graph(G);
24  { set n | n ∈ G ∧ n.color1 = cyan • n }
25
26  function Blue(G: set⟨Node⟩): set⟨Node⟩
27    reads G; requires graph(G);
28  { set n | n ∈ G ∧ n.color1 = blue • n }
29
30  function Pink(G: set⟨Node⟩): set⟨Node⟩
31    reads G; requires graph(G);
32  { set n | n ∈ G ∧ n.color2 = pink • n }
33
34  function Red(G: set⟨Node⟩): set⟨Node⟩
35    reads G; requires graph(G);
36  { set n | n ∈ G ∧ n.color2 = red • n }
37
38  predicate Next(G: set⟨Node⟩,X: set⟨Node⟩,Y: set⟨Node⟩)
39    reads G; requires graph(G);
40  { ∀ n,i • n ∈ G ∧ 0 ≤ i < |n.next| ⟹ ( n ∈ X ⟹ n.next[i] ∈ Y ) }
41
42  function Path(G: set⟨Node⟩,x: Node,y: Node,p: seq⟨Node⟩): bool
43    reads G; requires graph(G);
44  { |p| > 0 ∧ p[0] = x ∧ p[|p|−1] = y
45    ∧ ∀ i • 0 ≤ i < |p|−1 ⟹ p[i] ∈ G ∧ p[i+1] ∈ p[i].next }
46
47  function Cycle(G: set⟨Node⟩,x: Node,y: Node,p: seq⟨Node⟩,q: seq⟨Node⟩): bool
48    reads G; requires graph(G);
49  { Path(G,x,y,p) ∧ Path(G,y,y,q) ∧ |q| > 1 ∧ y.accepting }
```

A.2   Auxiliary Lemmas on Paths and Cycles

```
1    function KeyInvariant(G:set⟨Node⟩):bool
2       reads G; requires graph(G);
3    { ∀ s • s ∈ Blue(G) ∧ s.accepting ⟹ ¬∃ p • |p| > 1 ∧ Path(G,s,s,p) }
4
5    function NoPath(G:set⟨Node⟩,s:Node,t:Node,p:seq⟨Node⟩):bool
6       reads G; requires graph(G);
7       requires Next(G,Red(G),Red(G));
8       requires Next(G,Red(G),G − Cyan(G));
9       requires s ∈ Red(G);
10      requires t ∈ Cyan(G);
11      ensures NoPath(G,s,t,p);
12      ensures |p| > 1 ⟹ ¬Path(G,s,t,p);
13   { |p| > 1 ∧ p[0] = s ∧ p[1] ∈ p[0].next ⟹ NoPath(G,p[1],t,p[1..]) }
14
15   function NoCycle(G:set⟨Node⟩,root:Node,s:Node,p:seq⟨Node⟩,q:seq⟨Node⟩):bool
16      reads G; requires graph(G);
17      requires root ∈ Blue(G);
18      requires Next(G,Blue(G),Blue(G));
19      requires KeyInvariant(G);
20      ensures ¬Cycle(G,root,s,p,q);
21   { |p| > 1 ∧ p[0] = root ∧ p[1] ∈ p[0].next ⟹ NoCycle(G,p[1],s,p[1..],q) }
22
23   lemma NextCyan(G:set⟨Node⟩,s:Node,t:Node)
24      requires graph(G);
25      requires s ∈ G;
26      requires t ∈ s.next;
27      requires ∀ c • c ∈ Cyan(G) ⟹ ∃ q • Path(G,c,s,q);
28      ensures ∀ c • c ∈ Cyan(G) ⟹ ∃ q • Path(G,c,t,q);
29   { assert ∀ c,p • Path(G,c,s,p) ⟹ Path(G,c,t,p+[t]); }
30
31   lemma CycleFoundHere(G:set⟨Node⟩,s:Node)
32      requires graph(G);
33      requires s ∈ G;
34      requires s.accepting;
35      requires ∃ c,p • c ∈ Cyan(G) ∧ Path(G,s,c,p) ∧ |p|>1;
36      requires ∀ c • c ∈ Cyan(G) ⟹ ∃ q • Path(G,c,s,q);
37      ensures ∃ p,q • Cycle(G,s,s,p,q);
38   { assert ∃ c,p,q • c ∈ Cyan(G) ∧ |p|>1 ∧ Path(G,s,c,p) ∧ Path(G,c,s,q);
39      assert ∀ c,p,q • Path(G,s,c,p) ∧ Path(G,c,s,q) ⟹ Path(G,s,s,p+q[1..]);
40      assert ∀ q • |q| > 1 ∧ Path(G,s,s,q) ⟹ Cycle(G,s,s,[s],q);
41   } // this was very hard to prove and rather sensitive..
```

A.3   Main Method and Correctness Statement

```
1    method ndfs(root:Node) returns (found:bool)
2       requires graph(G);
3       requires root ∈ G;
4       requires ∀ s • s ∈ G ⟹ s.color1 = s.color2 = white;
5       modifies G'color1, G'color2;
6       ensures found ⟹ (∃ a,p,q • Cycle(G,root,a,p,q));   // soundness
7       ensures (∃ s,p,q • Cycle(G,root,s,p,q)) ⟹ found;   // completeness
8    { found := dfsblue(root);
9       assert ¬found ⟹ ∀ s,p,q • NoCycle(G,root,s,p,q) ⟹ ¬Cycle(G,root,s,p,q);
10   }
```

A.4   Blue Search

```
 1  method dfsblue(s:Node) returns (found:bool)
 2    requires s ∈ G;
 3    requires graph(G);
 4    requires types(G);
 5    requires s.color1 = white;
 6    requires Next(G,Blue(G),Blue(G) ∪ Cyan(G));
 7    requires Next(G,Red(G),Red(G) ∪ Pink(G));
 8    requires Pink(G) = {};
 9    requires Red(G) ⊆ Blue(G);
10    requires KeyInvariant(G);
11    requires ∀ c • c ∈ Cyan(G) ⟹ ∃ p • Path(G,c,s,p);
12    modifies G'color1 , G'color2 ;
13    decreases G − Cyan(G);
14    ensures types(G);
15    ensures old(Blue(G)) ⊆ Blue(G);
16    ensures Next(G,Blue(G),Blue(G) ∪ Cyan(G));
17    ensures Next(G,Red(G),Red(G) ∪ Pink(G));
18    ensures ¬found ⟹ s ∈ Blue(G);
19    ensures ¬found ⟹ old(Cyan(G)) = Cyan(G);
20    ensures ¬found ⟹ Pink(G) = {};
21    ensures ¬found ⟹ Red(G) ⊆ Blue(G);
22    ensures found ⟹ (∃ a,p,q • Cycle(G,s,a,p,q));
23    ensures KeyInvariant(G);
24
25  { s.color1 := cyan;
26    assert Path(G,s,s,[s]);
27    var i := 0;
28    while (i < |s.next|)
29    invariant types(G);
30    invariant Cyan(G) = old(Cyan(G)) ∪ {s};
31    invariant Pink(G) = {};
32    invariant i ≤ |s.next|;
33    invariant ∀ j • 0 ≤ j < i ⟹ s.next[j] ∈ Blue(G) ∪ Cyan(G);
34    invariant old(Blue(G)) ⊆ Blue(G);
35    invariant Next(G,Blue(G),Blue(G) ∪ Cyan(G));
36    invariant Next(G,Red(G),Red(G) ∪ Pink(G));
37    invariant Red(G) ⊆ Blue(G);
38    invariant KeyInvariant(G);
39
40    { var t := s.next[i];
41      i := i+1;
42      if (t.color1 = white)
43      { NextCyan(G,s,t);
44        found := dfsblue(t);
45        if (found) {
46          assert ∀ a,p,q • Cycle(G,t,a,p,q) ⟹ Cycle(G,s,a,[s]+p,q);
47          return;
48        }
49      }
50    }
51    if (s.accepting)
52    { assert s ∉ Pink(G);
53      found := dfsred(s,s);
54      if (found) {
55        CycleFoundHere(G,s);
56        return;
57      }
58      assert ∀ p • NoPath(G,s,s,p);
59    }
60    s.color1 := blue;
61    return false;
62  }
```

A.5   Red Search

```
 1   method dfsred(s:Node, ghost root:Node) returns (found:bool)
 2     requires graph(G);
 3     requires types(G);
 4     requires s ∈ G;
 5     requires root ∈ G;
 6     requires s.color2 = white;
 7     requires s = root ∨ s.color1 = blue;
 8     requires Next(G,Blue(G) ∪ {root},Blue(G) ∪ Cyan(G));
 9     requires Next(G,Red(G),Red(G) ∪ Pink(G));
10     requires Red(G) ⊆ Blue(G) ∪ {root};
11     requires Next(G,Red(G),G − Cyan(G));
12     modifies G'color2;
13     decreases G − Pink(G);
14     ensures types(G);
15     ensures ¬found ⟹ s ∈ Red(G);
16     ensures ¬found ⟹ old(Pink(G)) = Pink(G);
17     ensures old(Red(G)) ⊆ Red(G);
18     ensures Next(G,Red(G),Red(G) ∪ Pink(G));
19     ensures Red(G) ⊆ Blue(G) ∪ {root};
20     ensures Next(G,Red(G),G − Cyan(G));
21     ensures found ⟹ ∃ p,c • |p| > 1 ∧ c ∈ Cyan(G) ∧ Path(G,s,c,p);
22
23   { s.color2 := pink;
24     var i := 0;
25     while (i < |s.next|)
26     invariant types(G);
27     invariant old(Red(G)) ⊆ Red(G);
28     invariant i ≤ |s.next|;
29     invariant ∀ j • 0 ≤ j < i ⟹ s.next[j] ∈ Red(G) ∪ Pink(G);
30     invariant Next(G,Red(G),Red(G) ∪ Pink(G));
31     invariant Pink(G) = old(Pink(G)) ∪ {s};
32     invariant Red(G) ⊆ Blue(G) ∪ {root};
33     invariant Next(G,Red(G),G − Cyan(G));
34     invariant ∀ j • 0 ≤ j < i ⟹ s.next[j] ∈ G − Cyan(G);
35
36     { var t := s.next[i];
37       i := i+1;
38       if (t.color1 = cyan) {
39         assert Path(G,s,t,[s,t]);
40         return true;
41       }
42       if (t.color2 = white)
43       { found := dfsred(t,root);
44         if (found) {
45           assert ∀ p,c • Path(G,t,c,p) ⟹ Path(G,s,c,[s]+p);
46           return;
47         }
48       }
49     }
50     s.color2 := red;
51     return false;
52   }
```

On the Formal Verification of Optical Quantum Gates in HOL

Mohamed Yousri Mahmoud[1]([⊠]), Prakash Panangaden[2], and Sofiène Tahar[1]

[1] Electrical and Computer Engineering Deptartment, Concordia University,
Montreal, Canada
{mo_solim,tahar}@ece.concordia.ca
http://hvg.ece.concordia.ca
[2] Computer Science Department, Mcgill University,
Montreal, Canada
prakash@cs.mcgill.ca

Abstract. Quantum computers are expected to handle hard computational problems and provide unbreakable security protocols. Among different quantum computer implementations, those based on quantum optics and nuclear magnetic resonance show good advancement in building large scale machines. However, the involvement of optical and nuclear techniques makes their development very critical. This motivates us to apply formal techniques, in particular theorem proving, in quantum circuits analysis. In this work, we present the formalization of multi-inputs/multi-outputs quantum gates (technically called multi-modes optical circuits). This requires the implementation of tensor product over complex-valued functions. Firstly, we build a formal model of single optical beams and then extend it to cover circuits of multi optical beams, with the help of the developed tensor product algebra. As an application, we formally verify the behavior of the optical quantum CNOT gate and Mach-Zehnder interferometer.

Keywords: Quantum computing · Multi-modes · Tensor product · CNOT gate · Mach-Zehnder · Theorm proving · HOL light

1 Introduction

Quantum computers implemnt algorithms that would outperform classical machines, in particular for solving hard problems: a well known example is Shor's algorithm for integer factorization [10]. The new machine capabilities also offer powerful unbreakable security systems, e.g., [2]. Similar to classical machines, quantum ones consist of a new notion of a bit, called quantum bit (abbreviated as *qbit*), and a set of universal quantum gates, e.g., the Controlled NOT (the quantum counterpart of the classical NOT gate) [18]. The implementation of the quantum machine has been carried out in small scales using different means and technologies, such as ion traps [6] and quantum dots [11]. Many efforts are being invested for large scale machines [9], where optical circuits with the help of *Nuclear Magnetic Resonance* [20] and *Optical Nuclear Coupling* [7] are more reliable to implement such large scale computers.

© Springer International Publishing Switzerland 2015
M. Núñez and M. Güdemann (Eds.): FMICS 2015, LNCS 9128, pp. 198–211, 2015.
DOI: 10.1007/978-3-319-19458-5_13

The analysis and verification of this kind of optical quantum circuits and gates is very critical and faces some difficulties since traditional analysis techniques are ineffective. For instance, it has been proved that the simulation of a single time instance of a quantum system requires solving an exponential number of differential equations [4]. This motivates us to apply formal methods in this area, since the latter has enabled significant advancements took place in many engineering areas, e.g., analog systems designs [22], information theory [17], and sensor networks [3].

Recently, some developments for the formal verification of quantum optics has been conducted in higher-order logic (HOL) theorem proving [12] [14]. The main reason behind the choice of HOL is because of the high expressiveness it offers. Definitely, this comes at the expense of the full automation that HOL provers do not offer. However, HOL theorem proving still provides a good compromise compared to other automated formal techniques, such as model checking [1], that are unable to deal with the details of quantum systems. The application of abstraction techniques is not of much help as it would implicitly converge a quantum system to a classical one [21]. Frst-order logic is not suitable either since in most of the targeted quantum definitions and theorems there are quantifications over functions and predicates.

Based on [14], the formal model of one of the quantum computer gates, namely the optical flip gate, has been developed along with its verification [13]. However, the existing work is limited to single-input/single-output optical systems, which is technically called the single-mode optical beams theory. In this paper, we tackle the formalization of tensor product for complex-valued functions in order to allow the analysis of multi-inputs/multi-outputs systems, which is technically called multi-mode optical beams theory. As an application, we apply the multi-mode theory in the analysis of two quantum optical circuits: the Mach-Zehnder interferometer [16] and the Controlled NOT gate [19]. The former is a common circuit in quantum computing and quantum optics. The latter is a larger circuit, which is one of the universal gates of quantum computers. This shows the effectiveness of formal methods, especially in the case of complicated circuits with multiple connections. The verification of the two circuits is handled by two tactics that automatize most of the process, which removes a lot of burden from the interactive user, typically a system designer.

The rest of the paper is organized as follows: Section 2 briefly summarizes some basics of quantum optics. Section 3 deals with the formalization of L^2 space and single-mode theory. Section 4 contains the formalization of multi-mode and tensor product. Then, Section 5 discusses the formalization of the CNOT gate and the Mach-Zehnder interferometer and their verification, along with more elaboration about the tactics involved. Finally, we conclude the paper in Section 6 and provide hints to future work.

Note: the whole formalization presented here is implemented using the HOL Light theorem prover, and is freely available at [15].

2   Background

Any physical system has a mathematical model that describes its *state*. In classical physics, a system state can be deterministically evaluated at any time. However, in quantum theory, a system state has a probabilistic nature. In other words, a *quantum state* of a system, written as $|\psi\rangle$ [5], acts as a probability density function. Accordingly, the system state should satisfy the normalization condition (i.e., its integration over the real line is equal to one). In particular, in quantum optics theory, a state of an optical beam $\psi(q)$ is of type *real* $\rightarrow$ *complex* and satisfy the following condition:

$$\int_{-\infty}^{\infty} \psi^*(q)\ \psi(q)dq = 1 \qquad (1)$$

where q, in some physics interpretations, refers to the electric charges inside the optical beam [16].

A collection of such quantum states forms an inner product space, equipped with the Lebesgue integral as the inner product function. Formally, the inner product of two quantum states f and g is denoted as $\langle f|g\rangle$, and it is equal to $\int_{-\infty}^{\infty} f^*(q)\ g(q)dq$. A major consequence of this mathematical formalization of an optical beam is the consideration of light as a stream of particles, called photons, instead of the ray or wave nature as was believe in the classical theory.

Since quantum states form a linear function space, then there exists an infinite basis that spans such a space. In case of an optical beam, so-called *fock states* form the basis states, i.e., any $|\psi\rangle$ can be written as follows:

$$|\psi\rangle = \sum_n c_n |n\rangle$$

where c_n's are complex numbers such that $\sum_n c_n = 1$, and $|n\rangle$ is a fock state representing the existence of n photons inside the optical beam. Note that $|0\rangle$ is called the vacuum state, and describes the case of zero photons.

For a fock state, we are interested in a number of operations. An operator $\hat{a}$ is called the *annihilation* operator and another operator written $\hat{a}^\dagger$ is called the *creation* operator. These operators are adjoints of each other, i.e., $\langle \hat{a}\ n_1|n_2\rangle = \langle n_1|\hat{a}^\dagger\ n_2\rangle$, and their commutation is equal to 1, i.e., $\hat{a} ** a^\dagger - \hat{a}^\dagger ** \hat{a} = I$ (note that I is the unity function, and the multiplication $**$ is point-wise multiplication). The effect of these operators on fock states is described as follows:

$$\hat{a}|n\rangle = \sqrt{n}\,|n-1\rangle \ \text{ and } \ \hat{a}^\dagger|n\rangle = \sqrt{n+1}\,|n+1\rangle. \qquad (2)$$

Another important operator is the *number operator* $\hat{N} = \hat{a}^\dagger ** \hat{a}$, which returns the number of photons:

$$\hat{N}|n\rangle = n * |n\rangle$$

This shows that fock states are eigenvectors of the number operator.

Based on photon number operator, we can define the energy operator $\hat{H} = \frac{1}{2}\hbar\omega(\hat{N}+I)$, where ω is called the mode resonance frequency and $\hbar$ is the planck constant. The operator returns the amount of energy in a light beam. This formalization of energy inside an optical beam leads to the existence of energy in the vacuum state, i.e., in the absence of photons, the main source of energy in a beam. This is one of the interesting results in the quantum paradigm that does not have a classical counterpart.

All the above mentioned definitions, formulas and equations form the single-mode optical beams theory. This theory is suitable as long as we are dealing with systems that involve no more than one single beam. In order to tackle more general systems with multiple optical beams, we should consider the theory of multi-modes. The core idea is how to consider two independent optical beams (or particles), given that one has the individual physical description of each. For this purpose, we utilize the mathematical tool of tensor product. Let us assume the existence of two beams with quantum states $|\psi_1\rangle$ and $|\psi_2\rangle$, then we have a new quantum state $|\psi_1 \otimes \psi_2\rangle$ that describes both beams simultaneously. The new state satisfies the following properties:

$$|c * \psi_1 \otimes \psi_2\rangle = c * |\psi_1 \otimes \psi_2\rangle \text{ and}$$

$$|\psi_1 + \psi_2 \otimes \psi_3\rangle = |\psi_1 \otimes \psi_3\rangle + |\psi_2 \otimes \psi_3\rangle$$

For this kind of states, we need to develop suitable operators based on the existing ones. For instance, for two annihilation operators we will have a new tensor product operator $\hat{a}_1 \otimes \hat{a}_2$, where subscripts refer to the modes to which they belong. This operator when it is applied to $|\psi_1 \otimes \psi_2\rangle$, results in $|\hat{a}_1\psi_1 \otimes \hat{a}_2\psi_2\rangle$. It also satisfies similar properties such as tensor product of states, e.g., $(\hat{a}_1^\dagger + \hat{a}_1) \otimes \hat{a}_2^\dagger = \hat{a}_1^\dagger \otimes \hat{a}_2^\dagger + \hat{a}_1 \otimes \hat{a}_2^\dagger$.

In the following sections, we will present the formal aspects of the theories presented in Section 2, where we elaborate more on the details of the higher-order logic implementation.

3   Single-Mode Formalization

As we described in Section 2, the set of quantum states lies in the inner product space of square Lebesgue integrable functions. In [14], the quantum states space was defined axiomatically as an inner product space of the functions of type A $\rightarrow$ complex. In this formalization, we instantiate A to be real, since the electric charge q is of type real. Thus, we define a new type bqs : real $\rightarrow$ complex which stands for beam quantum state. Based on the new type, we can then define the notion of space of complex-valued square integrable functions L^2.

We start by formally defining the notion of the set of square integrable complex-valued functions, namely sq_integrable:

Definition 1.
new_specification ["sq_integrable"]
  ∀f. f ∈ sq_integrable ⇔
1   f complex_measurable_on (: real) ∧
2   (λx. ||f x|| ^{2}) real_integrable_on (: real)

Since we are dealing with complex-valued functions then the square of a function f means the multiplication of f(x) by its conjugate f(x)*. This is equivalent to the norm square of f(x), as presented in Line 2. There is another mandatory condition to form a subspace of these functions, which is the complex measurability [8]:

Definition 2.
f complex_measurable_on s ⇔
  (λx. Re (f x)) real_measurable_on s ∧
    (λx.Im (f x)) real_measurable_on s

Note here that the measurability and integrability are over the whole real line (i.e., from $-\infty$ to ∞). We refer the reader to [8], where more information about measure theory can be found. Next, we define the inner product function over the elements of space sq_integrable as follows:

Definition 3.
r_inprod f g =
1   complex(real_integral (: real) (λx : real. Re((f x)* * (g x))),
2   real_integral (: real) (λx.Im ((f x)* * (g x))))

The above definition states that the inner product of two square integrable functions f and g is a complex value, whose real part is the real integral of the real part of f * g (see Line 1), and its imaginary part is the real integral of the imaginary part of f * g (see Line 2).

Now, we move to the most important step, namely to prove that these definitions form a linear space and the associated r_inprod function is its inner product. Formally, we need to prove the following set of properties according to [12]:

Theorem 1.
is_cfun_subspace sq_integrable ∧ ∀x. x ∈ sq_integrable ⇒
real (r_inprod x x) ∧ 0 ≤ real_of_complex (r_inprod x x) ∧
(r_inprod x x = Cx(0) ⇔ x = cfun_zero) ∧
∀y. y ∈ sq_integrable ⇒ cnj (r$_i$nprod y x) = r_inprod x y ∧
(∀a. r_inprod x (a%y) = a * (r_inprod x y)) ∧
∀z. z ∈ sq_integrable ⇒ r_inprod (x + y) z = r_inprod x z + r_inprod y z

where cfun_zero is a function that always returns zero regardless of the input parameter, % refers to scalar multiplication.

The proof details of above theorem is complex and outside the scope of the paper. We refer interested readers to [15] for proof scripts, where they can find more details. According to the above shown properties, we can prove the following result, which is a conjunction of them:

Theorem 2.
is_inner_space (sq_integrable, r_inprod)

Now, we have all ingredients to formally implement the single-mode (see Section 2):

Definition 4.
is_sm sm $\Leftrightarrow 0 < $ w sm $\wedge$
1   is_hermitian(sq_integrable, r_inprod) (anh sm)(cr sm)
2   $\wedge$ anh sm com cr sm $= I \wedge$ is_qst (vac sm)
3   is_eigen_pair (h sm) (vac sm, Cx(planck $* \frac{(w\ sm)}{2}$))

where a single-mode **sm** consists of the creator **cr**, annihilator **anh**, resonance frequency **w** and vacuum state **vac**. Line 1 assumes the adjointness between creator and annihilator, where is_hermitian is defined as follows:

Definition 5.
is_hermitian $(s, inprod)$ op$_1$ op$_2$ $\Leftrightarrow$
   is_inner_space $(s, inprod) \Rightarrow$
      $\forall x\ y.$ inprod x (op$_2$ y) = inprod (op$_1$ x) y

Line 2 in Definition 4 assumes the commutation between the same operators and Line 3 assumes the relation between the vacuum state and the energy operator, where is_eigen_pair is defined as follows:

Definition 6.
is_eigen_pair op $(v, \mu) \Leftrightarrow$
   op v $= \mu\%$ v $\wedge$ (v $\neq$ cfun_zero)

Recall that a single-mode field at a fock state $|n\rangle$ means that the light stream contains exactly n photons. Such states are quite important since they form the basis of the single-mode quantum states space. Accordingly, we define fock states as follows:

Definition 7.
fock sm 0 = vac sm $\wedge$
   fock sm (SUC n) = get_qst(cr sm (fock sm n))

where get_qst f $= \sqrt{\text{r\_inprod f f}}\ \%$ f, i.e., returns the normalized version of a square integrable function, which is typically a quantum state.

For the given definition of the fock state, we prove the effect of creator and annihilator on fock states as presented in Section 2:

Theorem 3.
$\forall n$ sm.is_sm sm $\Rightarrow$
   (cr sm) (fock sm n) = Cx(sqrt((SUC n)))%fock sm (SUC n) $\wedge$
   $\Rightarrow$ (anhhsm) (fock sm (SUC n)) = $\sqrt{\text{SUC n}}\ \%$ fock sm n

In the next section, we will present the multi-mode formalization which is the main tool, in addition to single-mode, to formally verify the CNOT gate and the Mach-Zehnder interferometer.

4   Multi-Mode Formalization

The core idea of the Multi-Mode formalization is based on the development of the tensor product between states and operators. Before we present the general definition of quantum states tensor product, we will show an example of the tensor product of only two states. Given a quantum state $|n_1\rangle$ of an optical beam, in one of the interpretations of quantum mechanics, this state (i.e., the complex valued functions) is a probability density function which provides the probability of the number of photons inside the optical beam. Now, if we have another beam with state $|n_2\rangle$, the function that describes the joint probability of the two beams is the point-wise multiplication of $|n_1\rangle$ and $|n_2\rangle$. Hence, we define the tensor product of two quantum states as follows: $\lambda y_1\ y_2.\ |n_1\rangle\ y_1 * |n_1\rangle\ y_2$. To generalize for n beams, we define the tensor product recursively as follows:

Definition 8.
tensor 0 (modes : bqs^N) = K(Cx(1)) $\wedge$
   tensor (SUC n) (modes) =
      (λy : A^N.((tensor n modes) y) $*$ (modes\$(SUC n)) (y\$(SUC n)))

where modes is a vector of size n that contains n modes. The base case of the zero modes is a trivial case; it only guarantees a terminating definition. We then define the tensor product of operators as follows:

Definition 9.
is_tensor(tens : cops^N $\rightarrow$ (real^N $\rightarrow$ complex) $\rightarrow$ (real^N $\rightarrow$ complex)) $\Rightarrow$
   $\forall$(ops : (bqs $\rightarrow$ bqs)^N) (modes : bqs^N) n. is_linear_cop (tens ops)$\wedge$
   tens ops (tensor n modes) = tensor n(lambda i.(ops\$i) (modes\$i))

where ops is a vector of operators defined on the single-modes, and tens ops is the tensor product. Note that the resulting new operator is only applicable to the tensor product of states. That is why we define it in a predicate form in order to restrict its functionality. For this definition, we prove the following crucial property of the operators tensor product, associativity:

Theorem 4.
$\forall$ ten ops1 ops2 n modes.
   is_tensor ten $\Rightarrow$ ten ops2(ten ops1 (tensor nmodes)) =
   ten ((λ i. (ops2\$i) o (ops1\$i))) (tensor n modes)

where o refers to function composition.

As we will see later, an optical quantum circuit accepts single-modes as inputs, however, the circuit operation itself runs in multi-mode. Thus, we need to develop a function to embed (or express) a single-mode operator in a multi-mode fashion. For this purpose, we define the following function:

Definition 10.
pos (tens : cops^N $\rightarrow$ (A^N $\rightarrow$ complex) $\rightarrow$ (A^N $\rightarrow$ complex)) (op : cops) m =
   tens (lambda i. if i = m then op else I)

The concept of pos (or positioning) is to place a given operator in a specific mode (based on its order in the input list) and leave the other modes with the identity operator. Now, we will utilize the development of multi-mode to define a very important optical element, of which many quantum circuits are built.

Beam Splitter in Multi-Mode

A beam splitter is a device that takes a beam of light and partly transmits it and partly reflects it, thus splitting the beam into two beams. The remarkable feature of quantum mechanics is that a *single photon* can be split by a beam splitter.

In its standard definition, a beam splitter consists of two-input/two output ports. We can recognize each port (or optical mode) by the creator and annihilator operators, as shown Figure 1:

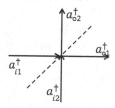

Fig. 1. Beam Splitter- Standard Inputs and Outputs

The beam splitter then relates input modes with the output modes according to the following matrix representation:

$$\begin{pmatrix} \hat{a}_{o1}^{\dagger} \otimes I \\ I \otimes \hat{a}_{o2}^{\dagger} \end{pmatrix} = \begin{pmatrix} \mathbf{T}' & \mathbf{R} \\ \mathbf{R}' & \mathbf{T} \end{pmatrix} \begin{pmatrix} \hat{a}_{i1}^{\dagger} \otimes I \\ I \otimes \hat{a}_{i2}^{\dagger} \end{pmatrix} \tag{3}$$

with the following relations between the coefficients :

$$|\mathbf{R}'| = |\mathbf{R}|, \ |\mathbf{T}'| = |\mathbf{T}|, \ |\mathbf{R}|^2 + |\mathbf{T}|^2 = 1,$$

$$\mathbf{R}^*\mathbf{T}' + \mathbf{R}'\mathbf{T}^* = 0, \ \text{and} \ \mathbf{R}^*\mathbf{T} + \mathbf{R}'\mathbf{T}'^* = 0.$$

These coefficients are of type complex and represent the reflectivity and transitivity in some sense. We now have the quantum mechanical description of the beam splitter, and thus we can develop its formal version as follows:

Definition 11.

```
1 is_beam_splitter(p1, p2, p3, p4, ten, i1, m1, i2, m2, o1, m3, o2, m4) ⇔
2    is_sm i1 ∧ is_sm i2 ∧ is_sm o1 ∧ is_sm o2
3    ∧ w i1 = w i2 ∧ w i2 = w o1 ∧ w o1 = w o2 ∧
4    vac i1 = vac i2 ∧ vac i2 = vac o1 ∧ vac o1 = vac o2 ∧
5    pos ten (cr i1) m1 = p1*% pos ten (cr o1) m3 + p2*% pos ten (cr o2) m4
6    pos ten (cr i2) m2 = p3*% pos ten (cr o1) m3 + p4*% pos ten (cr o2) m4
```

Note that the formal definition of beam splitters relates the inputs operators in terms of the outputs operators (see Line 5 and Line 6), to the contrary of the theoretical definitions presented earlier in Equation (3): This form is practical for the analysis of the circuits, as we will see later, since the goal is to generate the output states from the input states. Thus, the parameters {p1,p2,p3,p4} are the inverse of the matrix presented before. In Line 1, the parameters {m1,m2,m3,m4} define the order of each mode in the whole circuit. In the case of a circuit of only two inputs/two outputs, the possible values of these parameters are 1 and 2. Line 2 and Line 3 ensure that the four modes are proper single modes, and working with the same frequency and vacuum state (i.e., the state of zero photons).

Now, we have the full tools to tackle any circuit that consists of beam splitters, and generate the corresponding output of this circuit.

5   Quantum Optical CNOT Gate

In this section, we will tackle the formalization of the universal quantum CNOT gate. Before this step, we will study the formalization of a simpler circuit, namely *Mach-Zehnder* Interferometer, in order to illustrate how the mathematics work in these kind of circuits, which also applies for the larger circuits, e.g., the CNOT gate.

5.1   Mach-Zehnder Verification

The most interesting use of the beam splitter is to combine it with mirrors that reflect the incident photon. The configuration shown in Figure 2 is called a *Mach-Zehnder* Interferometer. There are two beam splitters labelled BS_1 and BS_2. The grey objects shown are mirrors. The photon is shown as a wavy line. The photon incident at BS_1 is split in the manner we have described above, where each beam splitter is working according the matrix $\frac{1}{\sqrt{2}} \begin{pmatrix} -i & 1 \\ -1 & i \end{pmatrix}$, and each mirror produces phase shifts of i over creation operators.

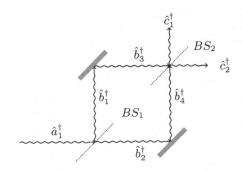

Fig. 2. Mach-Zehnder Interferometer- Inputs and Outputs

Accordingly, we have the following transformation between the different creations operators:

$$\mathbf{a}_1^\dagger = \tfrac{1}{\sqrt{2}}(i\mathbf{b}_1^\dagger + \mathbf{b}_2^\dagger)$$
$$\mathbf{b}_1^\dagger = i\mathbf{b}_3^\dagger$$
$$\mathbf{b}_2^\dagger = i\mathbf{b}_4^\dagger$$
$$\mathbf{b3}_1^\dagger = \tfrac{1}{\sqrt{2}}(i\mathbf{c}_1^\dagger + \mathbf{c}_2^\dagger)$$
$$\mathbf{b4}_1^\dagger = \tfrac{1}{\sqrt{2}}(\mathbf{c}_1^\dagger + i\mathbf{c}_2^\dagger)$$

Given that only one photon incidents at the input mode $\mathbf{a}_1^\dagger$ (see Figure 2), then the state of the input modes is $|1\rangle \otimes |0\rangle$. According to Equation (2), this is equal to $\mathbf{a}_1^\dagger \otimes I(|0\rangle \otimes |0\rangle)$. Carrying out the above transformations of the field operators all the way to the end, the output modes state becomes equal to $i\mathbf{c}_1^\dagger \otimes I(|0\rangle \otimes |0\rangle)$, i.e., the photon will leave from the vertical port of BS_2 (see Figure 2). In the following, we see how to formally prove this result along with the formal definition of the Mach-Zehnder interferometer.

Before we present the theorem that verifies the above result, we have to define the notion of mirror, similar to what we have for the beam splitters:

Definition 12.
mirror(ten, i1, m1, o1, m2) $\Leftrightarrow$
  pos ten(cr i1) m1 = i % pos ten (cr o1) m2

The following theorem shows the formal structure of the above circuit, and proves that if we receive a photon at the horizontal input of the interferometer, then it will leave at the vertical output of the interferometer:

Theorem 5.
$\forall$a b d.
  is_tensor ten$\wedge$
1 is_beam_splitter $(-\sqrt{\tfrac{1}{2}} * ii, \sqrt{\tfrac{1}{2}}), -\sqrt{\tfrac{1}{2}}, \sqrt{\tfrac{1}{2}} * ii,$
    ten, a\$1, 1, a\$2, 2, b\$1, 1, b\$2, 2)$\wedge$
2 mirror(ten, b\$1, 1, b\$3, 1) $\wedge$ mirror(ten, b\$2, 2, b\$4, 2)$\wedge$
3 is_beam_splitter $(-\sqrt{\tfrac{1}{2}} * ii, \sqrt{\tfrac{1}{2}}), -\sqrt{\tfrac{1}{2}}, \sqrt{\tfrac{1}{2}} * ii,$
    ten, b\$3, 1, b\$4, 2, c\$1, 1, c\$2, 2)
4 $\Rightarrow$ tensor 2 (lambda i. if i = 1 then fock (a\$1) 1 else vac) =
5   ii% tensor 2 (lambda i. ifi = 1 then fock (c\$1)1 else vac)

Lines (1-3) provide the structure of the circuit in Figure 2 with the same modes naming. Line 4 describes the input modes, where we have one photon at mode $\mathbf{a}_1^\dagger$ and nothing elsewhere. Line 5 provides the corresponding output modes, where we obtain one photon at mode $\mathbf{c}_1^\dagger$ and nothing elsewhere.

Now, we will move to a more complex circuit, where we will focus on the formal results obtained rather than the proof steps.

5.2   CNOT Gate Verification

Similar to classical computer, the basic component of the quantum computer is the quantum bit (or *qbit*). A quantum bit is a quantum system with two basis states $|0\rangle$ and $|1\rangle$. However, in contrast to its classical counterpart, the state of a qbit is not only $|0\rangle$ or $|1\rangle$, but can be a mix. Indeed, such a state can be expressed as $|\psi\rangle = \alpha|0\rangle + \beta|1\rangle$, where $|\alpha|^2 + |\beta|^2 = 1$. There are a number of operations that can be defined over these qbits. In this paper, we are interested in the Controlled NOT gate. It is a two inputs/two outputs gate, namely *control* and *target* signals. The gate semantic is to invert the target bit whenever the control bit is equal to one, and nothing changes as long as the control bit is equal to zero. The control bit is always transmitted as is. In other word: if the possible input is $|\psi\rangle = \alpha|00\rangle + \beta|01\rangle + \gamma|10\rangle + \eta|11\rangle$ then the output is $|\psi_o\rangle = \alpha|00\rangle + \beta|01\rangle + \gamma|11\rangle + \eta|10\rangle$.

In quantum optics, this gate can be implemented using five beam splitters [19], as given in Figure 3, where each of the control and target qbits is repre-

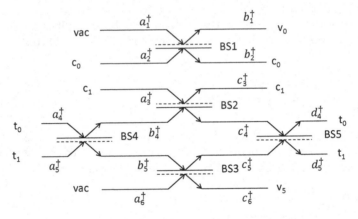

Fig. 3. Controlled NOT gate optical implementation

sented using two optical beams, and each of the beam splitter follows the matrix $\begin{pmatrix} \sqrt{\eta} & \sqrt{1-\eta} \\ \sqrt{1-\eta} & -\sqrt{\eta} \end{pmatrix}$. For BS4, BS5 η is equal to $\frac{1}{2}$, and for the rest it is equal to $\frac{1}{3}$. The encoding of such four beams is as follows: applying a single photon to c_0 is equivalent to setting the control bit to zero, and applying the photon to c_1 is equivalent to setting the control bit to one (same rule applies for the target bit). In Figure 3, *vac* refers to vacuum state, i.e., we do not apply any photons at these ports. For the output modes, v_0 and v_5 are dummy signals and do not have any semantic.

Now the formal definition of such circuit is included in the following theorem:

Theorem 6.
∀a b c d.
  is_tensor ten ∧
1 is_beam_splitter $(\sqrt{\frac{1}{3}}, \sqrt{\frac{2}{3}}, \sqrt{\frac{2}{3}}, -\sqrt{\frac{1}{3}},$ ten, a\$2, 2, a\$1, 1, b\$2, 2, b\$1, 1)$ ∧
2 is_beam_splitter$(\sqrt{\frac{1}{2}}, \sqrt{\frac{1}{2}}, \sqrt{\frac{1}{2}}, -\sqrt{\frac{1}{2}},$ ten, a\$4, 4, a\$5, 5, b\$4, 4, b\$5, 5)$ ∧
3 is_beam_splitter$(\sqrt{\frac{1}{3}}, \sqrt{\frac{2}{3}}, \sqrt{\frac{2}{3}}, -\sqrt{\frac{1}{3}},$ ten, b\$4, 4, a\$3, 3, c\$4, 4, c\$3, 3)$ ∧
4 is_beam_splitter$(\sqrt{\frac{1}{3}}, \sqrt{\frac{2}{3}}, \sqrt{\frac{2}{3}}, -\sqrt{\frac{1}{3}},$ ten, b\$5, 5, a\$6, 6, c\$5, 5, c\$6, 6)$ ∧
5 is_beam_splitter$(\sqrt{\frac{1}{2}}, \sqrt{\frac{1}{2}}, \sqrt{\frac{1}{2}}, -\sqrt{\frac{1}{2}},$ ten, c\$4, 4, c\$5, 5, d\$4, 4, d\$5, 5)$ ⇒
6 $|010100\rangle = \frac{1}{3} * (|\underline{010100}\rangle + \sqrt{2} * |101000\rangle$
7    $+ \sqrt{2} * |100001\rangle + |011000\rangle + |010001\rangle + \sqrt{2} * |100100\rangle)$

Lines (1-5) represent the formal structure of the CNOT gate in Figure 3. Note that we used the bra-ket notation [5] in the formal theorem for simplicity, in the actual code all states are written the same form as in the Mach-Zehnder example (see Theorem 5). The order of the output bits, on the right hand side of Line 6 and Line 7, is $v_0, c_0, c_1, t_0, t_1, v_5$.

According to [19], the output of the circuit in Figure 3 is not exactly as desired: As one can notice from Line 6 and Line 7, in the case of the control bit is equal to zero and the target bit is equal to zero. The result on the right hand side contains many possibilities of different probabilities, among them the required (underlined) one with probability $(\frac{1}{3})^2$. Note that these unwanted possibilities do not contain at all any meaningful states, i.e., $|011000\rangle, |001100\rangle, |001010\rangle$. We can get rid of these unwanted outputs by a physics process called coincidence basis [19]. We also verify the case where the control gate is equal to zero and the target is equal to one. The result was compatible with the one presented in [19]. Similarly, we verified the case of the control is equal to one. For example in case of $|001100\rangle$, the following theorem shows the result:

Theorem 7.
tensor $|001100\rangle = \frac{1}{3} * (|001010\rangle - \sqrt{2} * |002000\rangle - |001001\rangle +$
  $\sqrt{2} * |000200\rangle + |000101\rangle + |000110\rangle + |000011\rangle)$

The formal analysis of these two optical circuits would not have been possible without the development of the following tactic: MULTI_MODE_DECOMPOSE_TAC which is responsible for passing the creator operator in/out to/from the different modes. As its name suggests, it acts like decomposing multi-modes to many single modes that can be dealt with using the single-mode theorems.. The key lemma, on which this tactic is built, is:

Theorem 8.
∀p q f x.(p x ⇒ f x = q) ⇒ (if p x then q else (f x)) = f x

This lemma typically reduces multi-mode to single-mode, whenever all possible conditions (in the if statement) reduce to the same predicate.

Besides above tactic, we have developed a few other, such as CFUN_FLATTEN_TAC, which takes the whole formula to complex level, at final stage of the proof, to handle some algebraic simplification to finalize the proof. Without these tactics the verification of Mach-Zehnder and CNOT would be lengthly and complicated. Interested readers can check the HOL script of these tactics at [15], and see how they are utilized in the proofs.

This interesting result concludes the whole formalization by showing the effectiveness of formal methods, in particular with large circuits with a large number of connections and variables. Note that this circuit is working on 6 modes in each step, with the actual number of single modes (including intermediates) equal to 16.

6   Conclusion

Quantum computers are expected to outperform classical machines in certain cases, and provide powerful and unbreakable security systems. Among many implementations, quantum optical circuits with the help of nuclear optical coupling and nuclear magnetic resonance showed good advancement in building quantum machines at large scale. Thus, the quantum computer development became very critical. In this paper, we have studied the applicability of formal methods, in particular of HOL theorem proving, for the formal analysis and verification of quantum optical computers. The presented work includes the formalization of optical single-mode and multi-mode that helped in the analysis of quantum gates. As an illustrative application, we presented the verification of the Mach-Zehnder interferometer and Controlled NOT gate. Throughout our development, we have experienced a number of difficulties. We had a problem to find one clear definition of many quantum concepts. Physics books present the same idea from different perspectives and each considers some implicit assumptions. To deal with this problem, we focused our axiomatic definitions on the common ground of the different physics resources. The usability and readability of definitions and theorems are another challenge, where in the first versions of our development, we had lengthy definitions and theorems due to the high number of variables that control the quantum process. For this situation, we tried to remove irrelevant variables (which is a kind of low-level abstraction) that do not affect the quantum natures of systems. We also enhanced the proving process by developing dedicated tactics. This facilitates the reasoning about potentially similar circuits and gates and removes the burden of tedious steps, in particular with large circuits that have a high number of modes (i.e., optical beams). As a future work, we are targeting the formalization of more complicated quantum gates, e.g., the Hadamard gate [19], and enhancing the whole verification process to be more automated.

References

1. Baier, C., Katoen, J.P.: Principles of Model Checking. MIT Press (2008)
2. Brassard, G., Crepeau, C., Jozsa, R., Langlois, D.: A quantum bit commitment scheme provably unbreakable by both parties. In: Proceedings IEEE Annual Symposium on Foundations of Computer Science, pp. 362–371 (1993)
3. Elleuch, M., Hasan, O., Tahar, S., Abid, M.: Towards the formal performance analysis of wireless sensor networks. In: Proceedings IEEE International Workshop on Enabling Technologies: Infrastructures for Collaborative Enterprises, pp. 365–370 (2013)
4. Feynman, R.: Simulating physics with computers. International Journal of Theoretical Physics 21, 467–488 (1982), doi:10.1007/BF02650179
5. Griffiths, D.J.: Introduction to Quantum Mechanics. Pearson Prentice Hall (2005)
6. Haeffner, H., Roos, C.F., Blatt, R.: Quantum computing with trapped ions. Physics Reports 469(4), 155–203 (2008)
7. Jones, J.A.: Quantum computing: Optical nuclear coupling. Natural Photonics 5(11), 513 (2011)
8. Kolmogorov, A.N., Fomin, S.V., Fomin, S.V.: Elements of the Theory of Functions and Functional Analysis. Dover books on mathematics, vol. 2. Dover (1999)
9. Ladd, T.D., Jelezko, F., Laflamme, R., Nakamura, Y., Monroe, C., O'Brien, J.L.: Quantum computers. Nature 464, 45–53 (2010)
10. Lomonaco, S.J.: Quantum Computation: A Grand Mathematical Challenge for the Twenty-first Century and the Millennium. American Mathematical Society (2002)
11. Loss, D., DiVincenzo, D.P.: Quantum computation with quantum dots. Physical Review A 57, 120–126 (1998)
12. Mahmoud, M.Y., Aravantinos, V., Tahar, S.: Formalization of infinite dimension linear spaces with application to quantum theory. In: Brat, G., Rungta, N., Venet, A. (eds.) NFM 2013. LNCS, vol. 7871, pp. 413–427. Springer, Heidelberg (2013)
13. Mahmoud, M.Y., Aravantinos, V., Tahar, S.: Formal verification of optical quantum flip gate. In: Klein, G., Gamboa, R. (eds.) ITP 2014. LNCS, vol. 8558, pp. 358–373. Springer, Heidelberg (2014)
14. Mahmoud, M.Y., Tahar, S.: On the quantum formalization of coherent light in HOL. In: Badger, J.M., Rozier, K.Y. (eds.) NFM 2014. LNCS, vol. 8430, pp. 128–142. Springer, Heidelberg (2014)
15. Mahmoud, M.Y.: Formal verification of optical quantum gates - HOL Light script (2014), http://hvg.ece.concordia.ca/code/QGates/
16. Mandel, L., Wolf, E.: Optical Coherence and Quantum Optics. Cambridge University Press (1995)
17. Mhamdi, T., Hasan, O., Tahar, S.: Formalization of entropy measures in HOL. In: Interactive Theorem Proving. LNCS, vol. 6898, pp. 233–248. Springer, Heidelberg (2011)
18. Nielsen, M.A., Chuang, I.L.: Quantum Computation and Quantum Information: 10th Anniversary Edition. Cambridge University Press (2010)
19. Ralph, T.C., Langford, N.K., Bell, T.B., White, A.G.: Linear optical controlled-not gate in the coincidence basis. Physics Review A 65, 062324 (2002)
20. Verhulst, A.S.: Optical pumping experiments to increase the polarization in nuclear-spin based quantum computers. PhD thesis, Stanford University, CA, USA (2004)
21. Yamashita, S., Markov, I.L.: Fast equivalence-checking for quantum circuits. In: IEEE/ACM International Symposium on Nanoscale Architectures, pp. 23–28 (2010)
22. Zaki, M.H., Tahar, S., Bois, G.: Formal verification of analog and mixed signal designs: A survey. Microelectronics Journal 39(12), 1395–1404 (2008)

Author Index

Printed in the United States
By Bookmasters